Growing Up In Public

Edited by Chris Charlesworth
Cover designed by Robert Fairclough/Four Corners
Book designed by Four Corners
Picture research by Glen Marks & Dave Brolan

ISBN 0.7119.3002.3
Order No. OP 46820

Exclusive distributors:

Book Sales Limited,
8/9 Frith Street,
London W1V 5TZ.

Music Sales Corporation,
225 Park Avenue South,
New York, NY 10003, USA.

Music Sales Pty Ltd.,
120 Rothschild Avenue,
Rosebery, NSW 2018, Australia.

To the Music Trade only:
Music Sales Limited,
8/9 Frith Street,
London W1V 5TZ, UK.

Printed in Great Britain by BPCC Hazells, Aylesbury, Bucks

Every effort has been made to trace the copyright holders
of the photographs in this book but one or two were
unreachable. We would be grateful if the photographers
concerned would contact us.

A catalogue record for this book is available from the
British Library.

DEDICATION
To my parents

LOU·REED
Growing Up In Public

PETER·DOGGETT

OMNIBUS PRESS
LONDON · NEW YORK · SYDNEY

ACKNOWLEDGEMENTS

I'D FALLEN FOR THE RAVE REVIEWS THAT greeted 'Mistrial' in 1986, and been gravely disappointed. When the publicity campaign for 'New York' in January 1989 bragged that Lou thought this was his best ever record, I remembered the words of Mandy Rice-Davies: "Well, he would say that, wouldn't he?" It was a new label, a new deal, a new record to be sold. After three years of silence, and the three before that of creative anonymity, another Lou Reed record was neither here nor there.

That was until I heard it. Like everyone else, I was impressed by the artistic ambition of 'New York', its lyrical verve, its humour and imagery. Where did it come from? How could the man who thought 'Mistrial' an appropriate response to the 1980s have channelled so much experience into one record.

The seeds of this book were planted then. 'New York' sent me back to the rest of Reed's back catalogue, not just to the accepted glories of The Velvet Underground and the glam-rock era, but also to the dark and challenging work of the late seventies and early eighties. Faced by the critical commonplace that Reed was a genius of the sixties and a sorry wastrel thereafter, I was pulled by the need to set the record straight, to shout from the rooftops that his career was - as Lou had always claimed - one long autobiographical novel, an uncompromising record of personal loss and growth.

Although Reed's time with The Velvet Underground has been documented in print, no-one has ever attempted to survey his entire career with the same degree of sympathy. Contrary to popular belief, Reed and the Velvets were not the lucky recipients of some freakish spark of the imagination, which then lay dormant until it was miraculously rekindled on 'New York'. Reed's work is actually one seamless tapestry of exploration and nerve, which has its antecedents in the New York art scene of the sixties and the proud literary history of his homeland. That's off-limits for most rock criticism, which tends to see music as enjoying a direct line to the streets, but baulks at any notion that it might fit into wider artistic movements. Lou Reed has never made any secret of the fact that it is literature, as much as rock'n'roll, which has been his choice of weapon.

Facts are easy enough to assemble but what really matters is perspective. I was lucky enough at an early stage of this project to be put in touch with Glen Marks, who had both at his fingertips. As a keen follower of Reed's career since the early Seventies, Glen has marshalled an impressive collection of information, memorabilia, gossip and researched knowledge - probably unequalled in the world - without which this book would have been much less substantial.

More importantly, Glen was an endless fund of theories, ideas and speculation. Sometimes these notions coincided with mine, sometimes not, but the stimulus was a lifeline at times when it seemed that Reed's career was too bizarre to assimilate. For a man who has long harboured a wish to write his own account of Reed's life and work, Glen took my invasion of his territory with exceptional grace. It's a cliché to say the book could not have been written without him but for once the cliché is true.

Elsewhere Louise Cripps acted as a one-woman support team while I was writing this book, for which I am once again extremely grateful. I still don't think she likes 'Metal Machine Music' though. Mark Paytress does, and his enthusiasm for the avant-garde has resulted in some heated discussions over the last five years, most of which I have won only because I was wielding the editorial red pen. He read parts of the work in progress, and provided an informed view of the music and art that time (and the mainstream) forgot.

Chris Charlesworth not only edited the manuscript but back in 1977 bought two of Lou Reed's many black and white televisions, neither of which worked particularly well. He was able to bring his recollections of the people and places involved in the New York Seventies scene to this book. Johnny Rogan has proved to be an enthusiastic and expensive telephone correspondent over the last five years, and although a mere novice in the ranks of Lou Reed alumni, his refusal to let lazy thinking pass without contempt has been a long-distance source of inspiration every time I dare pick up a pen. Debbie Pead read much of the manuscript, and many of the ideas thrown around inside this book were first aired during our conversations sometime over the last 15 years.

Brian Hogg proved, as ever, to be the person who has exactly the information I wanted on the day I wanted it, and also inspired me to listen to Archie Shepp and Ornette Coleman. John Platt and Eva Hunte offered useful ideas on Andy Warhol, while some of Clinton Heylin's theories about Lou Reed were provoking, and others provoking but unprintable. Mention should also be made of Nicki Pritchard and Linda La Ban for friendship and support; and the staff of the University of London Library, the Hayward Gallery, the New York Museum of Modern Art, the Library of Congress in Washington and, of course, *Record Collector*. Finally, I am indebted to Andrew Dean, the first person to play me The Velvet Underground. Neither of us knew then what was in store.

Peter Doggett

INTRODUCTION

"I've had more of a chance to make an asshole out of myself than most people, and I realise that. But then not everybody gets a chance to live out their nightmares for the vicarious pleasures of the public."
(Lou Reed, 1979)

IN 1980, LOU REED MARRIED FOR THE second time. Four months later he released an album entitled 'Growing Up In Public', an uncomfortable merging of lyrical self-analysis and ersatz black music stylings. The record did not herald one of Reed's sporadic periods of acceptance by a mass audience; as a media event, it passed almost unnoticed. For Reed, however, it was a talisman of hope: a deliberate farewell to a decade in which he had paraded his private ghouls in the public arena. Reed's virtual disintegration during the Seventies began as a controlled chemical experiment, in which he tested the limits of his psyche and physique; eventually the sorcerer's apprentice could no longer hold down the forces which he had conjured up, and Reed's life became a desperate effort to muster substance out of strife.

Almost by instinct, Reed continued to function as an artist; it was what he *did,* whether he was master of his senses or not. Working in an idiom where success was measured by commercial acceptance, however, he found himself increasingly marginalised. What the public wanted was a freakshow, the sight of a matchstick-legged, leather-clad buffoon reeling across the stage, scarcely conscious of where he was or why. "They wanted to see me die," Reed remarked in a moment of sensibility, and the compelling drama of his flight into the abyss easily upstaged the altogether more subtle pleasures of his artistic output.

Looming over him were the masks he had created - the legacy of The Velvet Underground, the uncompromising and consciously perverse art-rock band which Reed had led in the Sixties, and which had become an essential piece of every namedropper's armoury; the figure of the Transformer, sexually ambiguous, unashamedly camp, inviting his audience to take that endless walk on the wild side; and mightiest of all, the

Rock & Roll Animal, Reed's most durable creation, a reservoir of every dubious value enshrined in the holy trinity of sex, drugs and rock'n'roll.

Under this triple threat, the private Lou Reed - the creative writing graduate who won awards for his poetry, the novelist who forced his characters into lyrics rather than prose, the obsessive chronicler of the speech and scenarios of the New York streets - lay ignored. Throughout the Seventies, Reed was reviewed as a case history rather than an artist. The adopted saint of a generation of rock critics, Reed disappointed his would-be champions by resolutely refusing to conform to their expectations. We see public figures through the opaque glass of the media, and the Lou Reed of the Seventies was caricatured as a misfit, forever failing to live up to other people's fantasies.

By 1979, Reed had regained some measure of control over his career and his personal life. Dark hints about his consumption of drugs and alcohol remained, however, and his sexuality - which had coloured his view of the world from the first Velvets' album onwards - was now an open book. Reed confessed publicly that he was gay, that he had always been gay, and that his well-publicised attempts at heterosexual conformity had been predestined not to succeed. A little over a year later, Reed was married, a liaison that survives to this day. He disavowed drugs, abandoned alcohol after attending AA sessions, and severed his links with the rock media. After touring to promote the 'Growing Up In Public' album that summer, he announced that he would no longer perform onstage. His next record, the alternately bleak and tender 'The Blue Mask', unveiled an artist in absolute command of his gifts; to promote it, he stage-managed a series of press conferences whereby no-one could come too close.

During the Seventies, Reed had fashioned an anarchic, near-dependent relationship with the rock writer Lester Bangs: trading insults and double shots of Johnnie Walker Black, the couple fuelled a succession of bizarre confrontations which came close to dissolving the barrier between artist and admirer, and leaving both awash in a sea of alcohol and pills, mumbling incoherently at the ceiling. Bangs took the roller-coaster of excess to its final destination; Reed cut his ride short.

Cleaned-up, and remodelled as a trim, professorial figure, Lou gradually returned to the world, issuing a run of modest, calculated albums that presented their creator as a short story writer in song, offering vignettes of adult life from the perspective of the amused voyeur. Eventually, too, he returned to the road. Gone were the shambolic monologues, the grotesque parodies of drug abuse, the sense of a life on the line: in their place Reed substituted a tight, workmanlike formalism as carefully constructed as the rest of his new persona.

The contrast - the remaking of an *enfant terrible* into a respectable elder statesman of rock - was almost too dramatic to grasp. After fifteen years of public exhibitionism, the revived Reed was defiantly restrained. Yet his reconstituted stage personality allowed him to stake claim to the whole of his past. The archetypal voice of experience, he could perform ambiguous celebrations of drug addiction and transvestism with the distant air of the survivor. "I was all these things," he seemed to say, "and I have learned to outlive them."

At the end of the eighties, after three years of virtual artistic silence, Reed re-emerged with a pair of albums that set the seal on his new image. 'New York' was a conscious effort to make a grand statement about modern city life, slyly presented as a novel-in-music which lived up to all the pretensions of its advance billing. At the same time, Reed renewed a two-decades-dormant collaboration with John Cale, which produced a tribute - part mock-autobiography, part confessional regret - to their mentor, the artist Andy Warhol. 'New York' reclaimed the present, 'Songs For Drella' the past; suddenly Reed was being treated with the respect, and awe, due an artist who had fulfilled every hint of promise he had dangled in the public's face over the previous twenty-five years.

The effect of the double impact of 'New York' and 'Drella' has been to revive Reed's status as A Major Artist - albeit with a career reduced to a brief list of accepted masterpieces that runs from the first Velvet Underground album and parts of the second, through 'Walk On The Wild Side' and 'Street Hassle' in the seventies, to his most recent work.

What this simplified recap of his progress ignores is any sense of growth or decay, any notion of the organic nature of artistic creation. Many artists achieve greatness for a fleeting moment, and then spend a lifetime sweating to recapture a feeling that originally arose from grace rather than hard labour. Others, a far more select band, have greatness constantly within their grasp. Lou Reed belongs to the latter category, and the story of his three decades as a creative artist reveals a constant flight back and forth between success and failure, with each step into the unknown countered by the painful threat of losing the path.

But Reed is not only an artist: he is a performer who chose for a decade or more to make his life part of the performance. A former student of both journalism and acting, Reed has constantly been aware of the need to create an effective image, and to play the part with authenticity. Under strain from chemical abuse and the tangle of his personal relationships, he discovered in the mid-Seventies that the image-mask was almost impossible to dislodge. The New Man - sexually, artistically, visually at odds with its predecessor - is a creation that Reed has found much more easy to control.

Beneath the mask lies the artist; and much of this book is devoted to unveiling him, to tracing the history of his creativity, its sources and inspirations, the evidence which supports Reed's claim to be a major American writer. But the mask itself is also worthy of study. Few popular figures have moulded as extreme a persona as Lou Reed between 1966 and 1980; fewer still have fallen so deeply under the spell of their own media manipulation. Reed's transformation from sexual outlaw into contented husband is either one of the most dramatic conversions since Saul's fateful encounter on the Damascus road; or it's as subtle and convincing a piece of conjuring as any sleight of hand by Harry Houdini. In a way, the truth is irrelevant. What matters is the journey - the path from middle-class boyhood, through the wildest excesses of the rock circus, to the settled life of the American poet - and the way in which Reed has chronicled his progress.

ONE

IN JULY 1975, LOU REED ISSUED 'Metal Machine Music', his seventh album as a solo artist, and his first double set. Side one tripped the listener headlong into a sea of noise, a bewildering assault on the senses that at first made evaluation impossible. From the left speaker issued the incessant howl of overloaded amplifiers, bursting out a wall of feedback that dipped and soared in intensity. Over the top swirled a mass of ear-stretching treble sound - at one moment echoing the tormented wail of a wounded animal, at another cascading in a savage parody of a psychedelic trip. Slowly the frantic burbling of random notes took on a faint air of order, as the distant shape of exotic scales formed and just as quickly dissolved into mayhem.

From the right speaker, in delicate counterpoint, came a second wave of howling, interrupted by bursts of hiss as the machinery sprang desperately to life. The effect was like having your eardrums syringed while a pneumatic drill crunched through a metal surface beside you, and a flock of rabid seagulls swooped around your head.

After sixteen minutes the noise ceased. Turn the record over, and it began again - the musical Tower of Babel whirling ever faster, broken by shrill cries that belonged in some dark mingling of the torture chamber and the dentist's surgery. And so it continued, across this side, and the whole of another record - two albums of unrelenting, vicious sound, the threatening soundtrack of electronic machines driven past their limits of control.

The artist who issued this record was at the commercial pinnacle of his career. Emerging from a year of camouflage, recuperating from the nervous exhaustion which had forced him to quit The Velvet Underground on the brink of some measure of success, he had found himself a cult figure, at last given credit for artistic developments which had originally been scorned. He capitalised on this sudden notoriety by writing a song which traded explicitly on his relationship with Andy Warhol's avant-garde circus, and was duly rewarded with his first hit single. His new-found status as the poet of perversity - 'The Phantom Of Rock' was the cunning label applied by his record company - allowed him to follow through with a concept album that told a sorry tale of addiction, obsession and suicide. Then he toured America with a guitar-heavy band of sessionmen, churning out brash parodies of his Velvet Underground trademarks, and found that the public demanded two live albums documenting the experience. Between them, he manufactured 'Sally Can't Dance', a sly mixture of self-mockery and frank confessional that was packaged like a soft porn mag and greeted as an exhibition of sleaze. For the first time in his life, Lou Reed was not only playing popular music but also enjoying real popularity.

Perhaps 'enjoying' was overstating the case, however. Outside the sales charts, Reed was showing every sign of self-destruction. Already renowned as the grim chronicler of drug addiction, Reed began to live out the grossest implications of his songs in real life. Onstage, he produced a syringe, pumped up a vein and proceeded to inject himself with drugs - or not, as it was difficult to see from the stalls. Either way, it didn't really matter. Reed could scarcely tell the difference himself: observers noted that he stumbled incoherently across the stage, while in private he alternated between dark periods of silence and the incessant babbling of a mind beyond control. His once chubby features took on a deathly pallor; his limbs grew stick-like and weak; his hands shook; his left eye, always prone to laziness, veered alarmingly out of sync as if contemplating an existence of its own.

When it seemed as if his body could take no more, and his name was being prepared for the obituary columns, Reed began to put on weight. He toured Europe, was hit in the face by a brick during the first song of a performance in Rome, and was forced to abandon his next shows having apparently suffered "a nervous collapse". Completing 'Metal Machine Music', he set out on another exhausting transcontinental trek, to be followed by a sweep across Europe as part of an ill-conceived multi-artist festival package.

In New Zealand, the wire broke, and Reed's career tumbled to the ground. "Physical inability" had prevented him from completing his concert arrangements reported the *Wellington Evening Post,* "Reed had a personal problem of such magnitude that he was unable to perform". Promoter Ron Blackmore elaborated: "Reed had a very very personal problem that should never have damned well happened. It's so personal and serious that I can't even tell you about it off the record. If you could imagine what it is like to get a call from the other side of the world and be told that your mother was not only a drug addict but a hooker, and that she'd hooked some of your friends, then you might be able to understand how he was feeling."

Back in America, RCA Records released 'Metal Machine Music'. It was subtitled 'An Electronic Instrumental Composition', albeit in type that was dwarfed by the picture which Reed had chosen for the front cover. It showed the artist frozen in awkward, distracted pose, his emaciated body clad in studded black leather, his hair bleached blond and cut severely to the shape of his head, his eyes as ever hidden beneath the insectile wrap of impenetrable shades. The shot echoed the cover of

'Rock And Roll Animal', the first of the overblown live albums that turned Reed into a superstar. And on the back the promise was explicit: framed by a single spotlight, Reed stood onstage, arms perched camply on hips, displaying a full set of darkly painted fingernails.

Maybe some of Reed's stadium followers, having swilled beer and quaaludes to prepare themselves for the show, did follow these clues too strictly and delude themselves that they were buying another concert album. But it seems unlikely: no sooner was the record in the shops than the press reacted. 'Metal Machine Music' received universal derision - aside from the ever-loyal Lester Bangs, whose *Creem* review greeted it as "the greatest album of all time". But people read Bangs as a humorist, not a guide, and everyone knew he worshipped at Reed's feet. The rest of the media, depending on their attitude to Lou, treated it as a jest too far, or used it as an excuse to slice his reputation to shreds. Even the trade mag *Billboard,* always sympathetic to the lamest product in its efforts to boost commercial activity in the industry, was forced to admit: "Recommended Cuts: None".

Not in business to finance failure, RCA began an exercise in damage limitation. The presses were halted; both the stereo and quadrophonic mixes of the album were effectively removed from distribution. In Britain, the album was cancelled. RCA imported a batch of unwanted American copies for the benefit of the curious and prurient; otherwise, as an RCA spokesman euphemistically put it, "We'll just let it wash through the system in a low-key way."

In New York, the *Village Voice,* forum of the artistic and radical communities, printed what was said to be a statement of regret from the artist: "A lot of people may feel ripped off," Reed allegedly said, "and I understand and apologise for this." But the damage was done: within weeks, Reed's manager Dennis Katz, a staunch supporter throughout the troubled years of commercial success, terminated their relationship.

Strangely, Reed reacted to this tempest with apparent insouciance. Journalists expecting to be faced by a personality in the final stages of disintegration were startled to find the artist combative, confident, and anything but regretful. "I didn't apologise for it," he told *Melody Maker*'s Caroline Coon. "If you read the apology - well, I don't talk the way the apology was written. The apology the record company put out was meant for rock dealers."

In place of the apology came the apologia. "I've got something here that I mean by heavy metal," he boasted. "I had to wait a couple of years so I could get the equipment, now I've got it and it's done. I could have sold it as electronic classical music, except that it's heavy metal, no kidding around." The album was "probably one of the best things I ever did... I find it very relaxing." And to Lester Bangs he explained how he had submitted the album to the head of RCA's classical division: "He loved it. He said we really must put it out. I said no way, because it seems hypocritical, like saying, the really smart, complicated stuff is over here in the classical bin; meanwhile, the shit rock and roll goes over here where the schmucks are." Bangs tracked down the elusive Red Seal man, by this time the former head of the label, and reported that he had viewed Reed as... "not too well connected with reality. But I had to handle him with kid-gloves because he was an artist in whom the company had a long-term commitment. I couldn't tell him it was just a bunch of shit."

By this stage, however, Reed was in full flight - boasting that each side of the album clocked in at precisely sixteen minutes and one second, to preserve its conceptual unity; crowing that the album contained "frequencies that are dangerous... they're illegal to put on a record"; avowing, to anyone who dared to question the artistic content of the piece, that he had laced his feedback howl with the melodies of classic composers: "There's all kinds of symphonic rip-offs in there, running all through it, little pastoral parts, but they go by like - bap! in five seconds. Beethoven's Fifth, or Mozart... The Glass Harp... Eroica. I used pretty obvious ones. But there's about seventeen more going at the same time. It just depends which one you catch."

Suitably impressed, the writers proclaimed that they had followed Reed's advice, and that maybe 'Metal Machine Music' was, after all, a piece of classical art. Well, maybe. It's certainly true that within the frantic atonal gabble of noise, there were snatches of melody - some Eastern in flavour, some hinting at 1967 experimentalism like Pink Floyd's 'See Emily Play', and some, no doubt, replicating the more subtle cadences of the giants of serious German music.

The effect was strictly coincidental, however: throw enough random notes into the air, and the ear will want to translate some into recognisable tunes. The more notes are available for consideration, the more 'difficult' you can imagine this classical composition to be.

A more blatant source of inspiration was the world of the avant-garde, as Reed acknowledged to Lester Bangs: "I've been thinking about doing it ever since I've been listening to LaMonte Young. I had also been listening to Xenakis a lot." Two names we'll return to in a later chapter, and to whom Reed had been introduced by fellow Velvet John Cale. What Reed neglected to mention was that Cale had prefigured the 'Metal Machine Music' sound, with Lou's aid, as early as 1965; while the impression of a myriad melodies fighting for attention had been achieved by that doyen of the avant-garde, John Cage, who overdubbed dozens of harpsichords playing different pieces simultaneously.

Reed's assertion that each portion of his composition lasted for a second over sixteen minutes was equally shaky, as anyone with a stopwatch could determine. Three of the four sides do endure for something near to the announced time, but the fourth runs out of steam after less than fourteen minutes - though Reed did make sure that the needle drifted across the final millimetres of the record into a locked groove, which repeated the closing moments of hiss and distortion as long as the electricity supply was maintained.

In a conscious effort to present 'Metal Machine Music' as a single, unified composition, Reed not only left the individual sides untitled, but offered his own perverse parody of classical liner notes. His first piece of published prose for more than three years, the 'Metal Machine Music' 'Notation' was a remarkable combination of arrogance, bluster and inadvertent confessional. The prose was fractured and ungrammatical, full of clauses and phrases left marooned in mid-sentence, their meaning unclear. The subject shifted from Reed's complaints about the tedium of most heavy metal, to the symmetrical genius of his creation, to pathetic puns on his own album titles, to incoherent babblings about the gap between drug "professionals" (like Reed himself, of course) and "those for whom the needle is no more than a toothbrush". Besides constant reminders that "No one I know has listened to it all the way through including myself... I love and adore it. I'm sorry, but not especially, if it turns you off... Most of you won't like this, and I don't blame you at all. It's not meant for you." Reed cemented élitism in his final line, the classic boast of the amphetamine head: "My week beats your year."

There were other overt drug references, albeit imprecise ones: "The agreement one makes with 'speed'. As way of disclaimer, I am forced to say that the possible negative contra indications must be pointed out... hypertense people etc. possibility of epilepsy (*petit mal*), psychic motor disorders, etc., etc., etc." The front cover referred the record buyer to two handbooks of pharmaceutical medicine; the back displayed the chemical make-up of an amphetamine-based concoction.

Why would Reed so blatantly reveal that 'Metal Machine Music' was inspired as much by chemicals as by classical conceits? For the same reason, perhaps, as he allowed his brainchild to be packaged between photographs taken a year or so earlier, portraying an artist inevitably linked in the public eye with severe mental and physical disorders. Gradually, Reed began to let some of the answers slip. He hinted, for instance, that one impetus behind the project had been to break his managerial links with Dennis Katz. "It was a giant fuck-you," he explained to Lester Bangs. A year later, caught off-guard at a Ramones CBGBs show by the correspondents of *Punk* magazine, Reed went a stage further: "I put out 'Metal Machine Music' to clear the air and get rid of all those fucking assholes who show up at the show and yell 'Vicious' and 'Walk On The Wild Side'."

By 1977, another piece of the puzzle had been uncovered; Reed told Allan Jones, "It was all so BORING. Then along came 'Metal Machine Music'. It was like a bomb. The idea was good in itself, but for the full impact you had to go through all the motions of execution." And finally, when the critics thought they had spotted the belated renaissance of Reed's muse on 'Street Hassle', Lou let down another veil: "There were rumours that I couldn't stand tours because I was on dope and my mind was going. I put out 'Metal Machine Music' precisely to put a stop to all of it. It wasn't ill-advised at all. It did what it was supposed to do."

"To put a stop to all of it": that's what motivated 'Metal Machine Music'. Nine years earlier, Bob Dylan found himself locked into an enervating series of contractual commitments - one murderous tour after another, each one greeted by the seething rage of folk purists unable to think beyond the iconic status of Dylan's acoustic guitar. After the tours loomed a TV spectacular, another album, a film, a novel, more tours - and then Dylan fell off his motorbike. He was dead, rumours suggested, or brain-damaged; finally, it was established that he had broken his neck. There *was* a motorbike crash; there *was* a neck injury; but the rest served Dylan with an appropriate excuse to break the headlong, amphetamine-fuelled progress of his career.

Reed entered 1975 a captive of his own careless image-mongering. Grown lazy and cynical on the easy fruits of success, he had succeeded in persuading the world that he was a drug-raddled fool; then, for precarious months, he tottered on the edge of confirming his own mythology. The New Zealand incident - the "personal problem of such magnitude that he was unable to perform" - was a hiccup in Reed's relationship with his partner of several months, Rachel, who, rest assured, reappears later in our story. A night of separation merely confirmed Reed's dependence; built into a full-blown psychodrama, it allowed him to slip out of the rest of his tour.

'Metal Machine Music' broke another section of the straitjacket. It effectively sabotaged Reed's commercial standing, which was based on music which he hated, and which in one case - 'Lou Reed Live' - he had attempted to prevent being released. Yet at the same time it won him endless publicity, on his terms: anxious to watch Reed slip down for the third time, the press allowed him rein to lay waste to his image as the Rock & Roll Animal, and recreate himself as the champion of the avant-garde. Appalled by what he viewed as commercial misjudgement, manager Dennis Katz fled the sinking ship.

Meanwhile, Lou Reed had already begun work on 'Coney Island Baby', an album that demonstrated such artistic control that it was impossible to imagine its creator had ever relinquished the barest hold on reality.

Moreover, Reed, as a longterm admirer of LaMonte Young's Dream Music, and a man of immense humour, particularly when aimed at the music industry, relished every agonising second of 'Metal Machine Music' - an album which does, after all, repay repeated listening without exploring any areas previously unknown to the avant-garde. The most commendable aspect of the entire project, however, was Reed's very survival. He designed the album to deflate a myth, at the risk of ending his career. The myth dissolved, right on schedule, and the album merely added to another legend: that of Reed as an artist who lived every second of life to the extreme. Far from registering him for a mental institution, 'Metal Machine Music' left Reed ahead of the game, the master of media manipulation - free to pursue his real career aims, as a rival to William Shakespeare.

TWO

"My expectations are very high... to be the greatest writer that ever lived on God's earth. In other words I'm talking about Shakespeare, Dostoevsky. I want to do that rock and roll thing that's on the level of The Brothers Karamazov... *starting to build up a body of work. I'm on the right track. I think I haven't done badly. But I think I haven't really scratched the surface. I think I'm just starting."*
(Lou Reed to Paul Morley, 1979)

"I always wanted to be a writer and I went to college to prepare myself for it. See, that's where I'm coming from. If you have my interests and my kind of academic background, then what I'm doing is not really an unlikely thing to do." (Lou Reed, 1982)

LOU REED CHOSE TO WRITE IN THE rock tradition, which at the moment when he began his career with The Velvet Underground, in 1965, was teetering on the verge of broadening its horizons to take in some of the concerns and imagery of literature, art and film.

The popular song traditionally takes the form of an unsent letter - an outpouring of the heart too revealing and romantic to be exposed in everyday conversation, serving the same function as the message inside a greetings-card. On that level, maturity is measured by the wittiness of the song lyrics, with the faintly cynical tricks and turns of a Cole Porter attracting the greatest kudos. Rock and roll, as an artform aimed at working-class teenagers, reduced these conventions to their lowest common denominator: teen ballads stripped Porter's arch asides down to a basic "I love you/do you love me too", while the quintessential rock and roll song was Little Richard's 'Tutti Frutti', a litany of jive talk topped by an exuberant wail of "awopbopoloobopawopbamboom". Words were reduced to their ancient role as pure expressions of feeling: Little Richard's cry meant nothing on the page, and everything in performance.

The exception, and it's an all too familiar road for rock historians, was Chuck Berry - a man maybe a decade older than most of his competitors in the rock field, who with the unwavering eye of the novelist was able to create the world of teenage America through the accumulation of minor but telling details.

As his autobiography revealed, Chuck Berry had his own views about prose styles, but he had no output for them in the Fifties. Until rock merged with the folk tradition in the early Sixties, no-one else thought far beyond romance as a suitable subject for song. You could create mini-dramas and soap operas, like Goffin and King, Barry and Greenwich, Shadow Morton; you could even hint at personal insecurity, like John Lennon ('There's A Place') and Brian Wilson ('In My Room'). But it was Bob Dylan - the next step in rock's traditional canon - who first introduced some measure of adult life into rock and roll.

Though folk music became a haven for those who wished to reject the crass commercialism of mid-twentieth century Western civilisation, it was rooted in the oral tradition, of ballads handed down through the generations, gaining narrative twists with each retelling. In the folk heritage, there was no need for categorisation into 'popular' and 'serious'. At its purest, folk music was the music of the people, their means of exploring subjects too delicate to be raised in speech, of celebrating behaviour out of bounds in everyday village life. Songs centred around the essentials - birth and death, lust and loathing, murder and guilt. As communication between villages, towns and eventually countries became commonplace, so taboos were erected around the playpen of popular culture. Bourgeois society gradually eviscerated all mention of sex and death, viewing them as primaeval forces ill-suited to the veneer of civilisation. In place of sex, society conjured up the myth of romantic love, stripped it of the idealised force it had held in the Middle Ages, and promoted it as a sop to the discontent of the working-classes.

Popular music thus fractured into two strains - the folk tradition, which held true to the earthiness of mediaeval ballads; and a more sophisticated and formularised pop tradition, which viewed music as an antidote to the cares of everyday life. Where working-class culture remained strong - eventually, where poverty robbed people of the opportunity to participate in the bourgeois mass media - so the folk tradition continued to grow, producing a diversity of country-based styles in the American south, and the black equivalent, the blues, in the shanty-towns and ghettos that stretched from the cottonfields to the Chicago meat factories.

These surviving working-class styles were discovered in the late 1950s and early 1960s by American college students - literate enough to want music which went beyond romantic clichés, and politically educated into basic identification with the plight of the poor and underprivileged. So was born the folk revival, whereby songs that reeked of history and ambiguity were reduced to tokens of social awareness by performers who smoothed over their rough edges and stripped away the life-force that had helped them to survive.

At the same time, the romantic attitude of the Beat movement - a group of writers who captured the directionless ennui of middle-class youths unable to squeeze themselves into the neat pigeon holes prepared by their elders - helped to recreate the idea of the troubadour. Woody Guthrie, eternal champion of the dispossessed, was one role model here; another was Jack Kerouac, whose *On The Road* provided a map for anyone too confused to draw their own. The mythic status of the drifter, always on the move to another town, never still long enough to gather society's shackles, manifested itself in the hero-worship of actors like James Dean and Marlon Brando; and it persuaded a generation of folksingers that the old tradition of songs and causes could be extended into the nuclear age.

Bob Dylan emerged as the standard-bearer of the new folk music, concealing his comfortable bourgeois background and recreating himself as a hobo, an orphan, a runaway, companion of the dustbowl singers and the blind blues guitarists, friend to the poor and to the victims "bent out of shape by society's pliers". When he began translating his facsimiles of Woody Guthrie into potent political messages, Dylan was greeted as the poet of the human rights crusade; his songs became anthems, totem-poles of liberal attitudes.

Dylan's reading of the Beat writers went further than Kerouac, however, and it was the gushing word-fountains of Allen Ginsberg's poetry that inspired his next move. Fuelled by increasing use of amphetamines, Dylan transferred his landscape from the political arena to the growth of his own consciousness. Overtly rejecting the protest movement with the song 'My Back Pages', Dylan combined his own flood of imagery with the rock and roll backbeat, and in 1965 issued two albums, 'Bringing It All Back Home' and 'Highway 61 Revisited', that redefined the boundaries of what could be achieved in the popular song.

Dylan's achievements have been much fêted elsewhere; Paul Williams' *Performing Artist* is a useful place to start. For Lou Reed, however, working eight hours a day as a hack songwriter for Pickwick Records, Dylan's adventures of 1965 aroused envy and no little contempt. A decade later, Reed sniffed: "Dylan was NEVER around for me. But he did have a nice flair for words that didn't mean anything. They were just marijuana throwaways." It's true that as Dylan approached his own crisis in 1966 his wordplay became more and more self-referential; while his admirers tried to unravel the code, Dylan exploded across the four sides of 'Blonde On Blonde', and then re-emerged clear of amphetamines, and with his imagery stripped to the bone.

Little of Reed's work betrays the direct influence of Dylan's scatter-shot imagery. But the very fact that Dylan had emerged out of New York, and had succeeded in forcing the complexity of modern poetry within the constrictions of the rock and roll form, must have inspired envy, and an urge for competition.

Before Dylan, nothing in popular music convinced Reed that he could combine his obsession with New York rock and roll, and his burning ambition to be a writer. At first the two themes ran side by side; Reed attended college, and then spent his nights alongside friends like Sterling Morrison, churning out three-chord covers of the latest hit songs. Meanwhile, Reed began to write poetry. "The *New Yorker* rejected me," he recalled in 1974. "That's when I wanted to be a New Yorker poet. I used to get *Writer's Market* which told you all the books that take poetry, like *The Kenyon Review, Hudson Review, Paris Review,* but later it dawned on me, who wants to be published in these magazines, anyway?"

At college, Reed studied Creative Writing under the poet and story writer, Delmore Schwartz; he read the philosophy of Sartre, Hegel and Kierkegaard; and he was introduced to the literary tradition of his own country.

"USA is the slice of a continent. USA is a group of holding companies, some aggregations of trade unions, a set of laws bound in calf, a radio network, a chain of moving picture theatres, a column of stock quotations rubbed out and written in by a Western Union boy on a blackboard, a public library of old newspapers and dogeared historybooks with protests scrawled on the margins in pencil... But mostly USA is the speech of the people." (John Dos Passos, *USA*)

"One of my strong points is that I'm good at dialogue. I can make it sound like something someone said. A lot of my stuff sounds like the way people speak, when in fact it's not. It's sort of a polished version of the way people speak." (Lou Reed, 1984)

Bending and shaping conventional rock dialogue to reflect the lessons he had learned in college, Reed necessarily had to take a stance in the critical debate which had dominated American literary culture in the twentieth century. He came down on the side of naturalism, a cause which was rooted in Europe in the late nineteenth century, and had inspired a tradition of American writers ever since.

Throughout the nineteenth century, novelists debated the relationship between life and the way it was described on the page. The goal was 'realism', the reproduction of society's nuances and strata through the creation of characters who would represent every section of present-day existence. At its furthest extreme, realism had a political impetus, parodied by the Russian Communist Party's insistence that its authors write Socialist Realism, in which puppet-like figures played out the inevitable triumph of the Marxist ideal over the doomed representatives of bourgeois capitalism. At its subtlest, realism allowed the writer to shape a view of society by the cunning juxtaposition of opposing social forces - the landowners, the reformers and the pioneer railwaymen of George Eliot's *Middlemarch,* for instance, or the aristocracy and the peasantry in Tolstoy's *Anna Karenina.*

The French novelist and social campaigner Emile Zola was the theoretician of a movement which narrowed the margins of the debate. He assumed that fiction had a social purpose, that the need to write was inseparable from the wish to change society. His books - written in a style which he coined as 'naturalism' - focused on working-class French life in the closing years of the last century, exposing the appalling conditions endured by miners, the poverty of farmers dependent on the whims of bourgeois landowners. In his hands, however, the class struggle took on an almost elemental nature. His hero-victims railed vainly against the vicissitudes of the climate, human nature, and an unseeing God. Pitted against forces too mighty to resist, they were ground into the dirt. We can change people's circumstances, Zola seemed to say, but we can never change their fates.

It was this air of primaeval struggle that attracted a dynasty of American writers, from Theodore Dreiser to Hubert Selby Jnr. Books like Frank Norris's *The Octopus,* Upton Sinclair's *The Jungle* and Dreiser's *An American Tragedy* epitomised the tradition: each sent a quixotic innocent into battle against overpowering economic forces, and each ended with the common man crushed beneath irresistible wheels, unable to alter the inexorable progress of capitalist society. In each case, romantic love merely heightened the pace of the tragedy; the hulk of industrial civilisation could not be diverted by mere human needs.

Alongside the portrayal of social upheaval, the naturalists sought to convey the sounds and sights of contemporary America - Sinclair's 'Jungle' reeked with the mutilated carcasses of dead animals in the slaughterhouses of Chicago, while Dreiser's *American Tragedy* was played out against the ineluctable workings of the judicial system. Beyond the piling-up of descriptive details, the naturalists wanted to pinpoint the rhythms and cadences of American speech. Political rather than poetic in nature, Sinclair and Dreiser relied on the brutality of their narratives; the niceties of the spoken word were taken up by a more experimental, less pejorative class of American writers.

In the work of Ernest Hemingway, words - carefully selected to form short, precise sentences - were as important as action. For Gertrude Stein, they *were* action: through a process of repetition and wordplay, Stein recreated the manner, if not the content, of the spoken word, arriving at a form of truth by pushing the language to the limits of sense, and then treating as essential what remained.

James Joyce in Ireland, Ezra Pound in Italy, and T. S. Eliot within the walls of a London bank all moved beyond naturalism into what would eventually be classed as modernism. Shifting words out of context, inventing language to meet the demands of emotion, cutting away the narrative flow of prose and poetry, Joyce and his contemporaries suggested a meaning through and beyond words - as Picasso had found some deeper truth about the human body by dividing it into geometrical shapes and extending the ways in which reality could be represented.

The innovations of the avant-garde were attempts to come closer to the core of human existence, but the structures which they used merely drew barriers between their work and the general public. For a more literal translation of human speech, they could turn to the plays of Eugene O'Neill, whose caricatures of negro language were revolutionary at the time, and now appear patronising and sarcastic. John Dos Passos's mammoth *USA* trilogy used a device he called 'The Camera Eye' to offer brief monologues or dialogues in the common tongue. Thirty years later, Lou Reed's favourite writer, Hubert Selby Jnr., extended this mode to give a voice to the underclasses of New York - concocting page-long, rambling sentences full of the casual expletives and dead ends of every-day conversation. Some doubted whether this was literature, but it was the authentic voice of the streets.

As Reed himself noted earlier in this chapter, the point was not to reproduce the spoken word, with all its hesitations and repetitions, but to construct something that *looked* like the spoken word. As we shall see, he began with the first Velvet Underground album to examine the concerns of the New York street, but an authentic street language had to wait for a further decade.

Until then, Reed had a more extravagant desire: to use the predominant themes of American art in an artform previously restricted to cooings of teenage love. "I was very taken aback when people were surprised when The Velvet Underground consciously set out to put themes common to movies, plays and novels into a pop song format," he noted in 1982; and even then, eighteen years into his recording career, he was still being forced to explain, ever patiently, that writers don't always write about themselves. "I have songs about killing people," he told Mikal Gilmore in 1979, "but Dostoevsky killed people too. In reality I might not do what a character in my songs would do, if only because I'd be jailed. I've always thought it would be kinda fun to introduce people to characters they maybe hadn't met before, or hadn't wanted to meet."

Alone among the major rock lyricists, Reed has kept an emotional distance in much of his work - a device that has allowed him to deny personal involvement in songs that delve a little too close to the bone. Rather than equating the words with the singer, as you do automatically with Bob Dylan, Joni Mitchell or Neil Young, you have to stop and think: whose voice am I hearing? Where is Lou Reed in this song? "It's simply professional detachment," Reed explained when challenged about the apparent lack of morality in his work. "You could say I'm a voyeur, but I'm not. I'm just talking about what goes on around me. I've always been listening. The way things happen is the way they are. They're not necessarily about me, though. That's where everybody gets confused."

By stressing his role as a novelist in song, rather than a chronicler of his own mental processes, Reed has finally succeeded in persuading his listeners to accept subject matter that they would find intolerable if it was straight confessional. Occasionally, one can't help but wonder where the borderline lies, where Reed's fiction blends into autobiography. His lifestyle in the 1970s heightened such speculation, just as his calm, married status in more recent times has dampened it. By taking a non-committal stance on matters as extreme as drug addiction, murder, sexual ambiguity and mental cruelty, Reed has broadened the scope of the rock lyric, sharpened the edges of his own public image, and demonstrated a stunning ability to translate the least promising subjects into song. "My characters just squeak by," he explained in the late Seventies, and Reed has squeaked by with them. It's a method of working that has endless potential.

"You take the lyric and you push it a little forward so that it speaks

to you on a personal level and still keeps the beat, because I'm not talking about poetry reading. You can even make it a dialogue between men and women. That could keep you occupied for the rest of your life." (Lou Reed, 1979)

THREE

"Child labor! The child must carry
His fathers on his back.

But seeing that so much is past
And that history has no truth

For the individual
Who drinks tea, who catches cold,

Let anger be general:
I hate an abstract thing."

(Delmore Schwartz, 'The Ballad Of The Children Of The Czar')

LEWIS ALLAN REED WAS BORN IN Brooklyn, the largely residential borough of New York, on March 2, 1942. His official birthdate was long kept a mystery; in the early Seventies, RCA's press department admitted they were too nervous to ask the question. Many otherwise reliable rock encyclopaedias list his birthdate as 1943 or 1944, his birthplace as Freeport, Long Island, and his name as Louis Firbank. The suggestion - denied by no less an authority than Maureen Tucker - that Reed might have changed his name is fascinating in itself; such a manoeuvre always poses pertinent questions about family relations. In Reed's case, the questions arise regardless of his true identity.

According to Reed, his father was Sidney George Reed, his mother Toby Futterman. Their second child, a girl named Elizabeth, followed when Lewis was a small child; a second son was apparently born approximately a decade later.

Reed's mother was reputedly a former beauty queen; his father a legal accountant. As the family practice grew during the late 1940s, they moved from Brooklyn to Freeport on Long Island, a wealthier, predominantly middle-class area still under the thrall of New York, but considered a more pleasant place to live than the areas two or three miles west which were officially part of the city. Freeport lay on the Atlantic coast; along the shores of the Island ran miles of beaches, culminating in the notorious resort of Coney Island, which boasted a boardwalk that attracted teenagers of dubious repute from throughout the five Boroughs of New York. In a city whose suburbs were short on romance, Coney Island doubled as fantasy factory and recreation area; there was a famous Fun Fair overlooking the sea, rivalled only by the long-vanished amusements of Palisades Park.

In the darkest hours of his relationship with Seventies manager Dennis Katz, Reed referred to him publicly as a "kike", adding "If you ever wondered why they have noses like pigs, now you know". The author of these rather intemperate remarks was himself Jewish - "Aren't all the best people?" Reed remarked when he was called on the subject a few years later. Such is the mythic, tragic nature of the Jewish race in the twentieth century that it is difficult to resist theorising about the effect of growing up Jewish in a decade when six million of your fellows were annihilated in the gas chambers, and in a country where the Jewish lobby has often held effective control over East Coast politics. Despite this mixed status as a member of a persecuted élite, Reed has given little public indication of his attitude to his religion - beyond, at least, the vitriol he showed on the 'New York' album in 1989, when he lambasted presidential candidate Jesse Jackson both for his description of the city as "hymie town", and his dealings with the allegedly anti-Semitic followers of Black Muslim leader Louis Farrakhan.

Reed's own family relationship is easier to plot. "I didn't want to grow up like my old man," ran the chorus line of a 1980 song which had all the appearances of autobiography, though Reed rejected the connection. 'My Old Man' paints a distressing picture of a family dominated by a powerful father, while the mother soaks up the blows and remains a passive tool of her husband. 'Families', from 1979's 'The Bells', is equally uncompromising in its portrait of parent-child relations. And then, of course, there is 'Kill Your Sons'.

From the outside, however, there is little evidence to suggest that Reed's childhood was in any way abnormal. He followed sports, developing a lifelong affection for basketball; at high school, as the confessional opening to 'Coney Island Baby' reminds us, he tried out for linebacker on the school football team, only to finish up at right end when the coach - "the straightest dude I ever knew" - decided he was too lightweight for such a central role. Out of school, he underwent the traditional middle-class baptism of fire, enduring two years of piano lessons: "I was a tot - eight, ten, something like that. I just had a natural affinity for music. Playing the classical piano, I forgot all of it." Depending on the context, Reed was apt to dismiss this classical training as an imposition, or display it as his credentials for creating avant-garde masterpieces like 'Metal Machine Music': "I took classical music for fifteen fucking years, theory, composition, the whole thing," he claimed at the height of his career crisis in 1975. "One of these days I'm gonna pull my degrees out and say, 'Does that make me legitimate?'"

For the second generation of rock stars, the line from Dylan and The

Beatles through the Stones, The Who and Neil Young, the arrival of rock and roll in the mid-fifties was a declaration that the established order was not invincible. Andy Warhol was equally moved: in 1956, he drew a piece called 'Rock And Roll' to convey his excitement; and Warhol was already 27. The drawing showed a young woman seated beside a large valve radio, her head thrown back with feline pleasure, her mouth open in abandonment to the music, which is represented by random geometric patterns issuing from the radio. The message was simple: rock and roll brought instant relief. Reed used the same straightforward title for his own encapsulation of the same experience - repeating the figure of the young woman held entranced by what she hears coming over the New York stations, yet distancing himself from the experience by writing the song not around the classic rock and roll 12-bar changes, but actually in a non-standard tuning.

In interviews, Reed was more open about the impact that the new music had on his life. "I was influenced by everybody," he recalled, "by all the rock and roll I ever heard - the street groups, old fifties rock. I always liked all those really corny lyrics." As each succeeding week proved that the initial burst of rock records wasn't a fluke, Reed decided to put his two or fifteen years of music theory into practice. "I got a guitar, a Gretsch Country Gentleman," he told Steve Dupler in 1982, "and I paid somebody to teach me those first three chords. After that you're on your own, particularly at that time when you could play everything on the radio with those three chords."

Like kids everywhere from San Francisco to Sydney, Reed and friends reacted to rock's simplicity by attempting to reproduce it. They were more successful than most. Though the British music industry was still chained firmly under the control of four major labels, New York was a magical haven of independent entrepreneurs. Vocal groups literally sprang up on street corners, hassled for gigs at dances or clubs, waited in line outside the offices of local record companies. Hundreds of "typical teenage hoodlum bands", as Reed described his own outfit, won a brief stab at stardom, via a quickshot recording session and a thousand or so copies of their first '45. Reed's band was called The Shades; to single them out from the rest, they wore sunglasses and sequins. Reed's nasal baritone excluded him from the vocal front-line, but already he was writing songs on the guitar.

One of those primitive efforts, 'Leave Her For Me', duly appeared on one side of The Shades' first single - though the group became The Jades to avoid confusion with another local outfit of the same name. 'Leave Her For Me' ended up on the flipside of the record; it was the altogether more commercial 'So Blue', co-written by Lou and another member of the group, Phil Harris, which was scheduled for media attention. That song boasted typically inane teen lyrics, carried by the greasy vocals of the group; a prominent saxophone was their most startling innovation, behind which Reed played irrelevant guitar runs up and down the scale in a vain effort to seize the limelight.

Reed's own song shared the familiar C-Am-F-G structure of the era's vocal group hits, and The Jades' performance was as overdramatic as you'd expect from a band who knew this might be their only visit to a recording studio. The lyrics were slightly less predictable, however, already carrying the ironic tone that would become a Reed trademark. The opening lines, "Take away the oceans/Take away the seas", were conventional enough; but Reed continued with a lengthy litany of other objects which needed to be taken away, among them the sunshine and the rosebuds, the relevance of which wasn't apparently obvious. The monologue at the centre of the song - in its way as crass as Reed's parody of the genre on 'I Found A Reason' thirteen years later - gave the game away: "I lose all my judgement/I lose all my regard/To think only of nature/Seems so very hard". That regard/hard rhyme is appalling, of course, but the fact that 'regard' and 'nature' figure in consecutive lines suggests that Reed wasn't the ideal doo-wop composer; why, the boy was almost literate.

The Jades' single was issued on the Time label; unlike most of its competitors, it was then picked up by the major label Dot Records, who substituted another song, 'Belinda', for 'So Blue'. The single failed to break through, however, and Dot showed no further interest in the band. It was a disillusioning experience for a teenager, and Reed's stay with The Jades seems to have ended soon afterwards, though various line-ups continued to make records for ever smaller labels through to the early Sixties.

Doo wop - that blending of Inkspots harmonies and blues feel that dominated vocal group music in the late Fifties and early Sixties - was the authentic folk music of the New York underclasses. Its creators were, in that most patronising of words, 'ethnic' - either blacks, Puerto Rican Spanish, or Italian. Though the most thrilling doo wop records were mostly black, white working-class punks had a role model in Dion DiMucci - lead singer of The Belmonts, owner of one of rock's trademark voices, future heroin addict, and eventual star of a career resurrection that led him from religious revivalism back to the rock'n'roll which gave him his start. When Lou Reed ended up guesting on Dion's 1989 comeback record, the company used his quotes for their press ads: "We came from the same streets," Reed reminisced. "We probably threw rocks at each other's gangs." Well, perhaps, though gang warfare was more common on the streets of Brooklyn than in stolidly middle-class Freeport.

But there was still the radio, and in the mid-Fifties New York boasted a larger selection of stations and styles than any city in the world. Not only did Reed revel in the doo wop of The Diablos, The Jesters, The Solitaires and The Paragons; also crackling over the air came the rockabilly records made by poor 'white trash' from Tennessee and Texas, savage, eerie music by sharecroppers like Carl Perkins, Billy Lee Riley and Warren Smith, full of the casual violence of a Saturday night hoedown and the cheap thrills of a new pair of shoes or a red hot gal in a tight dress. Then there was Chuck Berry, a literate black man offering sly asides about white teenage life; Bo Diddley, boasting that he had brought the rhythms of the jungle to the inner city; Jerry Lee Lewis, licking his lips at any passing teenage girl.

New York airwaves also carried the sound of jazz - not just the free-flowing be-bop of Coltrane and Davis, and the jagged chordings of Thelonious Monk, but the downright weird, sometimes atonal improvisations of Ornette Coleman, Don Cherry and Archie Shepp. Reed was entranced by the simplicity of the three-chord rock song, the fact that such a predictable format could house so many variations and hooks; but the sea of possibilities suggested by free-form jazz was never far from his mind.

Lou's parents reacted with predictable confusion to their son's craving for music; all over the Western world, the birth of rock and roll was greeted with suspicion and scorn. They had other plans for their eldest child. "My parents were self-made millionaires," Reed explained in 1976. "On paper they were very rich. I know what it's like to have money. They would love me to take over their companies. It's tax law - it all has to do with numbers. If United Steel is your client you can save them millions."

As Reed endured adolescence, the dark shadow of his pre-mapped future loomed in the distance. So did the more complex nature of his sexuality. As he explained to Stephen Demorest in 1979, the recognition of his attraction towards his own sex came early, and so did the immediate attempts at subterfuge: "I resent it. It was a very big drag. From age twelve on I could have been having a ball and not even thought about this shit. What a waste of time. If the forbidden thing is love, then you spend most of your time playing with hate. Who needs that? I feel I was gypped."

In the late Fifties, there were no role models for young homosexuals, no stereotypes beyond the limp-wristed faggotry that was the target of every would-be football jock. In a decade when middle-class America had happily accepted Senator Joe McCarthy's claim that their country was swarming with hidden subversives, there was not likely to be much sympathy for anyone who stepped out of line. Hence the derogation of rock and roll as "nigger music", the naming of any teenager with an attitude as a "hoodlum", and the belief that every young man who saw other young men in his wet dreams needed psychiatric help.

In a poorer family, Reed might have had his homosexuality beaten out of him; that would no doubt have aroused sexual difficulties of its own. In Freeport, Long Island, they called in the professionals. Three times a week, the 17-year-old Reed received electro-shock therapy: "They put the thing down your throat so you don't swallow your tongue, and they put electrodes on your head. That's what was recommended in Rockland County then to discourage homosexual feelings. The effect is that you lose your memory and become a vegetable. I wrote 'Kill Your Sons' on 'Sally Can't Dance' about that. You can't read a book because you get to page 17 and have to go right back to page one again."

Though he didn't feel able to record the song until 1973, by which time it was simply another brick in his self-built image as a reservoir of extreme experiences, Reed actually wrote it nearly a decade earlier. John Cale remembers it being around when they formed The Velvet Underground, though never for public consumption. As released on 'Sally Can't Dance', the song broadened to take a potshot at his sister's suburban lifestyle, and to show off Reed's knowledge of tranquillisers and medication. But the original verse said it straight: "All your two-bit psychiatrists are giving you electric shocks/They say they let you live at home with mom and dad instead of in a hospital/Don't you know they're gonna kill your sons/Until they run away".

The humiliation of electro-shock therapy merely solidified Reed's distance from his family; the vitriol he employed for the next two decades when discussing his upbringing testifies to the trauma he endured. If quack psychology sees circumcision as an immediate association between sexuality and physical pain, then what would it have to say about a process whereby homosexuality is 'cured' through the application of electric current? Whatever the effect on Reed's psyche, the mental estrangement between father and son led Lou to search for leadership and guidance in a successive of patriarchal figures.

His education slightly delayed by the turmoil of his late teens, Reed did eventually run - not out on the road, like Jack Kerouac, but upstate to Syracuse University, where he arrived in the fall of 1961 ready to commence a Bachelor of Arts degree in English Literature and Philosophy.

The Germans call it *Bildungsroman* - the type of novel which describes a young man's (always a man's) voyage from the security of childhood into the ambiguous freedom of the adult world. In the classic form, the youth travels from a small village or town, caught in the innocence of a bygone age, to a city, where he discovers sophistication, in all its many disguises. Global media have robbed this journey of some of its ability to surprise, and the closest modern equivalent for the Western teenager is the experience of leaving home for the first time and going to college.

For Lou Reed, the pilgrimage took him merely two hundred miles from Long Island, North-West to the University of Syracuse, state capital of New York. In the true tradition of the genre, he left home with an ill-focused sense of anger; when he returned to live in Freeport more than three years later he had discovered a way to deal with his sexuality, a means of expressing his emotions in verse, a musical collaborator, and his first artistic father figure.

Reed's studies in philosophy took him from the Greeks to the French existentialists, via the tortuous dialectics of Hegel and the fear and loathing of Kierkegaard. Existentialism, with its live-for-the-moment idealism and dismissal of familiar gods, captured the imagination of Reed's entire generation; it would be facile to place too much emphasis on its influence. But by tearing down the tired beliefs of older generations, French existentialism gave a dual sense of the meaninglessness of existence, and the liberation and terror that knowledge brought - a mixed blessing reflected in the literature that swept the campuses in the late Fifties and early Sixties, the drama of Ionesco and his fellow absurdists, and the cool, reflective prose of Albert Camus, whose *Outsider* established the mood of the era.

Lou's literary courses took him from Latin poetry to the American novel, via Shakespeare, Dostoevsky and T. S. Eliot. More importantly, it introduced him to the writer who was to influence his entire career more than any other: the 48-year-old poet, author and critic whose life was a monument to shattered expectations, Delmore Schwartz.

"Delmore Schwartz was the unhappiest man who I ever met in my life, and the smartest - till I met Andy Warhol. He didn't use curse words until he was thirty. His mother wouldn't allow him. His worst fears were realised when he died and they put him in a plot next to her. Once, drunk in a Syracuse bar, he said, 'If you sell out, Lou, I'm gonna get ya.' I hadn't thought about doing anything, let alone selling out. Two years later, he was gone. I'm just delighted I got to know him. It would have been tragic not to have met him. But things have occurred where Delmore's words float right across. Very few people do it to you. He was one." (Lou Reed, 1978)

In one of his last 'official' portraits, Delmore Schwartz was photographed on a park bench in Greenwich Village. His jacket, buttoned too tight around his expanding waist, matches the tension of his pose - pretending nonchalance, Schwartz looks like a man awaiting the call to the electric chair. His eyes shift off to the right, anticipating trouble; the cast of his face suggests a man who has grown to expect defeat.

By 1962, when he took up his final post as a lecturer in the Creative Writing faculty at Syracuse, defeat had become a way of life for Delmore Schwartz. The publication of his first book, *In Dreams Begin Responsibilities*, persuaded critic Allen Tait to greet his work as "the only genuine innovation we've had since Pound and Eliot". In his mid-twenties, Schwartz had the literary world at his feet. Over the next decade, through a mixture of self-obsession and sheer obstinacy, he ruined his literary career, and set himself on the tortuous road to decline and Syracuse University.

His adulthood began in disappointment. His father died when he was in his teens, and Delmore had been led to believe he would inherit a fortune. The estate proved minuscule, and what little remained was slowly frittered away as Delmore pursued a vain course through the courts of the land in hope of financial salvation. His disastrous relationship with his mother, who had no time for Delmore or his literary ambitions, seems in classic Freudian fashion to have fated his many affairs with women. When his first wife left him in the early Forties, Delmore suspected a conspiracy: gradually, his paranoia created a giant cabal of whispering voices, which stretched from Governor Rockefeller of New York to John F. Kennedy and the Pope - plus, of course, all the critics and reviewers who greeted each new book of poems or stories with mounting disapproval.

From the start, Delmore Schwartz wrote about himself - expected of poets, frowned upon in fiction writers, especially when Delmore turned up in every story so thinly disguised. In tale after tale, he replayed the episodes of his past in hope of discovering a happy ending; then, as the past became too painful a subject, he used his work as a means of experimenting with the future, imagining what might happen if he pursued a particular course of action.

Completely absorbed in the fascinating details of his own life, Schwartz devoted years to an autobiographical poem called - like God's history of the creation of the world - *Genesis*. As the poem progressed, it began to ramble. From 1942, he started to drink to excess; then he added amphetamines to the cocktail, paying the familiar price by running from hyperactivity and compulsive behaviour to hideous bouts of fatigue. In 1952, he was treated as a speed addict; his condition led him through violent flurries of temper for a further five years until he was eventually hospitalised in 1957, suffering from what was gently diagnosed as "acute brain syndrome".

Because of his youthful brilliance, the sparkling charm of his conversation, and his pathetic fall from grace, Schwartz could always find luminaries on the literary scene willing to recommend him for lectureships. So it was in 1962 that novelist Saul Bellow and poet Robert Lowell combined to win him the post at Syracuse - where Delmore succeeded in being arrested within 48 hours for extreme drunkenness, and was beaten by local police when he refused to come quietly. The man who began to teach Lou Reed in the autumn of 1962 was no longer a creative writer, and his interest in his fellow authors often stretched more to their sexual habits than their work. But he could still command a room with his talk. Schwartz was increasingly erratic in the classroom, but off campus, at the Orange Bar - "the University of the bar", as Reed put it two decades later - he gathered a score of disciples around him, capivating them with his intimate knowledge of T. S. Eliot's bedtime habits, the genius of James Joyce, and his own sorry tale of lost inheritances and wives. As his biographer James Atlas also revealed, Schwartz's fantasies even stretched to a bizarre account of Queen Elizabeth II's exhibition of her knowledge of oral sex on the person of Danny Kaye - or, in less prurient mood, to the latest diabolic tricks performed by Nelson Rockefeller and his evil conspirators.

A Jew who hated to be thought Jewish, a Brooklynite who had turned to writing to escape from the New York suburbs, a poetic genius who had dampened his talents with alcohol and pills, a writer who combined philosophic flights with the voice of the city streets - Delmore Schwartz made an ideal role model for the young Lou Reed. He introduced him to James Joyce's *Ulysses* and Dostoevsky's *The Brothers Karamazov;* gave him signed copies of his own books of verse, which remain Reed's proudest possessions; taught him, like the naturalist writers that Lou loved, that a man's character was determined by the whims of fate and the crush of irresistible outside forces; even guided the young man's early attempts at poetic composition, as Ezra Pound had watched over T. S. Eliot's creation of *The Waste Land,* and Allen Ginsberg had edited the cascading pages of William Burroughs' *The Naked Lunch* into something approaching sense. Reed was one of a number of students who put forward poetry for a student anthology; Schwartz proudly edited the results, and even contributed an introduction.

In an essay titled *The Vocation Of The Poet In The Modern World,* Delmore composed his own requiem mass: "In the unpredictable and fearful future that awaits civilisation, the poet must be prepared to be alienated and indestructible - indestructible as a poet until he is destroyed as a human being." That was what he meant when he said "selling out"; though this was a grim message to a young writer, it must have given Reed a sense of the responsibility, power and awesome risk of digging poetry out of his own soul. *In Dreams Begin Responsibilities*, announced the title of his most famous short story - one which Reed later described as "one of my favourite pieces of writing of all time". Schwartz explained the nature of his dreams, and through his own savage journey into darkness he illustrated the full implications of responsibility. Emotionally estranged from his own father, Reed could do nothing but follow.

The concerns of Schwartz's work, and its means of expression, occur again and again in Lou Reed's own writing. The poet showed Lou how to write about himself; how to turn the rambling of native American speech into the concise rhythms of poetry; and how to use words "to verbalise the Thing... To seek the theme which every story shows", as Delmore described his methods in the poem *Examination Of Profession.*

But the final years of Delmore Schwartz's life also offered Reed an example to forget. Early in 1963, he spent several months in a sanatorium after he'd harassed public figures in New York about Rockefeller's conspiracy to destroy him. By June, he'd returned to Syracuse, but on campus he devoted more energies to chasing college secretaries than to teaching students. President Kennedy's death in November reduced him to a restless soul in torment; thereafter, he ignored his educational duties, and spent his hours in the Orange Bar. By dint of his literary reputation, he hung on at the university until January 1966, when he moved to New York - taking up residency at the Hotel Dixie in the faded glamour of Times Square. There Lou Reed, by now the leader of The Velvet Underground, prime exponents of what Delmore called "catgut music", paid a social call on his college mentor - only to be turned away at the door, Schwartz accusing Reed of being an agent for the CIA, yet one more strand in the universal conspiracy.

Six months later, at the Hotel Columbia on 46th and 6th, Schwartz became involved in a shouting match with a neighbour in the small hours of the morning. He then returned to his room to drag out his sack of rubbish, shuffled into the hall, and called the elevator. While it ascended, Schwartz suffered a major heart attack. His neighbours interpreted the groans as evidence of a burglary, and kept their doors bolted. By the time the ambulance arrived, Delmore was dead. His body lay unclaimed and unrecognised in the mortuary for two days. Eventually his family were tracked down, and Delmore was removed to the aptly named Schwartz Funeral Home in Greenwich Village, where he lay in state on the day of his funeral.

On that day in July 1966, Gerard Malanga accompanied Lou Reed to the viewing, and the memorial service. Afterwards, Reed sat in one of the two cars that followed the hearse to Cedar Park Cemetery in Westwood, New Jersey; and there master and disciple parted company - for the time being.

"I didn't care for the academic life at all. That's not to put it down - some people love it. But I didn't." (Lou Reed, 1982)

Delmore Schwartz hated "faggots"; he automatically suspected those he disliked of homosexual leanings. Lou Reed, meanwhile, found that Syracuse University gave him the opportunity to work through the ambiguous nature of his sexual feelings. Having survived electro-shock therapy on Long Island, he was not likely to be free of guilt when it came to manifesting his attraction towards his own sex. But, by his own account, at the age of nineteen he was able to carry out his first gay love affair: "It was just the most amazing experience. It was never consummated. I felt very bad about it because I had a girlfriend and I was always going out on the side - and subterfuge is not my hard-on. I couldn't figure out what was wrong. I wanted to fix it up and make it OK. I figured if I sat around and thought about it I could straighten it out."

In the same 1979 interview, Reed described the pain of "trying to make yourself feel something towards women when you can't". There's no sign that he 'came out' at college, though: even in the supposedly more liberal atmosphere of the Kennedy presidency, homosexuality was treated as a disease. It would be two years or more before he entered a milieu where expression of sexual needs was not only tolerated but demanded.

"Faggots" would also not have been welcomed in ROTC - mock-military cadet training into which Reed was dragooned as a normal part of his progress towards a Syracuse degree. He later claimed that this episode ended when he was busted from the cadets for threatening a superior officer with a revolver; that may have been youthful exaggeration, as there are more subtle ways of winning freedom from the cadet corps that don't involve the intervention of the State Police.

Despite his run-ins with the forces of law and order, and his distrust of the academic lifestyle, Reed eventually graduated from Syracuse with honours; his later insistence that he was sent down "well before graduation" was merely part of building a suitable rock'n'roll image. His education in the liberal arts set him up for a career in teaching, management or administration; but it was a younger profession which had already put in its claim for his future.

FOUR

REED'S EDUCATION AT SYRACUSE WASN'T entirely literary - or sexual. His Gretsch guitar accompanied him to campus; blaring out deafening chord patterns one afternoon while the college cadets drilled beneath his open window, Lou attracted the attention of a fellow literature student, Sterling Morrison, who recognised a kindred spirit.

Morrison, nearly six months younger than Lou, had been sent down from Illinois University for skipping ROTC training; he was staying at Syracuse with his schoolfriend, Jim Tucker, before beginning a course at City College in New York. He shared with Reed a middle-class Long Island upbringing, and a love for greasy rock'n'roll - a pantheon that ran the predictable course from rockabilly through R&B to the urban blues of Jimmy Reed. And they were both electric guitar players in an era when student musicians were supposed to carry chunky wool sweaters, a sheaf of traditional songs and an acoustic guitar.

Even Reed couldn't escape the sweaters: contemporary photos show him fronting a five-piece band, playing simple inversions of an E chord on his Country Gentleman, shirt collar tucked neatly beneath his pullover, hair cropped up the side and back, with just the hint of a side-burn hanging cheekily round his ear, and a thick tuft flopped across his forehead. His face is a study of quiet satisfaction; his mouth shows the vaguest hint of a proud smirk, the look of a 21-year-old who knows he is doing what he wants, and is quite aware that he is pissing other people off. A sax-player, dozy behind shades, waits for his cue on Reed's left; to his right, an earnest bass-player lets his tongue slip carelessly out of his mouth. This could have been L.A. (Lewis Allan) and The Eldorados, or Pasha and The Prophets; the leader was always Lou Reed, and more often than not Sterling Morrison was his sidekick. Morrison recalled in 1980: "Lou and I had some of the shittiest bands that ever *were*. They were shitty because we were playing authentic rock'n'roll. Lou and I came from the identical environment of Long Island rock'n'roll bars, where you can drink anything at 18, and everybody had phony proof of their age at 16."

By '63 and '64, Reed was a college fixture - leader of bands with a constantly updated repertoire of three-chord hits, churning out covers by The Kingsmen, Paul Revere and The Raiders, The Premiers, plus any-thing from New York with a classic doo wop feel and a street attitude. Sharing the same bands and songs were other musicians - Garland Jeffreys, a Reed acolyte a year younger than Lou, Nelson Slater, who reappears later in our story, and Felix Cavaliere, the future leader of The Young Rascals. While the college towns of New York and Boston pro-duced educated folksingers, Syracuse schooled a generation of American punk-rockers, each ready to mix the rhythmic pulse of Motown and Chess with the sly intelligence of the street-wise. Like Lou, some of them were able to live out their dreams on record: Cavaliere and fellow Syracuse undergraduate Mike Esposito, eventually a member of The Blues Project, issued a single called 'Saved'/'The Syracuse' on the Jag label around 1963; Lou may have been involved as a guitarist or produc-er. Another local musician, Peter Stampfel, began to put together an early line-up of The Holy Modal Rounders, whose off-the-wall merging of rock, folk, jug band and blues was to establish them as one of the pio-neers of the Greenwich Village rock scene around the same time that The Velvet Underground began their sonic adventures on St. Mark's Place. Lou himself copyrighted a song called 'Your Love' in March 1962, sug-gesting that he might have committed one of his college bands to vinyl.

Rock'n'roll wasn't Lou Reed's only musical playground at Syracuse. Given the chance to host a regular show on college radio, he named it 'Excursion On A Wobbly Rail' after a rambling piece of jazz improvisa-tion by Cecil Taylor. He also gave Ornette Coleman some rare airplay - "I used to run around the Village following Ornette Coleman wherever he played", he boasted in the late 1970s, when his interest in avant-garde jazz led him to form a touring band with Don Cherry. But mostly his radio show reflected his vintage loves - Sun rock'n'roll, New York doo wop, the familiar strength of three or four chords used as the basis for heartfelt expressions of love, anger and despair.

Even after graduation, Reed lived a double-life, caught between the sweaty, illicit stench of bars and rehearsal rooms, and the insidious pull of his voyage through literature and philosophy. Like many students, he viewed the end of his degree course as a crisis; outside was the real world, and the perennial promise of a career in legal accountancy. For the moment, Reed determined to remain a student. To that end, he signed up for post-graduate journalism studies; then, when that didn't work out, he switched to drama classes. "As an actor, I couldn't cut it - I couldn't cut the mustard, as they say," Reed recalled a decade later. "But I was good as a director." For a young man reeling with words and ideas, recit-ing someone else's lines was always likely to be a stultifying process. Directing, however, left room for interpretation; it also entailed control.

Given a free choice of the world's great drama, Reed elected to pro-duce *The Car Cemetery* (or *The Automobile Graveyard*) by Fernando Arrabal. Only translated into English in 1962, the extended one-act play typified the Theatre of the Absurd which - under the leadership of Eugene Ionesco - dominated 1960s avant-garde drama. At its most extreme, absurd theatre presented everyday actions, twisted into the bizarre without motive. It lacked surrealism's cutting edge of surprise; in the absurd, the absurd was all you expected. Surrealism always hinted that the transposition of sense and meaning had a purpose: absurdists suggested that all action, all speech was equally ridiculous.

Arrabal's play centred around the Christ-like passion of a musician, betrayed by his accompanist to the secret police who stalk the junkyard and its barren landscape of crushed and mutilated automobile hulks. The messianic role of the artist must have appealed to the would-be rock and roll star - as must the backdrop of sexual cruelty and empty prostitution which Arrabal sketched as a wry comment on the pointlessness of human relations.

Reed's own absurdist drama took a surreal turn at this point, when he was asked "by the Tactical Police Force of the city which housed my large eastern university to leave town well before graduation because of various clandestine operations I was alleged to have been involved in", as Reed wrote in 1972. The timing of this request was actually several months after Reed had graduated; the nature of his clandestine operations was presumably narcotics. Lou probably did nothing worse than get caught with a joint: whatever, he found himself back at home in Long Island, with the offer of an accountant's chair still open, and - as he was no longer exempt by being a student - the prospect of being drafted into the American services in Vietnam suddenly rearing up before him.

The call-up in the Vietnam War concentrated on the poor, and the black poor in particular; as a ROTC cadet, even a failed one, with a middle-class background, Reed could have expected to be submitted for officer training rather than a private's uniform. The conflict had yet to arouse a militant opposition; the scale of America's involvement in a local dispute between the communists of North Vietnam and the military government of the country's southern sector was still hidden, as successive Presidents Kennedy and Johnson assured their people that the U.S. was not becoming enmired in the struggle, merely sending advisers, observers and cheerleaders on behalf of democracy in its war against the evil empires of Marxism. Many rock'n'rollers did their two years of Army training and returned to their music careers; most never left the States, spending 24 months as Reservists, drinking, dreaming of women and listening to the changing face of the rock radio stations.

For Reed, military life was not an appealing option after the intellectual sustenance and rock'n'roll indulgence of Syracuse. He began "lining up medical proof" - like the hepatitis which he claimed to have caught from "a mashed-in Negro whose features were in two sections (like a split-level house) named Jaw", who had initiated the young student into the world of illegal drugs. Reed hinted that the exchange of "bad blood" sparked the disease; a year later he wrote a song detailing the emotional roller-coaster of mainlining heroin.

As it turned out, the hepatitis proved unnecessary. "I was pronounced mentally unfit, and have a classification that means I'll only be called up if we go to war with China", Reed boasted in 1972. "I did it well, I was only in the interview for ten minutes." The mere mention of homosexual leanings might have terminated Reed's interview that swiftly; at a time when they had their pick of a generation, the U.S. Army had little need for prospective officers who might seduce their men into bed rather than battle.

"I was working as a songwriter for Pickwick. We just churned out songs, that's all. Never a hit song - what we were doing was churning out these ripoff albums. In other words, the album would say it featured four groups and it wouldn't really be four groups, it would just be various permutations of us, and they would sell them at supermarkets for 99 cents or a dollar. While I was doing that I was doing my own stuff and trying to get by, but the material I was doing, people wouldn't go near me with it at the time. I mean, we wrote 'Johnny Can't Surf No More' and 'Let The Wedding Bells Ring' and 'Hot Rod Song'." (Lou Reed, 1972)

Within weeks of avoiding the draft, literature and philosophy graduate Lou Reed found a job at Pickwick Records - a New York budget label which specialised in dubious compilations, smothering a couple of semi-hit songs in a barrage of unfamiliar dross, or offering up cynical imitations of contemporary music trends with titles that sounded vaguely like something you'd heard on the radio. Pickwick wasn't interested in careers, just turnover. You weren't building an audience for the future, just persuading a kid to pull a dollar from his pocket when the album was on display. This was rock'n'roll by numbers - a sobering reintroduction to the music business for a man whose only previous encounter with the industry had ended in shattered ideals. This time, ideals didn't come into it. The instructions were to create pastiches, and to create them quickly. Quantity, not quality, was the Pickwick byword; the production line mentality of the factory floor translated into the semblance of art.

The entire Pickwick episode - this parable of innocent talent let loose among the sharks and spiders of entrepreneurial capitalism - is so suitable a schooling for Lou Reed that it is tempting to believe he invented the entire escapade. But the proof is there, strewn across a batch of Pickwick productions thrown into the shops in late 1964 and early 1965. Working in teams of four, roped together so that no-one would fall out of line, Pickwick's writers struggled to reproduce the sounds of the charts without infringing on anyone's copyright. Lou survived the course for a matter of months - he started work in late October 1964 and was gone by February 1965. But working with regular partner Terry Phillips, and pseudonymous songwriters Jerry Vance (alias Jerry Pellegrino) and Jimmie Sims (Jim Smith), he cranked out a series of songs which Pickwick rushed into the stores under a bewildering number of names.

Reed wrote more tunes than he recorded; songs like 'The Wild Ones', 'Oh No Don't Do It', 'What About Me?', 'Baby You're The One', 'Say Goodbye Over The Phone' and 'Bad Guy' were all written during the marathon sessions in the final weeks of 1964. Quite possibly these tunes crept out on long-forgotten compilation albums; meanwhile, other songs definitely did appear, though he didn't get to play on them, like Robertha Williams' 'Tell Mama Not To Cry' and 'Maybe Tomorrow', Ronnie Dickerson's 'Love Can Make You Cry', and Jeannie Larimore's 'Johnny Won't Surf No More'.

The last of these songs surfaced on an album entitled 'Soundsville' - recorded at Pickwick's tiny Coney Island studios on a pair of two-track recorders, in (so the company claimed) 'Stereo-Spectrum'. The album's gimmick was that it featured the sounds of today - the sounds of the West Coast, of Liverpool, of Nashville, of Hot Rod, even the sounds of the Campus (the delightful 'It's Hard To Be A Girl In A World Full Of Men').

Each song was credited to a different artist - or, as it transpired, a different combination of Pickwick staffers. And under the guise of The Roughnecks and The Beachnuts, Lou Reed's voice was heard on record for the first time. The Roughnecks offered the sounds of England - 'You're Driving Me Insane', to be exact, which opened with an unsettlingly tuneless buzz of guitars and then applied the unschooled, scratchy sound of The Kinks to some riffs refined from Chuck Berry. And over the dense, muddy instrumental came that voice - half-spoken, half-forced, droning out words that were supported by the eerie abandon of a rabble of partygoers in the background: "The way you rattle your brain/You know you're driving me insane".

For the sounds of Hot Rod, The Beachnuts concocted 'I've Got A Tiger In My Tank' - a petrol company's slogan turned into a cunning pastiche of Jan and Dean's 'Surf City', complete with soaring falsetto and Brian Wilson chord changes. Lou kept his voice out of the mix here, though his rhythm guitar churned faithfully in the background. But on The Beachnuts' other contribution, 'Cycle Annie', he reasserted himself - intoning a seedy tale of "a real tough cycle" who "just don't come any meaner". Reed chuckled to himself in excitement, before leading the primitive rhythm section through a convenient key change for the guitar solo, which mixed the sonic byplay of the surf sound with the first hints of his VU atonality. Filled with bizarre characters and a playful love of three-chord rock'n'roll, 'Cycle Annie' would have fitted just as well on 'White Light/White Heat'.

Pickwick left 'Soundsville' to sell itself to record buyers too naïve to realise that the sound of England might not necessarily have been made by Englishmen. 1964 had been dominated by the so-called British Invasion, whereby a generation of English teenagers produced their own exuberant facsimile of American rock and R&B, and sold it as an original sound to a country too effete to listen to the real thing. Reed and his friends - the ones who'd kept listening to the rock'n'roll and blues stations, who knew that American music hadn't died with Buddy Holly - resented the intrusion: "The Beatles were innocent of the world and its wicked ways," Lou recalled in 1972, "while I no longer possessed this pristine view. I, after all, had had jaundice."

Beneath the media hype of all things British, American rock'n'roll continued to throw up a succession of dance crazes and earthy guitar songs in 1964. During one particularly frenzied Pickwick session, Reed and friends recorded 'The Ostrich' - a blatant parody of the ever-more-ridiculous dance routines foisted onto the nation's youth by TV shows like *Shindig* and *American Bandstand*. With instructions that demanded you "put your head upside your knees" and then step on it, 'The Ostrich' was an unlikely candidate for small-screen immortality. Nonetheless, Pickwick was sufficiently impressed by Reed's concoction to issue it as one of their rare excursions into the singles market - under the name of The Primitives, ironically shared with an equally uncompromising set of beatsters in England.

Listen to the record, and primitive is the only name that springs to mind, from the incessant bass drum thump to the piercing siren guitars, the demented whoop of the backing vocalists to the amphetamine stutter of Reed's vocal. It's like an invitation to partake in some dark, primaeval ritual, whose spirituality has been subverted by the insouciance and all-knowing irreverence of its leader.'Sneaky Pete', on the other side of the single, shared the same pre-musical feel - heightened by a lack of production awareness which buried Reed's two-tone guitar solo deep in the mix. Lou again took centre-stage - spouting the clichés of teenage drama as if the words were simply a gesture whereby he could express his delirium.

Remarkably, someone in the *American Bandstand* production team reckoned this was the stuff of the moment, and requested The Primitives' presence at a forthcoming TV taping. Pickwick was not set up to produce live performers; their confidence-tricks all took place on vinyl. But the opportunity was too rare to refuse. So Lou Reed and Terry Phillips set about completing a band - hitting upon a couple of musicians whom Terry met at a New York party, Tony Conrad and a Welshman named John Cale.

In this century, the avant-garde has devoted itself to the search for meaning in an increasingly complex world, and to stretching the boundaries within which that search can be carried out. 'Avant-garde' was originally a military term - the French equivalent to 'vanguard' - denoting those crack troops sent into the initial stages of the battle to create an opening for the mass forces to follow. The avant-garde's dilemma is that their advances all too often alienate the public. It's a risk which comes with the territory - the constant awareness that your experiments will be dismissed as irrelevant, and that only the passage of decades will prove whether you, or the sceptical masses, were right.

The sense that conventional ways of viewing the world are unequal to the task is what sparks the need to approach the problem from obtuse angles. In literature, for example, modernist authors like James Joyce and Virginia Woolf studied the findings of the early psychoanalysts, and came to realise that the objective, all-seeing vision of the nineteenth century novelist didn't match their own experience of life's tangled, subjective nature. In art, after the Impressionists had stressed the importance of personal interpretation of artistic vision, Picasso and his school dissected the physical world and emerged with a method of painting which reduced bodies and shapes to a collection of geometric forms. Exploding the traditional way of painting a face, Picasso achieved some insight into man's divided personality by reflecting that confusion in his art.

In music, the twentieth century began with a feeling that the scales and notes of Western composers were too restricting - that there was a deeper, more personal music to be found by breaking down the barriers of convention. Schoenberg threw away the comfortable melodic structures of previous classical composers, and proposed an unsettling twelve-tone scale as the basis for his work. The musical vanguard drew breaths of relief from his discovery that they could avoid the over-familiar melodic shifts of past centuries. Gradually, they settled into a free-for-all approach, in which every sound, no matter how it was produced, was equally valid within a composition. Dissonant noises, the clanking of machinery, the buzz of conversation - all these and more were incorporated into the symphonies of the new century.

The rapid growth in the science of electronics expanded the possibilities. Until the birth of the primitive gramophone in the final years of the last century, music was performed for an audience, and then lost in the realms of history. The fact that music could now be saved for posterity altered composers' perceptions. Electronic sound retrieval, on magnetic tape, revolutionised the process. As this century reached its mid-point, experimental composers like John Cage began to incorporate taped sound and music into their performances. The technology grew ever more versatile; often it was the composers, not the scientists, who were forcing the pace.

During the 1950s, Cage, the Greek composer Xenakis, the German Karl-Heinz Stockhausen and many more began to use the electronic process of tape recording not just as a means of transporting sound from one place to another, but as an instrument in itself. In the early Sixties, Terry Riley and Steve Reich (part of a generation of avant-garde composers born around the same time as Elvis Presley) pioneered the use of tape loops, creating an endless, repetitive landscape of sound over which they could either improvise, broadcast the ambient noises of the concert hall or studio, or else simply superimpose more tape loops.

The concept of repetition also inspired the American, LaMonte Young. His innovation was the single insistent sound - produced electronically or manually. Gathering around him a school of like-minded followers under the collective name of the Theatre Of Eternal Music, Young taped and performed lengthy musical pieces which either incorporated variations on a central drone, or else were made up of the drone itself, supported by visual accompaniment in the form of slides or lights produced by his wife Marian Zazeela. At his most conceptual, LaMonte Young belonged with the Fluxus group of musicians and artists flourishing in New York in the early Sixties, who reduced each work of art to a single, primal instruction - "bleed", for instance, or "die". His 'Composition 1960 No. 7', for instance, consisted of a single note and its harmonic fifth, with the instruction: "to be held for a long time". But Young understood the vital ingredient of performance, and encouraged his acolytes to express their emotions through a violent, often destructive attitude towards their instruments.

Into this fertile atmosphere came John Cale, a classically trained musician, born a miner's son in South Wales in 1940. At school, he learned to play the viola; after three years at college in London, he was awarded a Bernstein Fellowship to study music under Xenakis at Tanglewood, one of America's most prestigious music colleges. He seems to have spent little time there; within weeks he was in New York. There he fell under the spell of John Cage and his peers, taking part in a marathon performance of Cage's 'Variations' which won the attention of the *New York Times,* and becoming a performing member of LaMonte Young's Dream House ensemble.

Cale lived in a Manhattan apartment with another of Young's disciples, Tony Conrad - who owned an impressive collection of rock'n'roll records. The distance between Young's experimental use of sound and the playful energy of rock music caught Cale's fancy; as yet, though, there was no crossover point between popular music and the tightrope walks of the avant-garde.

John Cale was about to provide one. At a party, he and Conrad were introduced to Terry Phillips, who - hearing that they were musicians - announced that he was looking for a bassist, guitarist and drummer to complete a band he was putting together. Conrad suggested Walter DeMaria as a percussionist, and somehow the trio of classical students found themselves at Pickwick's Coney Island hit-faking factory. Waiting for them was the 22-year-old Lou Reed.

Reed demonstrated the simplicity of performing 'The Ostrich', using a droning open tuning - all six notes tuned to B, according to Cale - that struck immediate bells with the avant-garders. Lou, Cale, DeMaria and Conrad duly became The Primitives for a month - fulfilling the booking on *American Bandstand,* playing gigs up and down the East Coast at schools and shopping malls, even turning up in a piece in *Vogue* about this weird new dance craze that might just sweep the nation.

It didn't. Cale and Reed maintained the Pickwick connection long enough to write 'Why Don't You Smile' - a pastiche of The Kingsmen's 'Louie Louie' which was quickly recorded by The All Night Workers with a droning guitar accompaniment that suggested one or more of The Primitives had been on hand for the session. Then Reed left, the wiser for three months of intensive work in the studio, which left him with a speedy, even slapdash attitude towards recording that survived into The Velvet Underground.

Cale would have regarded The Primitives' episode as nothing more than a crazy adventure had he not heard Lou Reed's other songs. He initially rejected Reed's acoustic renditions of his own material - Cale had no truck with the Greenwich Village folk scene. But the words hit home.

At Pickwick, Reed had done little more than tweak the prevailing pop conventions. His latest work was no more related to the banalities of the pop charts than Cale's experiments into the avant-garde. Together, they were able to bridge the two - and to find, perhaps more by accident than design, the perfect setting for Reed's uncompromising, lyrical visions of New York life.

"I did go down Lexington - I did all the stuff then."
(Lou Reed, 1974)

"Rock fans have taken heroin thinking Lou took heroin, forgetting that the character in the song wasn't necessarily Lou Reed."
(Sterling Morrison, 1980)

'Heroin' was the first real Lou Reed song that John Cale heard. Junk had long been associated with the music industry; the jazz scene was rife with musicians who could only reproduce the exultation of their live performances by slipping a needle into their veins and letting the heroin slide into their systems. Few jazz songs flirted with the reality of addiction, though alcoholism was a more common subject. But within the blues and folk traditions, 'Cocaine' was a standard song; Bob Dylan was performing it in New York as early as 1962.

What distinguished Reed's song was the standpoint of its narrator. Previous drug songs either adopted a matter-of-fact tone - I use cocaine, what about it? - or else revelled in the pain and stigma of public knowledge. Reed's 'Heroin' was altogether more ambiguous. Over the simplest of rock and roll changes, from E major to A major, Lou set out the precarious existence of the junkie. "Heroin will be the death of me" struck the conventional pose, the knowledge that temporary thrills would soon be eclipsed. "I have made the big decision/I'm gonna try to nullify my life," Reed wrote, immediately undermining that knowledge.

It's difficult to separate the song, as words on the page, from the drama of its original existence as a Velvet Underground recording. On record, the music pounds frantically as the drug takes hold; on the page, the words resound more subtly in the mind. 'Heroin' is quite explicit, though, about the attractions of addiction - the sense of self-importance it brings, the sheer exultation of feeling the orgasmic rush spread through the body, making you feel "just like Jesus' son". "When the smack begins to flow/I really don't care any more," Reed sang, and in those words he sabotaged society's cosy taboo about drug use, just as William Burroughs had painted a heavenly nightmare in *The Naked Lunch*. Reed's lyrics welcomed the sacrifice of awareness, the chance to ignore the outside world and concentrate on the purely selfish shot of pleasure, regardless of the consequences. In its original form, the song at least began with a plea of diminished responsibility: "I don't know just where I'm going". In performance, Reed omitted the negative, and turned his trip into a willing descent into hell.

After 'Heroin', Reed must have played Cale 'I'm Waiting For The

Man', in which his junkie hero took the subway uptown to the centre of Harlem and risked the unwelcome attentions of the local inhabitants to meet his appointment with his dealer. Reed serves up the compulsion of the addict, and captures the sordid details of the encounter with a cameraman's eye - the way the dealer arrives late, offers a "sweet taste" of first-grade heroin and then passes over the required package, which may be cut from entirely different stock. And in the final verse, Reed swings the camera around, moving the scene forward - or back: the sequence is repeated every day - to the junkie's home, where he enjoys the brief satisfaction of the heroin rush and tries to ignore the craving that will drag him uptown tomorrow and every day thereafter.

In literature and film - remember *The Man With The Golden Arm* - these concerns were familiar by 1965. In rock, where the only hint of drug use came in Bob Dylan's sudden burst of amphetamine imagery that year, they shattered the conventions. Small wonder that Pickwick refused to record them, even on the trashiest of their cash-ins.

Cale was fascinated, however, both by the songs and the cocky, literate kid who had penned them. In return, he offered Reed the kudos of the avant-garde, and intellectual justification for the atonal drone which Lou had been working towards on his records at Pickwick. When The Primitives gave up the ghost, Cale and Reed continued to work together. Reed's college friend Sterling Morrison wandered conveniently back into his life at this point, and was dragooned into service - himself entranced by the possibilities of creating music that reduced the simple structures of rock'n'roll to a one-note tone. To provide the essential ingredient of rhythm, Cale enticed yet another of LaMonte Young's sidekicks: Angus Maclise, who bore a startling similarity to the mature Leon Trotsky, and had the same uncompromising attitude to art and life. Cale and friends introduced Reed to Young, and Lou became an enthusiastic disciple in his own right. "He was my teacher," he told performance artist Ondine, who remembered Young indoctrinating Reed's band for several months in the importance of atonality and repetition.

Their experiments were given practical purpose in the summer of 1965. While Lou Reed slowly assembled a collection of songs for the new band, Cale and Maclise arranged for the unit - sometimes known as The Warlocks (a name they unknowingly shared with the early Grateful Dead), sometimes more entertainingly, in view of 'Heroin', as The Falling Spikes - to provide soundtrack music for new work by the underground film-maker Piero Heliczer.

This commitment didn't usually involve recording; instead, the band accompanied screenings of silent shorts like The *Soap Opera*, grinding out cacophonous rhythmic guitar chords while lights flashed, slides were projected onto the wall, and a chorus of dancers whirled their limbs in apparent abandon. Unable, like most of the underground, to afford professional actors, Heliczer's films raided the local art community - Angus Maclise and LaMonte Young were perennial stars of his work. More pertinently, Heliczer shot a 16-minute silent film that summer called Venus In Furs - which he described obtusely as "a chess game under the bridge which becomes a Christmas party in Hell". The cast list included Angus Maclise, Lou Reed and John Cale, who together provided the soundtrack, in the form of Reed's own *Venus In Furs* and an instrumental rendition of 'Heroin'. CBS TV film cameras attended the filming, unwittingly capturing the first visual record of the formative Velvet Underground.

Inspired by LaMonte Young's mingling of noise and light, Heliczer's mixed-media presentations at the Cinematheque in Greenwich Village went under the title *Rites Of The Dream Weapon*. Ritual was the key: the constant thread of repetition in the music, the film and the lights produced a sense of the primaeval, of the dismemberment of societal conventions. Reed and his band were just a means to an end, part of a fiendish assault on the senses that was meant to strip away the manners of civilisation and reduce the audience to the status of laboratory animals, open to any suggestion the artist might concoct.

These performances allowed the band's classical and rock sensibilities to flow together; Reed, Cale and Morrison's blood brotherhood was sealed. But Angus Maclise sought a cleaner break from civilisation than the avant-garde could offer. A long-time adventurer into the occult, Maclise believed in the healing power of magic, and identified the transcendental spirit of the mystics of India as the solution to his dissatisfaction with urban life. In September 1965 he left New York for India; fourteen years later he died of malnutrition, having taken his ascetic vows to their logical conclusion.

Reed, Cale and Morrison wanted to remain in New York. With Maclise, they had already recorded a demo tape in the Ludlow Street loft which they shared for the rest of the year. Besides 'Heroin', they taped early versions of 'Venus In Furs', 'Black Angel's Death Song', 'Wrap Your Troubles In Dreams' and a song which Morrison later recalled as 'Never Get Emotionally Involved With Man, Woman, Beast Or Child'. Several copies of the tape were sent to England; none apparently survives today.

The new songs were every bit as extreme as 'Heroin' and 'Waiting For The Man' - more so, in fact. 'Wrap Your Troubles In Dreams' is slightly mysterious in origin: copyrighted as a Lou Reed composition in 1966, it was listed on Nico's début album the following year as a John Cale song. Either way, it aptly reflects the pair's determination to incorporate material from the literary underworld into the innocent playground of pop. The song begins as an idealistic wish-piece, only to turn into a horror movie as the blood seeps slowly into the white cloth of the opening verses. By its conclusion, the lyric is wading in excrement and confronting violent death - a stunning shift in mood which matched the flight from agony to ecstasy in 'Heroin'.

'Venus In Furs' was equally complex. Like Heliczer's film, it drew its title and its scenario from a notorious novel by Leopold von Sacher-Masoch, originally published in Germany in the early 1870s. Sacher-Masoch - whose name was borrowed many years later by the psychologist Krafft-Ebbing to describe the condition of enjoying pain - based his tale of compulsion and obsession on his personal experiences at the hands of Baroness Bogdanoff. Like his fictional protagonist, Severin, Sacher-Masoch gave himself entirely to the Baroness as a slave - utterly under her control, prepared at any time to accept the lash of the whip, administered in punishment or merely as a callous whim. In the novel, Severin humbles himself before his idol, Wanda, who dresses in furs whenever she chooses to exercise her totalitarian power. In return, she humiliates him, not merely by having him bound and flogged whenever she desires, but by instructing him to facilitate her own sexual liaisons with other men. Bound like husband and wife into this contract of control, Severin and Wanda grow into their roles of victim and savage dictator - until a beating from Wanda's lover shocks Severin into a recognition of his pathetic condition.

The novel is devoted to Severin's account of his torment, but only as told to, and therefore also told to us by, an outsider, who has his own dreams of a masterful woman who will manipulate his soul. Sacher-Masoch used the intervention of a voyeuristic narrator deliberately to cast doubt on the truthfulness of the tale. Is the book Severin's tale, or the narrator's fantasy about what Severin's tale might be? We are never told.

"I saw the book and just thought it would be a great idea for a song," Lou Reed explained in the early Seventies. "Now everybody thinks I invented masochism." After the twisted landscape of 'Wrap Your Troubles In Dreams', Reed's choice of raw material is intriguing enough. Equally fascinating is the way in which he deals with the subject. Reed shows us the whips, the boots, the relish with which Severin views the furs and the shiny leather; but the identity of the voice is unclear. At times, it is Severin speaking to Wanda, begging "Strike him mistress and cure his heart"; at others, Wanda commanding Severin to "Taste the whip". Reed asks us to identify with queen and minion, and allows us to share in the voyeuristic delight of choosing between them. 'Venus In Furs' is a cruel manipulation of fictional characters; and merely by watching we are as tainted as the controller of the whip, or the slave who begs to be shackled.

With its indecorous, vivid imagery, 'Venus In Furs' is far removed from the language of the street. Reed's writing was still divided between the poetic and the conversational, and 'Black Angel's Death Song' belonged to the first category. More than any other of his compositions, it offers direct homage to the influence of Delmore Schwartz, and before him to T. S. Eliot. The opening verses run with graphic, portentous snapshots of violence and destruction. But this is the work of a man more in love with the sound of words than their meaning, a poet unconstrained by the effort to communicate anything more than his own pleasure. Piling syllable upon syllable, Reed builds up an onomatopoeic wall of speech, revelling in his mastery over the language: "The rallyman's patter ran on through the dawn/Until we said so long to his skull-shrill yell/Shining brightly red-rimmed and red-lined with the time/Infused with the choice of the mind/On ice skates scraping chunks from the bells". It may be magnificent, but it is meant to blind the listener with sound, not capture an exact portrait in words. And at the end, Reed moves beyond language into what seems like a Buddhist chant, using the ultimate freedom from meaning as an exhibition of his own power.

Fronted by a poet who could paint shocking vignettes of squalid urban life, or fly off into a realm beyond words; boasting musicians equally at home with the three-chord purr of rock'n'roll and the thunderous drone of LaMonte Young's soundscapes; telling stories of sex, violence, obsession and terror; The Velvet Underground, though they had yet to adopt the name, were fully grown by the autumn of 1965. What they needed was a structure: a settled line-up, a name, a stage on which they could play out their experiments.

The name came first, when Tony Conrad picked up a battered copy of a paperback sex exposé called *The Velvet Underground* and brought it home. The line-up and the initial forum both came, indirectly, from *New York Post* critic Al Aronowitz. He managed a folk-rock band called The Myddle Class - in the aftermath of the Byrds, the 'y' was *de rigueur* - fronted by the husband of an early Lou Reed heroine, Carole King. Al offered the Velvets a support shot at an unlikely venue: Summit High School, Summit, New Jersey. To claim their $75, the band needed a percussionist - who emerged in the equally unlikely form of Maureen Tucker, sister of Lou and Sterling's college friend Jim.

Maureen recalled: "I can remember Lou coming to the house once when I was in 12th grade. Then Sterling went up to Syracuse to look around, he and Lou started playing, and that was kind of the beginning. The show came up at Summit High School and Angus Maclise was out, so they said, 'Let's get Tucker's sister, she likes to play drums'." Maureen worked as a computer operator; at night she would go home and play drums to her Bo Diddley records. The Velvets wanted her kit more than her; but she passed an afternoon audition with Lou, survived John Cale's initial aversion to playing with a female musician, and made it to the High School, where she laid her bass drum on its side and pounded it with a stick to achieve the African sound that Cale apparently wanted.

The date was November 12, 1965; The Velvet Underground had performed in public for the first time. Their repertoire was still restricted to a handful of Reed's songs, plus a selection of Chuck Berry covers, in deference both to Lou's personal tastes and Maureen's familiarity with Chicago R&B. Adapting to the new line-up, Reed and Cale soon discovered that they could each set off in different instrumental directions, confident that Morrison and Tucker would hold the song together. Gradually, the Velvets began to improvise, first within songs, then as separate pieces in their own right. 'Heroin' and 'Venus In Furs', Chuck's 'Roll Over Beethoven', and formless musical excursions without titles or scripts - it was this selection which the Velvets next offered to the patrons of the aptly titled Café Bizarre in the heart of the Village on West 3rd Street. There they were viewed first by Barbara Rubin and Gerard Malanga, then by their mentor, Andy Warhol.

"All the songs for the first Velvet Underground album were written before I ever met him. It's just that they happened to match his thing perfectly." (Lou Reed, 1976)

By 1965, Andy Warhol's 'thing' was being an entrepreneur. Bored with what he described as "repainting successful themes", he had abandoned his work as an artist the previous year, and devoted himself to gathering an entourage. Using them as puppets in his freakshow, he spiralled off into films, books, stage shows, happenings - all presented as Andy Warhol Productions, no matter how tenuous his involvement.

For Warhol, authenticity had never been a problem. Supporting himself as a commercial artist in the 1950s, he trademarked his work with a flourishing signature - drawn not by himself but by his mother. When he began to create 'serious' art, not that Warhol's art was ever entirely serious, he employed assistants. They began by preparing his materials, and ended by manufacturing Warhol's art themselves. Andy complained that his longest-serving disciple, Nathan Gluck, produced work which was more popular with clients and the public than his own. No matter: it was still Andy Warhol art - as personal a statement as films like *Andy Warhol's Bad* and *Andy Warhol's Frankenstein,* which were actually made by Paul Morrissey with Andy's vague knowledge and approval.

But a lack of authenticity was implicit in Warhol's philosophy of art. By the mid-Sixties he had become America's most famous visual artist, less for his graphic or portrait skills than for his enthusiasm in marketing his own genius. Warhol was known as the leader of Pop-Art, a genre he neither conceived nor introduced to the American scene. His achievement was to take a movement which had been propounded as an intellectual response to prevailing artistic trends, and to turn it into a frothy, cynical and utterly skilful piece of media manipulation.

Not that Warhol was a charlatan - far from it. Although his leisurely work-rate over the last two decades of his life suggested that he had created nothing more magnificent than himself, his early Pop-Art work, and his translation of his ideals into other fields, marked a definite progression. His triumph was to realise the potency of popular icons - anything from Marilyn Monroe to a Coke bottle, a car wreck to the bereaved Jackie Kennedy. Giving America back its everyday currency, and telling the country that he had created art, Warhol forced us to look again at the nature of the ordinary. In Andy's hands, anything might become important - anyone might become a superstar.

None of this would have been possible if Warhol had not first created a persona capable of carrying it off. In later years he picked bright young things to act out his fantasies. Before that, he chose himself. Snipping a final 'a' from his immigrant surname, Warhol transformed a proverbial ugly duckling - all bad skin and bald patches, ill at ease in company and gawkish to a fault - into a prototypical Sixties hero. When he elected to become a public being instead of an artist in 1963, he adopted a bright silver wig that was so fake everyone assumed it was his real hair. He heightened the oddity of his pale, almost translucent skin by wearing thick black shades and a leather jacket - the garb of a Brando or Dean and, after Andy, the image of the rock'n'roller as well.

At the same time, he submerged his own intelligence and enthusiasms, reinventing himself as a reflective surface against which others could shine. The new Warhol was inarticulate, stumbling through sentences laced with 'gosh' or 'gee', and attracting more attention through his curious silence than he had in the past when he spoke.

Looking back on the birth of the Factory scene from the ghost-ridden vantage of 1980, Warhol recalled: "Art just wasn't fun for me anymore. It was people who were fascinating and I wanted to spend all my time being around them, listening to them and making movies of them." The Factory - its very name an ironic hint that quantity not quality was the new watchword - was a hive of activity, some of it directed towards creating (in the widest sense) art. To Warhol's side flocked the men he called his 'A Team' or, more to the point, his "fags on speed". Warhol himself was homosexually orientated, though voyeurism pleased him even more. That way you could watch without becoming involved; he had learnt early in his romantic life that involvement merely brought pain. Warhol's camp followers, like Gerard Malanga, Ondine (Robert Olivio) and Billy (Linich) Name, offered him homosexual glamour, and the excitement of those who lived on speed time. Malanga acted as the Factory's social secretary, facilitating introductions between film makers and silkscreen artists, poets and rock stars; he was also a poet, an editor, and - in Warhol's films, at least - an actor. His looks were so striking that he seemed almost too perfect to be true - a bleached parody of the ideal American hero.

Ondine, stuttering and gushing his way through endless conversations, was Warhol's chief performance artist - frequently alienating his companions with his wilful behaviour, and then winning them back in an instant with an aside of gossip or self-parody. Billy Name chronicled the scene with his camera; he also designed the Factory's aluminium foiled interior, which blended perfectly with the silver bush of Warhol's hair. Like Malanga, he was a poet who became a renaissance man under the Factory régime of total artistic freedom.

In and out of the Factory flitted a succession of Superstars - Andy's half-ironic, half-sentimental name for the innocents who wandered into his orbit in the hope of achieving fame. And they did, many of them, simply for being where they were at the right time. Edie Sedgwick, for instance, was a model who became the face of 1965 in Warhol's hands: he groomed her to stand out in a crowd, and the pair formed a 'media couple' that summer and autumn, winning column inches wherever they chose to parade. Others roamed the same circuit - Ingrid Superstar, the Sugar Plum Fairy, and the omnipresent Brigid Polk/Berlin, answering incoming calls and taping all the day's conversations, each to be filed away neatly on shelves that overran her modest apartment.

To give his Superstars a setting, and to satisfy a craving for novelty that his work on canvas and silkscreen no longer gave him, Andy Warhol became a film mogul in 1963. His early work belonged to the margins of the Fluxus School, with a single, endlessly drawn-out action filling the frames of *Kiss* or *Eat*. *Sleep* devoted no less than six hours to footage of the recumbent John Giorno: at the height of Warhol's expansive period, he employed underground film master Jonas Mekas to film eight hours of lights being turned on and off through the night on the Empire State Building, and then presented the entire exercise uncut as *Empire*.

Besides their length, these films did little that hadn't been done by other New York film makers. But his notoriety brought them wide media coverage, and thus extended the potential marketplace for the avant-garde cinema. Other Warhol films indulged his passion for voyeurism, flirting with scenes of violence and sexual coupling. *Couch,* for instance, doomed itself to private screenings with its explicit footage of various positions and passions. Elsewhere, Warhol showed a cunning sense of humour. *Blow-Job* in 1963 concentrated entirely on the subject's face: the action that was causing his apparent ecstasy remained teasingly out of shot. This early short was a silent film; in the early weeks of 1966, Warhol made a longer, colour version of the same concept with sound, entitled *Eating Too Fast;* and among the spectators during the filming was Lou Reed.

Besides teasing, Warhol could also fake it on film. It transpired, for instance, that gathering six hours of footage for *Sleep* proved too diffi-cult: so Andy simply repeated some of the reels over and over again, rightly guessing that no-one would notice. We're back to authenticity again, and Warhol's overt dismissal of the concept - a decision that lies at the heart of his interpretation of the rules of Pop-Art.

"Any incentive to paint is as good as any other. There is no poor subject." (Robert Rauschenberg)

"I want to paint things the mind already knows." (Jasper Johns)

"I think everybody should be a machine... you do the same thing every time. You do it over and over again." (Andy Warhol)

After Picasso had dissolved the 'realistic' notion of painting into an explicitly subjective assemblage of patterns and forms, it was inevitable that art would progress towards the abstract. Once people and objects became coloured shapes, then you might just as well ignore the people and paint the shapes instead. Artists first explored the technical implica-tions of geometical abstracts; some then yearned for a more dramatic response to Western civilisation. So was born abstract expressionism, where the act of throwing a can of paint against a canvas became as valid an act as the subtle mixing of colour with a palette and brush.

Abstract expressionism was a liberation, both of technique and subject. But its distance from the real world led artists like Robert Rauschenberg and Jasper Johns to approach reality and unreality more openly. Rauschenberg was the theorist of Pop, devising intellectual justification for his subversion of familiar images. Inspired by the artistic nerve of

Marcel Duchamp, he took the debris of American life - police 'wanted' posters, photos, advertising slogans, comic strips - and then perverted them to make an oblique comment on the values of modern society.

Jasper Johns took the process further. He concentrated on America's equivalents to the standards behind which Roman legions marched into battle - the flag, the outline map of the nation, the very numbers and letters which constituted its means of communication. Merely by painting these Johns was highlighting their mythic force: by hiding their messages behind daubs of white paint, he subverted their natures into his own value-judgements about America. For Warhol, the social message was incidental. What mattered was the symbol. Take Leonardo's *Mona Lisa,* for instance: Rauschenberg borrowed this most familiar of classic paintings and repeated the image to emphasise that it was an object like any other. Warhol placed thirty miniatures of the work on a single canvas, and intended no message other than the title he gave his piece: *Thirty Are Better Than One.*

In an episode which has become legend, Warhol painted two Coca-Cola bottles - another image which he found in Rauschenberg. One he surrounded with abstract blurs of paint; the other stood starkly on the canvas. He showed both to dealer Emile De Antonio, who told Andy that the naked bottle was art, the other merely a pastiche. Warhol took his words to heart, and turned out facsimiles of soup cans, food cartons - telling the world that by calling them art he had made them art.

His work with silkscreen was less direct, though once again he used familiar cultural symbols - Elvis Presley, Marilyn Monroe, Superman - and repeated them, diminishing the force of their original meaning, yet consecrating them as totems of a new religion where fame was god.

At his blandest, Warhol presented a blank canvas on which others could paint their own interpretation. You decided whether the Coca-Cola bottle was an ironic comment on consumer values, an attack on the emptiness of capitalism, or a tribute to Warhol's preferred brand. Warhol simply stood there.

"If you want to know all about Andy Warhol, just look at the surface, of my paintings and films and me, and there I am. There's nothing behind it." (Andy Warhol, 1968)

"If you want to know what I am, look at the surface. Because I'm inside." (Lou Reed, notes to his 1975 tour programme)

"I'll be your mirror/reflect what you are." (Lou Reed, 1966)

Lou Reed fell in love with Warhol and his stance. Though he remained one of Andy's inner circle for little more than eighteen months, he continued to lionise Warhol for another decade. In the Factory, Lou found a laboratory where he could play - a test site for his artistic and sexual explorations, a milieu which provided endless fodder for his songs, and a protective environment through which he could bring his music to the world.

Reed chose at first to ignore the fact that his art and Andy Warhol's were often at odds. Look at the quotes a couple of paragraphs back, and at first glance they appear identical - Reed slavishly adopting one of Warhol's guiding principles as his own. Look again, and there's a major divergence. Warhol announces that beneath the surface of his work there is nothing; everything is surface. Reed says the opposite. Look at the surface, he says, because I'm inside, and I'm using the surface as a disguise.

Warhol subjugated his personality to the needs of his art. To all purposes, he ceased to exist as a human being in the mid-Sixties; when she shot him in 1968, Valerie Solanas was merely trying to live out the full implications of Andy's pose.

Reed, however, exists beneath and beyond his art. Warhol taught him how to paint on the surface, to use often shocking images to distract attention from the person of the artist. Warhol chose to become his work; Reed used his work as a cover for his personality, offering up a mixture of confession and observation. Just as the media fell for Andy's tricks, assuming that the man was as shallow as his public persona, so they tripped over the same wire a second time with Reed. Lou's songs reflected a world of amoral decadence and violence; that, they assumed, must be the life that Lou Reed led. Reed then intervened as the novelist, the distanced outsider who simply manipulated a cast of semi-fictional characters. It's purely coincidental, he seemed to say, that my creations toy with death and sexual perversion; that's what they are, and it has nothing to do with me. Having double bluffed his audience twice, the real Reed - not the Warholesque creation or the disinterested novelist - could hide in the confusion.

And confusion there was, and plenty, in the Factory during Reed's years as a denizen. Warhol's doctrine that work was better than play, and more work was better than less, spilled over in the lives of his entourage. Led by Andy to believe that they were important simply because they existed in his circle, they lent themselves willingly to a process of fearless documentation, all in the name of art. During the period between 1965 and 1967 there was always someone with a camera in hand, stalking through the Factory in search of a conversation, a confrontation or an intimate caress. Brigid Polk was everywhere with her tape recorder; anyone within the Factory walls might become an exhibit in Warhol's next chamber of horrors.

Warhol's newest film when Reed arrived at the Factory was *Vinyl,* the first movie adaptation of Anthony Burgess's *A Clockwork Orange* in which Gerard Malanga is submitted to the whims of torturers while in the background, unaware of the action, Edie Sedgwick smokes behind a screen. Her indifference was as shocking as the sado-masochistic rites; only later did it emerge that Sedgwick had not even realised she was in camera range. No matter: she was a Superstar, by virtue of being in the building, and Warhol exploited her to the full.

Reed watched the dramas and crises of Warhol's speed-fuelled followers unfold; sometimes he was the cause of them. Several participants have recalled that Reed was an object of desire for Factory men or women alike; Gerard Malanga's Secret Diary suggests that there was a constant flurry of jealousy and passion around Lou in 1966. More importantly, the Factory laid bare all the fantasies and taboos which Reed had been struggling to conceal since his days on Long Island. Here were sadists and masochists playing out their dreams for the camera. Transvestites roamed the Factory, rivalling Edie and her female counterparts in beauty. In a palace ruled by a gay voyeur, there were no rules: everything was sanctioned, except moralism.

The scenes and stars of the Factory peopled Reed's songs for another decade - not just 'Walk On The Wild Side', with its coy cameos of Factory acolytes, but a succession of mini-dramas featuring speed freaks and actresses, hoodlums and painters. Before the Factory, Reed had the scenarios for his songs; Warhol provided the cast and the telling details. Reed soon abandoned the sweaters and casual jackets he'd affected since leaving Syracuse, and took on the Factory image - Warhol's leather and shades. It became the Lou Reed look, and in its turn, the look of the rock New Wave; with its impersonal uniformity, it provided cognoscenti from guitarists to journalists with a common badge.

By remaking himself in Warhol's image, Reed was submitting himself to his master's voice. Like Delmore Schwartz before him, Andy represented an alternative to the middle-class upbringing Reed had endured on Long Island. Delmore invested Lou with the power of the word; Andy demonstrated the power of the image. And Andy had another power: his name. Warhol product attracted attention; the more extreme it was, the better. Andy loved simple rock'n'roll, the girl group records of the early Sixties, the manufactured Philadelphia teen idols of the late Fifties. He had no interest in the theories of LaMonte Young and John Cage, except insofar as they forced an audience to respond. In The Velvet Underground, Andy found a noise that was as unyielding as his own artistic credo. The Velvets found a sponsor who set no limits.

FIVE

AT THE CAFÉ BIZARRE, THE VELVET UNDERGROUND were booked to perform nightly through December 1965. The cafe patrons, expecting a variation on The Byrds or The Lovin' Spoonful, found the shrieking of John Cale's electric viola and the feedback howls of Lou Reed's guitar too discordant, and within a week the Velvets were asked to leave. As the legend goes, they were told they'd be fired if they played 'Black Angel's Death Song' one more time. They immediately obliged, and were dismissed on the spot.

By then, they had already been offered a management deal by Andy Warhol, so their rebellion was slightly dishonest. Warhol had been led to the group by Barbara Rubin, a familiar of the New York art and poetry scene, who'd invited Gerard Malanga to the Bizarre to check out this new band. Malanga brought along his whip, an essential prop in his pose as an exotic dancer, and felt sufficiently moved by the primal rhythms of the Velvets to join in. He passed on the word to Warhol, and the next night the entire Andy entourage arrived at the Café Bizarre.

Warhol and cohort Paul Morrissey had two projects in motion, both of which required music. The first was an Edie Sedgwick film retrospective, to capitalise on her iconic status in New York art circles; Andy intended to make it a mixed-media show, with Malanga's whip dance and a rock band rivalling his films for attention. The second was the offer to host a discotheque-cum-happening in a warehouse in Queens; again, a rock band was required. Warhol's Factory had already attracted visitors like Bob Dylan, The Rolling Stones and The Byrds; but he wanted a blank canvas which he could shape into a representation of his own world. With The Velvet Underground, little moulding was required.

Before the end of December, the VU signed a contract with Warhol, whereby he would finance the buying of new equipment and give them free rehearsal space; in return they would appear at designated Warhol events. Having garnered no interest in their initial demo tape, the Velvets agreed; and added to the mayhem in the Factory by rehearsing there night and day. On New Year's Eve, Andy took his entourage to the Apollo Theater in Harlem to see the James Brown Show, and then returned to the Factory in time to watch a CBS news report on underground film makers - featuring not only Andy Warhol but brief footage of the Velvets working with Piero Heliczer. It was a prescient omen for the New Year.

"Andy decided to throw Nico into the act because the Velvets themselves were not very charismatic onstage, and Andy wanted a spotlight on someone. So Andy threw her in on the act against the wishes of the Velvets, actually." (Gerard Malanga, 1978)

Actress and singer Tally Brown was Warhol's original choice to front the Velvet Underground. Professionally-trained, she moonlighted between off-Broadway theatre and the underground, mixing cabaret engagements in the Village with appearances in Warhol's improvised movies like Camp. Warhol approached her in the first week of 1966, and despite her lack of interest in rock'n'roll she agreed to meet the Velvets. She found Lou Reed "a fascinating, fucked-up guy", and spent an afternoon at his loft listening to fifties rock records in an attempt to gain a feeling for the music. When she realised that Lou expected her to perform with the Velvets that evening, she pleaded prior engagements, and left. Warhol bore her no malice; a few weeks later he called her up and said he was putting together a band called Children, which would be made up of female underground film makers, all of whom would play transistor radios instead of instruments.

Warhol doubtless viewed the Velvets in the same light, as a new toy he could manipulate at will. Hence the introduction of Nico - born Christa Paffgren in Germany on the verge of the Second World War, a former model and actress who had found herself in London in 1965, made records with Andrew Loog Oldham, been adopted by Brian Jones, entranced Bob Dylan, and was brought by him to the Factory. She arrived on Warhol's doorstep clutching an acetate of a song which she said Bob Dylan had written for her, called 'I'll Keep It With Mine'.

Nico was stunningly beautiful, in the idiom of the age - flowing blonde hair, perfect cheekbones, an icy, removed gaze. In photographs of the early Velvets, she looks as if she has arrived from another world, fallen by chance into this mêlée of amplifiers and leather jackets. And her voice - unashamedly Germanic, deep and almost entirely devoid of emotion - supported her appearance.

Wilful and determined, Nico immediately altered the balance of power within The Velvet Underground. "Poison is the essence of the performer," she once told Iggy Pop, and with her beauty and detachment she began to poison the Velvets' idealism. Lou Reed fell in love with her, and at the same time resented her for being foisted onto his group. When she switched her attentions from Lou to John Cale, their solidarity was weakened. Sterling Morrison watched from the side, amused; Maureen Tucker, adopting an image the exact opposite of Nico's, seems to have distrusted her from the start.

The Velvets' music was a conscious moulding of the avant-garde Cale tradition and Reed's poetic, violent rock'n'roll. Nico had no grasp of the subtleties of this relationship, and assumed she should become the band's sole vocalist. To keep Andy happy and Nico quiet, Reed wrote her a series of new songs - 'Femme Fatale' (actually inspired by Edie Sedgwick), 'I'll Be Your Mirror', 'All Tomorrow's Parties', 'Little Sister' (co-written with John Cale). And there was 'I'll Keep It With Mine', which the Velvets did their best to sabotage at every opportunity, apparently resenting its composer's standing in the eyes of Warhol, Nico and Edie Sedgwick.

The Velvet Underground And Nico - immediately highlighting the rift between band and singer - made their first public appearance at Delmonico's Hotel in New York, on January 8, 1966. Before an audience composed almost entirely of psychiatrists, attending a business convention, The Velvet Underground performed ear-damagingly loud renditions of Reed's songs, with Nico offering occasional vocals, and then fell into an improvised period of free-form noise - Cale slicing at his electric viola, Reed and Morrison forcing agonised screeches of feedback from their guitar amps, while Tucker pounded monotonously on her bass drum behind them. The band stood beneath huge chandeliers in the hotel ballroom, while Gerard Malanga rehearsed his whip dance, and Edie Sedgwick weaved between them in a figure-hugging dress.

The show was filmed by Jonas Mekas and photographed by Billy Name; but it was only the beginning. Back at the Factory, Warhol filmed a couple of reels of the band rehearsing with Nico; the footage ended when the New York police arrived to investigate the noise. The film became another Warhol presentation, *The Velvet Underground And Nico: A Symphony Of Sound;* eventually the band would perform with the movie projected over them. Around the same time, Andy signalled Lou Reed's acceptance into his domain by making him the subject of one of his *Screen Tests* - three-minute shorts focusing on the cool gaze of a Factory citizen.

Lou Reed and John Cale played a more substantial role in Warhol's *Hedy The Shoplifter,* an ironic replaying of the fall from grace of Hollywood star Hedy Lamarr. Shot in February 1966, the movie subverted the implications of its title by refusing to follow the action out of camera shot. Cale and Reed were among those who improvised Ms Lamarr's sorry tale; more importantly, they also created the soundtrack.

Like their work with Piero Heliczer, the *Hedy* music was a cacophony of feedback and distortion, which began in vaguely symphonic form with a portentous landscape of sound, shifting elegiacly into claps of thunder, and broken by occasional squeals from Reed's guitar. After a brief interlude of near-silence, the noise returned - now translated into a piercing treble howl, like the sound of an animal undergoing dissection before death.

Reed and Cale retained this idiom as their private province, while The Velvet Underground were moulded into part of Warhol's mixed-media mayhem. In February 1966, Andy appeared on educational New York TV, coyly introducing his band to the world. Later that month, he presented them in his first fully-fledged 'happening' at the Film-Makers' Cinematheque on 41st Street - the same venue where the Velvets had already worked with Heliczer. The Velvets' noise was powerful enough; but at its height, the Warhol experience was more than a rock concert. In front of the band, Gerard Malanga and Mary Waronov swept whips through the air in a S/M parody of go-go dancers. Behind them, on a giant projection screen, loomed the image of Edie Sedgwick, as Warhol ran *Vinyl, Bitch, Restaurant* - any of the sheaf of movies he'd assembled in mid-1965 by letting the cameras roll as the Factory workers played out melodramas and fantasies. Framing the stage was a lights show - not the languorous shifting of colours and shapes favoured by the early psychedelic bands, but a harsh, hypnotic rhythm of strobes that compounded the sense of disorientation.

"In our show," Lou recalled a decade later, "the guy who was doing the lights - Danny Williams - he committed suicide eventually. He would sit up for hours at the Factory, with seven strobe lights, and use himself as a test subject. That's why John and I used to wear sunglasses when we played. We didn't want to see it."

For an audience, it was a devastating, sense-destroying experience, which was repeated across America for the next year. Andy christened the show *Up-Tight,* and in early March he took it on the road to Rutgers University in New Jersey. There was a change of personnel that night; Edie Sedgwick had fled the nest and signed with Bob Dylan's manager, Albert Grossman, convinced that she would marry Bobby (who in fact had secretly married in November 1965) and star in a major Hollywood picture alongside him. In her place at Rutgers was Ondine, making a one-night-only appearance as a dancer and exotic vision.

From New Jersey, the circus moved to the University of Michigan Film Festival in Ann Arbor, and then back to New York, where Warhol negotiated a residency at a hall called the Dom on St. Mark's Place in the East Village. Surrounded by ethnic restaurants and dance clubs, with hookers and junkies littering the streets, the Dom became the home of what Paul Morrissey rechristened the Exploding Plastic Inevitable. Supported by the Fugs or the Holy Modal Rounders, the Warhol crew played the Dom for a straight month, with a sense of camaraderie that stretched as far as a communal earnings system and shared billing for the entire cast. But at the end of April 1966, Warhol lost the lease; and the EPI broke off while the Velvets began to make their first professional recordings. Financed by Warhol, the band spent three nights at a cheap studio on Broadway, taping initial versions of most of the songs that would appear on their first album, plus 'Wrap Your Troubles In Dreams', 'Little Sister' and Reed's 'Get It On Time'.

A week later, the entire EPI package migrated to California, where the Velvets appeared before the West Coast rock aristocracy at the Trip in Los Angeles. High on psychedelics, David Crosby of The Byrds announced: "It's like eating a banana nut Brillopad"; but the typical reaction was more muted. The band were booked for four weeks, supported by The Mothers Of Invention, but after three nights the Sheriff's office closed the venue down. The Musicians' Union insisted they still be paid, and the VU spent the money at TT&G Studios in Los Angeles, re-recording 'Heroin', 'All Tomorrow's Parties', 'Waiting For The Man' and 'Venus In Furs'.

Thereafter they hung out in the Hollywood Hills, before moving up the coast to San Francisco to play two nights at Bill Graham's Fillmore West, again with The Mothers. Sterling Morrison recalled that they revo-lutionalised the Fillmore light show, though Graham had already been staging mixed-media events in San Francisco for around six months. But rock's future king of promoters took an immediate dislike to the Velvets' New York cool, and Lou Reed responded by badmouthing the West Coast scene for the next two years.

In San Francisco, Reed met Steve Sesnick, a club owner and manager who recognised in Lou "somebody putting out messages that I found interesting". Discussing business deals, record companies and percent-ages, he planted the first seeds of suspicion in Reed's mind that Andy Warhol's management of the Velvets might not be entirely altruistic.

Back in New York in June, Lou contracted hepatitis and was con-signed to the Beth Israel Hospital. Andy started fishing for record deals, and John Cale assumed total leadership of the band in preparation for six nights at Poor Richard's in Chicago. Without Lou, Cale became lead vocalist and guitarist, Tucker switched to bass, and original Velvet Maclise, briefly back from India, played drums. Maclise wanted to rejoin the band, but was nixed by Reed as soon as he recovered. Ironically, it was one of these Reed-less shows that was filmed by independent moviemaker Ron Nameth; he captured Cale dragging the Velvets through a restrained, doomy rearrangement of 'Heroin', and 'Venus In Furs'.

While Lou was out of action, Andy Warhol found the Velvets a record label. Atlantic's Ahmet Ertegun loved the band, but refused to let them issue 'Heroin', while Elektra, home of many of the leading figures on the New York folk-rock scene, liked the songs but hated the drone that accompanied them. Eventually it was Tom Wilson, former producer of Bob Dylan and champion of The Mothers Of Invention, who signed them to MGM's Verve label. The Mothers' double album was recorded and released within weeks; the Velvets' LP, complete by August 1966, did not appear until March 1967. Reed's contempt for the music business hierarchy, and for Mothers' leader Frank Zappa, doubled by the day.

In the event, the Velvets' first appearance on record came not through MGM, but via ESP-Disk. They issued an 'Electric Newspaper' edition of the *East Village Other* in late 1966, to mark the dual event on August 6, 1966, of Hiroshima Day, and the wedding of President Johnson's daugh-ter, Luci. The Velvets' contribution, juxtaposed against radio coverage of the wedding service, was entitled 'Noise' - a loop of feedback and viola howl, over which the band tuned up, crashed atonal chords, rattled per-cussion and stuttered with no real sense of rhythm. The contrast between the banality of the radio pundits, and the sensory assault of the music, was as close as the band came to social satire.

In August 1966, the Warhol dream factory was still in full flow, as Andy supervised the making of his most famous movie, *Chelsea Girls.* Set in the Chelsea Hotel, a favoured haunt of artists and musicians, it collected together vignettes from previous Warhol films, as well as new footage - each reel spotlighting a different Factory employee, in discussion or repose. The only member of the Velvets to appear in the movie was Nico, who was filmed cutting her hair; but the group did provide accompaniment for the reel subtitled *The Gerard Malanga Story,* creating another tableau of noise and distortion that acted as an ironic counterpoint to the rambling, inconsequential dialogue and erratic camera-work.

Chelsea Girls was first screened within a month of being shot: faced with seven hours of film, Warhol decided to divide the footage between two screens and projectors, which would run simultaneously side by side. Reed filed this idea away for future use; and also offered his own slightly cynical view of the film in a song he wrote for Nico later that year, which offered snapshots of the *Chelsea Girls* stars (except Nico). "Here they come now/See them run now", he wrote slightly contemptuously at the end of each of the verses which labelled and filed Warhol's actors away for posterity. Six years later he repeated the exercise on 'Walk On The Wild Side'.

October 1966 found the Velvets back at the Dom - to discover that it had been bought by Albert Grossman and renamed the Balloon Farm. The EPI performed there for a week or so, but then quit, mourning the loss of the original Dom atmosphere. In their place, Andy Warhol presented the début of Nico, solo artiste - singing to the pathetic accompaniment of a tape of guitar backings recorded by Lou Reed, who didn't want to appear with Nico in person. The tape was soon discarded, as first Tim Buckley and then Jackson Browne took its place.

For the next few months, Nico drifted in and out of the Velvets, who saw out the year on a cross-country trip that took them from Massachusetts to Cincinnati, up into Canada, back to Detroit (where they supported The Yardbirds, whose guitarist Jeff Beck asked Lou to show him the chords to 'Waiting For The Man'), and back into New York. In Cincinnati, a fan made a 90-minute tape of the band's show, half of which was devoted to two lengthy pieces of improvisation - one presumably what Sterling Morrison called 'The Nothing Song', the other (known as 'Melody Laughter') opening with Nico intoning a Middle Eastern call to prayer, before Reed eventually lost patience and began playing with feedback, and the band set off into an approximation of the riff which would soon become 'Sister Ray'.

In New York, the Velvets - or rather John Cale, working under the name of The Velvet Underground - taped 'Loop', which was used on a flexidisc included in the December 1966 issue of *Aspen* magazine. Though Reed failed to make the comparison, 'Loop' was a prototype for 'Metal Machine Music': Cale set his amplifiers howling in a recurrent rhythm of crescendos and troughs, and then built over this volcanic noise a second layer of dissonant sound. More structured than Reed's later effort, Cale's 15-minute recording had a complex, logical form which clearly displayed his avant-garde heritage. And, again like Lou, Cale ended the piece with a locked groove, leaving the final bass notes pumping vainly towards a climax doomed to remain out of reach.

In the final weeks of 1966, MGM finally agreed to issue a Velvet Underground record. For anyone who had heard the band with the EPI, the single was destined to be a shock. 'Sunday Morning' opened with the tinkling of a zylophone over a simple bass riff, before John Cale's viola entered, muted to sound like a distant orchestra of strings. Finally came the vocal - breathy, sexually ambiguous, not immediately recognisable as Lou Reed, or indeed as a man at all. The sole track produced by Tom Wilson during the album sessions, 'Sunday Morning' brilliantly intercut the band's garage-flavoured rock sound (Maureen's drumbeat, Lou's crackly solo) with an artier, almost ethereal atmosphere. Wilson mixed Cale's viola during the solo so it sounded like a trumpet, introduced a piano wandering gently under the vocal, and set up Lou's ironic twist - this gentle, almost languorous song was about urban paranoia.

On the flip was 'Femme Fatale', Lou's song for Edie which became a theme song for Nico. No professional producer touched this track - the guitar was overmiked into distortion, the Velvets' defiantly flat backing chorus sounded pinched and thin, and towards the fade, Lou's guitar veered gradually out-of-tune as Cale's viola chopped across the rhythm of the song.

'Sunday Morning' hovered on the edge of the *Cashbox* Top 100 chart, and persuaded MGM to free the Velvets' album. With hindsight, it's difficult to cut the record away from its legend; at the time, another legend - that of Andy Warhol - intervened between the band and their music.'The Velvet Underground And Nico' was the album's title; but the cover advertised Andy Warhol, not the Velvets. In a brilliant piece of Pop-Art fakery, Warhol designed a cover which featured a bright yellow banana, curved phallicly across the sleeve. 'Andy Warhol' ran the title beneath it, in the printed signature Andy had adopted as his own. Above the banana was printed 'Peel it and see'; and if you scratched and pulled at the stalk, the paper did indeed peel away to reveal not a phallus but - a pink banana.

On the back was a beautiful colour still of the Velvets in concert, whip dancers before them, a giant celluloid Lou projected over their heads. (Originally this photo featured a superimposed portrait of performance artist Eric Emerson; he sued, and MGM were forced to airbrush him out.) Above this picture, and five brilliantly evocative solo portraits by Paul Morrissey, ran the album title - and beneath, in identical type, the words 'Produced by Andy Warhol'.

Though he occasionally visited the studio during the sessions, Warhol no more produced the record than Bob Dylan did. His credit denoted, like a movie mogul, that he had financed the project; and also that the Velvets, like the rest of the Factory organisation, were Warhol's property, puppets he could jerk or let fall at whim. By the time the record was released, Lou Reed and John Cale were already querying their status. But the record, despite its photos from Warhol's EPI extravaganzas and review cuttings crediting him with the inspiration, was Lou Reed's vision. John Cale provided the instrumental co-ordination, the atonality which took it out of the rock mainstream; but the songs reflected no-one's philosophy other than Lou's.

Despite the lack of basic record production values - and there's a sharp divide between the songs recorded in New York and those taped a month later in California - 'The Velvet Underground And Nico' has an intensity and single-mindedness of vision that marks it out as a work of genius. The band's frenzied assault on their instruments behind Lou's jabbering 'Black Angel's Death Song' was the familiar sound of the Exploding Plastic Inevitable; they repeated it on 'European Son', a two-verse throw-away given epic status by the ferocity and length of the instrumental coda. After Reed has spat out his meaningless lyrics, there's an explosion that seems to herald the coming of a black hole, ready to suck the song inside it. A bottle shatters, in stereo, and then the pace doubles as Reed and Morrison's guitars speed towards no destination in particular, simply for the pleasure of the ride. Reed and Morrison dedicated the song to Delmore Schwartz - for no other reason than that Delmore had hated vocal music, and 'European Son' had the shortest lyric on the album.

At the other extreme, Reed and Cale provided the most delicate of settings for Nico's 'Femme Fatale' and 'I'll Be Your Mirror'. The latter began as a two-line encapsulation of Warholism, and turned into the most tender of love songs, addressed to someone hiding themselves from the world in case someone should see the Scarlet Letter stitched across their chest.

Nico also intoned 'All Tomorrow's Parties', further evidence that Reed maintained a healthy irony towards the social whirl of the Factory scene. Beginning the lyric with the second half of a sentence, Reed made it sound as if he was eavesdropping on a conversation; later he used the conscious grammatical inversions of poetic language for almost the last time: "A blackened shroud, a hand-me-down gown/Of rags and silks a costume". Under it all ran LaMonte Young's patented drone, suggesting that, after all, one party was just as boring as another.

Reed's rock roots dominated the rest of the album - stealing the opening riff from Marvin Gaye's 'Hitchhike' for 'There She Goes Again', which boasted the memorable chorus line "You better hit her"; powering 'Run Run Run', a Warhol movie in four verses, with a Bo Diddley backbeat; and making 'Waiting For The Man' as much a celebration of the music as a calm description of the drug scene by pushing the band through a frenetic, yet controlled, rhythm, with John Cale stabbing viciously at his piano before the bass set off on a trip of its own, and Reed chuckled to himself as he waved it goodbye.

'Heroin' remains the most startling moment on the album, however. Whereas Cale's live performances in Chicago had retained the steady pace of the opening bars throughout the song, Reed's arrangement ebbed and flowed in line with the spreading of the heroin through the bloodstream. Throughout the album, Maureen Tucker's bass drum acts as a heartbeat tracing the emotional and physical condition of the narrator; and on 'Heroin' it pounds alarmingly as the spike enters the vein, only to slow to a steady pulse as the system takes the invading drug under control.

Over seven minutes long, 'Heroin' is everything The Velvet Underground ever promised to be. Cale's demented viola bridges the gap between sanity and madness; Reed's vocal has the breathless excitement of the innocent at sea, as he revels in the high-wire walk between life and death; and the lyrics reflect reality in all its complexity, ignoring the softer options of cliché or lapsing into incoherence.

Andy Warhol, unwitting yet calculating 'producer' of this masterpiece, proudly announced that 'The Velvet Underground And Nico' was a counterpart to his movie of *Chelsea Girls*. He obviously didn't understand the album. Like Andy's movie, the LP offered a picture of reality; but there the similarity ended. Warhol's work was the creation of a non-judgemental artist; whatever happened before the cameras was automatically art, simply because Andy Warhol said so. Lou Reed and John Cale's work was subtler, and more 'artistic', than that. It accepted the shaping and guiding hand of the creator, the awareness that reality had to be selected, presented and interpreted before it could achieve any lasting significance. In a way, both Warhol and Reed kept true to their manifestos. *Chelsea Girls* was a film made up of surfaces; 'The Velvet Underground And Nico' hid its real message beneath the crust. The aura of perversion, chemical abuse and total liberation from taboos drew people in; but rather than pandering to the lowest aspirations of his characters, Reed used their experiences as a map that uncovered the routes to heaven and hell, and left the choice to those who listened. With this record, the Velvets outlived their usefulness to Andy Warhol, and vice versa; and they showed up the clinical emptiness at the heart of Warhol's world.

Early in 1967, Lou Reed stormed into the Factory and announced: "So she photographs well in black and white. I'm not playing with her anymore." 'She' was Nico, who had been subjecting Lou to another of her romantic powerplays, or else demanding that he write a fresh batch of songs for her to sing. After the Dom debacle, Reed had agreed to support Nico in another solo venture, at Stanley's Bar in the Village. Between shows, he, Cale and Morrison would walk down to Max's Kansas City, which had become the house club for the Warhol crowd. The three musicians now lived in separate apartments in the East Village, all around East 10th Street, and they offered a united front to the world. Maureen Tucker, meanwhile, came in from the Island on request, but otherwise took little part in the boys' social scene.

Despite the strains induced by Nico's tantalising affairs with one and then the other - plus half the folkies in the Village - Cale and Reed were still a mutual appreciation pact. "John idolized Lou," Paul Morrissey recalled. "He thought anything Lou said was wonderful." In return, Reed continued to respect Cale's musical judgement, even allowing John to contribute lyrics to 'Black Angel's Death Song'.

The Velvets' reputation had by now spread through the international avant-garde. Michelangelo Antonioni requested their presence for his film *Blow-Up* in London, but the financing of the operation proved too difficult, and he used The Yardbirds instead. Meanwhile, the Velvets returned over and over again to the same venues - Provincetown, Rhode Island, or Michigan University in Ann Arbor. In New York, however, their base and hometown, they refused to appear after a brief season at the Gymnasium Club on the Upper East Side. MGM had been unable to persuade the leading pop stations to accept advertising for such a controversial album, so the VU punished the city by their absence.

The Gymnasium engagement coincided with the making of *a,* the first and only work of fiction published under Andy Warhol's name. Its status as a novel was dubious: the book supposedly recounted 24 hours in the amphetamine-lagged day of Ondine, told through verbatim transcriptions of his conversations in person and on the phone. The book was Billy Name's idea, so he was given the task of transcribing it. He structured it into chapters - each one defined by the length of a 30-minute audio tape. Apart from Ondine, few of Warhol's circle were identifiable in the book to outsiders: Warhol, for instance, appeared as 'Drella', Brigid Polk as 'The Duchess'. Towards the end of the 24 hours, Lou Reed appeared, discussing the forthcoming Gymnasium show, and Ondine's planned contribution.

a wasn't published until 1968, taking advantage of the recent publicity Andy Warhol had gained by being shot. Warhol planned a regular five-yearly update, but *b* was abandoned in the early Seventies when Warhol was unable to find anyone interested enough in being its model. The book plays a minor role in the Lou Reed saga - except that he took to describing it as his favourite book in the mid-Seventies, both as a gesture of love towards Warhol and a means of confounding anyone who had actually tried to read it.

a was one of Warhol's final gestures of art-as-pure-documentation. After completing a rough cut of **** (alias *The 24-Hour Movie*), he abandoned such expansive forms of art, and made increasing forays into the mainstream, pushed more by the bullets of Valerie Solanas than by a real shift in artistic philosophy. *Andy Warhol's Index,* an ambitious publishing concept completed in the summer of 1967, marked a step along the way. Less a book than a celebration of the Factory, it printed interviews with Andy and his clique, and was packaged with a number of Warholesque objects - among them a balloon, eight labels (four of them blank, four of them with Warhol's name - spot the difference), a plastic bag, a selection of pop-up drawings (including one showing a castle peopled by Andy's entourage), and finally a flexidisc. This record was decorated with a photo of Lou Reed, clad in the Factory uniform of impenetrable shades; when you played it, you heard an inane interview with Nico, while the Velvets' album played in the background.

The cosy family presented in *Andy Warhol's Index* was actually on the verge of collapse. The constant bickering between Reed and Nico over who should front the group had been resolved when Nico flew to Ibiza - ostensibly to settle there, though she was back at the Dom within a fortnight. After a nostalgic appearance with the Exploding Plastic Inevitable at Steve Paul's Scene Club in New York, Andy Warhol took most of his hangers-on to the Cannes Film Festival, where he was intending to launch *Chelsea Girls* onto the international market. The Velvets, meanwhile, headed to Boston, where they were booked for a two-day gig at the Tea Party - a club operated and owned by Steve Sesnick, whom the band had met in California a year earlier.

Though there had been no documented link between Sesnick and the Velvets during that time, it's obvious that Lou and Steve had been in contact. Sesnick had already sent a copy of 'The Velvet Underground And Nico' to Beatles' manager Brian Epstein, in the hope of winning some kind of publishing or managerial contract. Epstein was interested, but by this time too lost in a haze of alcohol, acid and sleeping pills to decide what day it was, let alone add to his artist roster. When this avenue closed, Sesnick decided he would manage the Velvets himself.

To achieve this end, the relationship between Reed and Warhol had to be fractured. Stage one was to banish Nico, who arrived in Boston in time for the shows, only to be refused leave to play. "Lou likes to manipulate women, to programme them," Nico recalled nearly two decades later, "and he tried to do that with me." Sesnick raised the promise of the Epstein connection, the constant bookings he could offer in Boston, and the mammoth efforts he would invest on the Velvets' part; he also no doubt flattered Reed by singling him out as the leader of the pack. Reed remembered the radio ban on their album in New York, the fracas over the Eric Emerson cover photo (which had forced MGM to whip the record out of the shops almost immediately after it went on sale), and the fact that 'The Velvet Underground And Nico' had barely registered on *Billboard*'s Top 200 chart.

By the time Warhol arrived back from Cannes, Reed was waiting to break the news - the Velvets wanted to end their contract. Warhol was predictably hurt: "He called me a rat," Lou noted years later. "It was the worst thing he could think of." But rather than tie up the Velvets in litigation, Warhol simply tore up their contract. When he had lost Edie Sedgwick a year earlier, the arrival of Nico and the Velvets had been more than adequate compensation. When the Velvets left, his avant-garde corporation lost its soundtrack. For the rest of 1967, Warhol reheated old ideas, and pondered the future with vague foreboding.

Reed allowed a few weeks to pass, to let feelings cool, and then signed with Sesnick. The initial omens were promising: the band landed a rare TV spot on *Upbeat*, a Cleveland rock show: rather than promote their album, they unveiled a new song, a rather laboured boogie called 'Guess I'm Falling In Love' that borrowed its main lyrical idea ("fever in my pocket") from Bob Dylan's 'Absolutely Sweet Marie'. The song was one of several which the band rehearsed in concert that summer, in readiness for the upcoming sessions on their second album. Towards the end of 1966, Reed, Cale and Morrison had laid down some rough demos of four songs in Reed's loft - 'It's Alright, The Way That You Live', a conventionally sentimental love song that was hinged around the same simple chord changes as half the first album; 'Sheltered Life', a jazz piece that mocked its narrator as an out-of-towner innocent of the delights of the big city, and featured some enthusiastic kazoo solos by John Cale; 'I'm Not Too Sorry', with Lou bidding a perfectly happy farewell to a lover; and 'Here She Comes Now', an intricate drone over which Lou improvised lyrics while John Cale played ragas on his viola.

Only one of these songs survived into 1967, although Lou rediscovered and sharpened up 'Sheltered Life' a decade later for 'Rock And Roll Heart'. Lacking from them all, apart from 'Here She Comes Now', was a sense of mystery or drama. The lyrics simply existed, telling everyday stories in language that had no voice behind it. Having exposed some of his deepest taboos on the Velvets' first album, Lou was unable to find a means of moving beyond them. When the band broke a series of Boston Tea Party gigs to return to the studio in New York, they sacrificed lyrical invention and concentrated on reaching new horizons with their music.

The summer of 1967 is fated to go into history as 'the summer of love', suggesting that the world was blessed with a sudden aroma of peace and elected to use flowers instead of guns as its method of communication. This may have been true in small areas of California, London and New York, but elsewhere the world operated as usual. Without wishing to be crass, 1967 was also the summer of the Six-Day War, the Vietnam Conflict, riots in black ghettos across America - anything but universal love and understanding.

More exactly, 1967 was the year that youth culture discovered hallucinogenic drugs. "I used to take acid," Lou Reed confessed in 1978, but two years earlier he expressed his doubts about the validity of the psychedelic experience: "You discover the universal truth in four hours, forget it in the fifth, and in the sixth you're hungry." Reed and the rest of the Warhol clique preferred to gamble with amphetamines, grabbing the 36 hours of insane energy and then praying to postpone the comedown by shovelling more pills into their systems. While the rock élite celebrated their discovery of God in a blade of grass, or more accurately a tab of acid, The Velvet Underground chose to record an album that was a testament to the roller-coaster cycle of speed.

Given Reed's attitude towards the West Coast acid-freaks and hippies, it would be logical to assume that he shared none of the optimism of that innocently blinkered summer. But Jackson Browne, then a teenage folk guitarist supporting Nico on record and at the Dom, remembers otherwise: "Lou, who always had this incredible menacing scowl on his face, wouldn't say more than one or two syllables because that was how Andy was. But he's a sweetheart underneath. We got to rapping and he turned out to be this great person." Lou told Browne about the recent 'be-in' hippie celebration in San Francisco, and revealed that he'd been to the simultaneous event in New York. "The way he described it, you realised there was a place for all that inside of him," Browne recalled. "He loved seeing Central Park full of people all just high and loving each other. You don't think about that when you think of all those Warhol people."

Little of this benevolence towards the human spirit surfaced on 'White Light/White Heat', the Velvets' second album. The title track was a riotous ride through the mind of a speed freak, stuttering in joyful incoherence, and indulging in some oedipal fantasies along the way. 'I Heard Her Call My Name' bristled with the same rampant energy, beginning and ending with some of the most terrifying and unrestrained guitar playing ever put on record - a helter-skelter tumble round the possibilities of the instrument that moved beyond tones and scales into the realm of physical pain.

Miraculously the band kept this dark passion under control, careering back into a song which captured all the exuberance and liberation of the greatest rock'n'roll, and laced it with the eerie confidence of the serial killer.

The perversity which that song hinted at was unveiled in 'Lady Godiva's Operation', which began innocently enough as the portrait of a Factory transvestite, and then achieved genuine horror by suggesting, but never quite revealing, the nature of the surgery being practised upon him/her. Cale's lugubrious Welsh voice intoned this song, with Reed playing character parts as the doctor and victim. And it was Cale who recited 'The Gift', a macabre Reed short story that borrowed the title of a piece by Delmore Schwartz. In Delmore's tale, the gift was an offering from angels hovering midway between good and evil. Reed went straight for the skull with the chainsaw that dissected the hapless Waldo Jeffers, an innocent let loose in the cynical world of modern romance. Inspired no doubt by Warhol's split-screen presentation of *Chelsea Girls*, Reed juxtaposed Cale's matter-of-fact recitation against 'The Booker T', an instrumental chug of no fixed direction which the band had been performing live for several months.

The seventeen minutes of 'Sister Ray' dominated the album. Reed recalled: "It was built around this story that I wrote about this scene of total debauchery and decay. I like to think of Sister Ray as a transvestite smack dealer. The situation is a bunch of drag queens taking some sailors home with them and shooting up on smack and having this orgy when the police appear. And when it came to putting the music to it, it just had to be spontaneous. We turned up to ten, flat out, leakage all over the place. That's it. They asked us what we're going to do. We said we're going to start. They said, who's playing bass? We said there is no bass. They asked us when it ends. We didn't know. When it ends, that's when it ends."

Cut in one take, as the band knew they would never capture the same ferocity twice, 'Sister Ray' is one of those rare pieces of extended rock music that justifies its length. Reed's lyrics read like an amalgam of episodes from Selby's *Last Exit To Brooklyn,* but the words were never the point - "I did my best to drown the lyrics out," Sterling Morrison revealed. While stray phrases like "sucking on my ding-dong" and "I'm searching for my mainline" topple out of the mix, what hits home is the noise - four people searching for the ultimate musical high, a sound that grows organically out of itself and takes over the direction from the performers, deciding to go where it wants to go. It's the same loss of individual personality, the sense of adventure, unity and wholeness, which the acid-rockers like the Dead and the Airplane were searching for in San Francisco. But The Velvet Underground turned it inwards, creating an agonising tension and violence that incited the listener to mirror the random cruelties of the song's characters.

Occupying one side of the record with 'I Heard Her Call My Name', 'Sister Ray' helped conceal the fact that 'White Light/White Heat' lacked the conceptual unity and poetic vision of its predecessor. It's a stunning record, but one that adds nothing to the lyrical impact of 'Heroin' and 'Venus In Furs'. It merely stretches those portraits to their ultimate sonic extreme, offering coy horror stories as a sop to anyone seeking voyeuristic cheap thrills.

'White Light/White Heat' is also, by technical standards, the worst produced record in rock. It was ostensibly produced by Tom Wilson, who may have been in control for 'Here She Comes Now', which has all the sonic clarity of 'Sunday Morning'. But the title track, 'Sister Ray' and 'I Heard Her Call My Name' are enmired in distortion, to the point where it's difficult to separate the Velvets' noise from the harsh ambience of the studio. Today that's all part of the record's charm, and a clean digital remix would be an abomination. In 1967, it doomed the album to commercial failure. With an album unplayable on the radio, and a songwriter apparently struggling for a direction, the Velvets saw out 1967 in some disarray. At the close of the year, they wandered back into the studio, but halted the sessions after they'd taped nothing more than a backing track for 'Guess I'm Falling In Love'.

The aura of their début album was briefly recaptured in the autumn of 1967 when Reed, Cale and Morrison ended their feud with Nico and performed on her début album, 'Chelsea Girl'. Reed picked electric guitar behind Nico's ominous vocal on the title track, while 'Wrap Your Troubles In Dreams' was reprised from the band's early live repertoire. 'Little Sister' marked John Cale's début as a lyricist, while Cale also contributed 'Winter Song'. But producer Tom Wilson sacrificed the purity of Reed and Cale's bare backing tracks by allowing arranger Larry Fallon to festoon the album with baroque strings and woodwind - no doubt intended to heighten the glacial atmosphere, but actually serving to undercut Nico's uncompromisingly flat vocals. "If they'd just have allowed Cale to arrange it and let me do some more stuff on it," Reed complained. "Everything on it - those strings, that flute - should have defeated it. But with the lyrics, Nico's voice, it somehow managed·to survive. We still got 'It Was A Pleasure Then' on, they couldn't stop us. We'd been doing a song like that in our beloved show; it didn't really have a title. Just all of us following the drone. And there it sits in the middle of that album."

'It Was A Pleasure Then' was a direct descendant of one of the improvisations which the band had played at Philadelphia the previous autumn ('Melody Laughter') - Arabic scales, meandering guitar, hints of feedback, and over it all, Nico wailing like an ancient seer. For the last time, it caught the spirit of the original Velvet Underground. Two years after the group had invented their first free-form soundtrack to a Piero Heliczer, they waved farewell to their avant-garde credo; and in doing so they turned over the entire responsibility of the band to Lou Reed.

SIX

"I love Lou, but he has what must be a fragmented personality, so you're never too sure under any conditions what you're going to have to deal with." (Sterling Morrison)

"Lou was starting to act funny. He brought in this guy called Sesnick - who I thought was a real snake - to be our manager, and all this intrigue started to take place. Lou was calling us 'his band' while Sesnick was trying to get him to go solo. Maybe it was the drugs he was doing at the time. They certainly didn't help." (John Cale)

"You can recognise an amphetamine user by the odd hours he keeps. Depending on how much is being used there will be unaccountable mood spasms: joyful and confident; anxious and irrational, with out-breaks of temper." (Andrew Tyler, *Street Drugs*)

WITH STEVE SESNICK EGGING HIM on, Lou Reed gradually eroded the Velvets' democratic foundations during the early months of 1968. Sesnick and Reed decided where the band should play, which effectively meant a surfeit of gigs at the Boston Tea Party, broken by occasional visits to California, Cleveland and Canada. They also masterminded a subtle shift in the band's musical axis, away from explorations of sound towards investigations of the human spirit under strain from obsession and guilt.

In April, John Cale married Betsey Johnson, a fashion designer who had - at Reed's insistence - designed suede outfits for the band. In the classic rock'n'roll tradition, however, the intervention of a woman whom Cale regarded as a creative equal upset the balance of the male hierarchy. Johnson later apportioned herself part of the blame for the Velvets' split; simply by distracting Cale out of Reed's orbit, she must have represented a threat.

Two months later, in a Californian hotel, Reed and Sesnick discovered that Andy Warhol had been shot. Valerie Solanas, an occasional visitor to the Factory, finally gave voice to the silent fear that touched several of

Warhol's team, when she stepped unannounced out of the office elevator to suggest that Andy was controlling her mind, and then fired several bullets into his chest. Solanas was instantly caught and - to Reed's disgust - given a sentence that by the mid-Seventies allowed her back out on the street, uttering renewed threats against Warhol's person.

Warhol, meanwhile, heard the hospital doctors announce he was going to die, and though he didn't - not yet - he never quite believed in the reality of his own recovery. His health continued to suffer from his wounds, which leaked pus and blood through his shirt if he over-exerted himself. And his spirit remained in the hospital. The new Warhol was a security freak, with the open doors of the old factory locked shut, cameras and spyholes watching every visitor to his domain, and Andy gradually gave up the company of unpredictably erratic and brilliant speed freaks for the gentler sport of celebrity hunting. Liz Taylor, after all, knew how to behave.

"I was scared to call him," Reed recalled of Warhol's long hospitalisation, "and in the end I did and he asked me, 'Why didn't you come?'" Already tinged with guilt, Reed's relationship with his former mentor grew ever more complex after his shooting. Father figures weren't meant to be mortal; so Reed distanced himself from the reality that death could claim Andy Warhol by avoiding the sight of his mortality. "I really love him," Lou confessed on many occasions, and the emotion was always reciprocated by Andy. But there was also an inhibition on both sides, an awareness that some boundary of behaviour had been breached.

A few weeks after the shooting, Maureen Tucker and Sterling Morrison received frantic phone calls from Reed begging their presence at a band meeting at the Riviera Café in the West Village. When they arrived, there was no sign of John Cale. Instead, Reed announced that Cale was being ousted; if Tucker and Morrison objected, then the band was finished. "Finally I weighed my self-interest against Cale's interests and sold John out," Maureen Tucker remembered.

Sterling Morrison was equally equivocal: "I told Lou I'd swallow it, but I didn't really like it. I'd have to say Lou bumped John because of jealousy. John and I always knew that he really wanted some kind of recognition apart from the band." Other observers blame "ego" - Reed's ego.

The decision gave Reed absolute power, but over a shattered kingdom. Cale's oblique vision and stunning improvisational talent had matched and spurred Reed's more traditional musical vision. Without Cale, The Velvet Underground became a vehicle for Lou Reed's songs; but they lost the three-dimensionality that fuelled their most experimental music.

Ironically, Cale's departure seems to have unlocked a key in Reed's psyche, enabling him to write songs more lyrical, tender and insightful than ever before. Cale had provided the soundtrack to Reed's searing revelations of sexual violence, chemical abuse and romantic obsession. Relieved of the burden of matching Cale's thunderous soundscapes in words, Reed discovered a more subtle way of expressing his feelings. He began to examine emotions from opposing sides, to realise the complexity of personal relations, to look beyond power as a solution to affairs of love and lust. The contradiction is that this empathy with the outside world was achieved by a Napoleonic gesture of manipulation, forcing his compatriots to cast out one of their number or lose everything they had worked towards for the last three years.

Cale went quietly enough, playing his last VU shows at - where else - the Boston Tea Party in September 1968. Four days later, the band appeared at La Cave in Cleveland with a new bassist - Doug Yule. Doug had a conventional rock background, with the Boston band Glass Menagerie, who'd supported the Velvets earlier that year; Steve Sesnick sang his praises to the rest of the band, who noted with approval that he was young, pretty and companionable, and therefore unlikely to challenge Reed's mastery.

Almost immediately, the Velvets went into the studio. Earlier in the year, they'd twice begun recording projects but aborted them. February 1968 saw them record 'Stephanie Says', a gentle, ambiguous ballad about a woman known to her friends as "Alaska". The band approached the song with a lightness of touch that suggested they might have been getting quietly mellow before the session - a feeling heightened by the sheer stoned silliness of the other track they recorded that day. 'Temptation Inside Your Heart' had Lou sounding like Woody Allen on reefer as he spouted one-liners like "electricity comes from other planets" while the rest of the band whooped up some falsetto harmonies.

Three months later came Cale's swansong, 'Hey Mr Rain', a simple Reed ditty ranged over a droning viola. Placid and undemanding, it satisfied neither Reed's poetics nor Cale's invention.

The band began to record their third album, 'The Velvet Underground', at TT&G in Los Angeles, the same studio where they'd completed 'The Velvet Underground And Nico'. This time, ironically, Reed welcomed the presence of another vocalist, allowing Doug Yule to sing the more complex lyrics in a gentle, emotionless voice that cunningly undercut their message - just as Lou had contrived. More contrivance was to follow. Reed later described the third album as "a complete synopsis of worldly sin", and hinted that it had been a concept album before its time. Its subject, he claimed, was "far, far more perverse than the other two albums"; Candy, its central character, was apparently the girlfriend of the junkie who'd been the narrator of the first two Velvets' albums. He even went so far as to construct a plotline which linked all the songs together as a mutual exploration by Candy and her friend of the limits of love and salvation.

But Reed's novelisation was too glib for a record which unveiled a new style of lyric writing. For the moment, he sacrificed the seamy street sagas of the earlier albums, and also trimmed down the consciously poetic language of 'Venus In Furs', 'Black Angel's Death Song' and 'Lady Godiva's Operation'. Instead, he reduced his lyrics to a series of puzzling aphorisms, little gems of moral guidance touched with cynicism.

The music had changed, too. Reed's sinuous lead guitar was briefly allowed its head, but the fundamental sound was sober and gentle, carefully holding back from emotion. The shift in landscape from the unhinged experimentation of 'White Light/White Heat' to the placid colouring of 'The Velvet Underground' was greeted by some of the band's core of followers as a betrayal - the first time Reed had to face the relentless logic of disappointed fans.

'Candy Says' set the tone - muted guitar playing delicate arpeggios, a whispered lead vocal from Doug Yule, and some soft doo-wah backing voices borrowed from the most sentimental arm of the Fifties vocal groups. It was the first time Reed had released one of his 'Says' songs, which made the bold statement in their titles that this wasn't Lou himself speaking. Candy may have been Candy Darling, who grew to hate her body sufficiently to become a transvestite and then die of cancer fuelled by the silicon implanted in her breasts. But the song did more than hint at Candy's dissatisfaction with her male gender: it explored the notion that experience would bring understanding, "maybe when I'm older". 'The Velvet Underground' is, to borrow William Blake's oft-quoted title, a collection of Songs Of Innocence And Experience; and 'What Goes On' elects for the latter, crying that only total dislocation of the senses can create personal freedom. It's a notion supported by the chemical stimulation behind 'Beginning To See The Light', where Reed stays as high as he can, to avoid the question, "How does it feel to be loved?"

Much of the album tries to deal with that puzzle. 'Some Kinda Love', coated in Reed's most angular, tense guitarwork to date, tells us that "no kinds of love are better than others". The beautiful images of 'Pale Blue Eyes' lead to the same conclusion; "If I could make the world as pure and strange as what I see", Reed wishes, and the juxtaposition is quite deliberate. The single repeated verse of 'That's The Story Of My Life' repeats the lesson: wrong and right, says Billy, are one and the same. And just to prevent the class from becoming too predictable, Reed follows this trilogy with a simple request for Christian salvation in 'Jesus': "Help me in my weakness/Cause I'm falling out of grace".

The album's theme is summarised by the innocent voice of Doug Yule on 'I'm Set Free': "I'm set free to find a new illusion/I've been blinded by hate so now I can see". Vision and illusion, freedom and restriction, good and evil - Reed sets endless pairs of opposites in motion, and leaves them to wear each other down. No response to life is any more valid than any other; and as the eternal observer, the uninvolved creator of his confused cast, Lou can simply walk away.

Two songs remain, but neither really belongs to the rest of the album - though they do cast ironic shadows over what has gone before. What's startling about most of 'The Velvet Underground' is the way in which Reed passes such complex and demanding issues before our eyes in so few words, and with such a minimum of musical support. But the sense of unresolved drama which Reed constructs in his songs is also the reason that the album remains alive in a way that other, more transparent work does not. 'The Velvet Underground' is not just an unsolved mystery; it's a mystery that can never be solved.

And so is the album's penultimate track - a 'Murder Mystery', to be precise. This one track contains more words - spewing out of two speakers simultaneously, in an obvious tribute to the double screens of Warhol's *Chelsea Girls* - than the rest of the album put together; and all of them are reduced from meaning to sound by the babble from the other side of the room.

'Murder Mystery' is a sustained wordplay, which was printed in 1972 in the literary journal *Paris Review* as a Lou Reed poem. That transcript omitted many lines from the song, however - not because Lou had rewritten it, I reckon, but because the poor fool given the task of copying the words off the record couldn't keep up. The song alternates fast and slow sections, involving recitations from all four members of the band; after several minutes, this format breaks, leaving a childish piano riff clanking in the background while two sets of words compete to drown each other out. And what words: even in its truncated, printed form, 'Murder Mystery' is a stunning piece of work, impenetrable to any easy attempt at understanding, but resounding with puns, wordplay, assonance, dissonance, the entire calendar of the poet's diary. Like a nightmare, the phrases hang just outside the reach of meaning; any flurry of words that does make a distant brand of sense is immediately contradicted or obscured by its neighbour.

'Murder Mystery' may just have been Reed reminding himself not to trust the power of words. What follows is pure bathos: Maureen Tucker, already devastatingly off-key in her contributions to the previous track, chanting her way through 'Afterhours', a coy nightclub ditty that asks us to "say hello to Never", but probably has no deeper message other than the blues cliché that the night time is the right time. The Athens band REM, avowed disciples of the Velvets, often closed their shows with this song on tour during the late Eighties.

Not surprisingly, 'The Velvet Underground' failed to bring any relief to the band's commercial situation. Maureen Tucker later described their financial state as "dire", and the deliberate non-production of the record - emphasised when Lou rejected the album's original mix and redid the job himself, leaving the sound even flatter than before - couldn't help that. Reed was obviously not concerned, for he chose not to record 'I Can't Stand It', a fixture in their live shows by late 1968, and just the kind of jokey, off-the-wall song that might have reached the mainstream radio stations.

Lou had now moved out of Greenwich Village to the Upper East Side; Sterling Morrison remembers his flat as being a scene of "isolation and despair", devoid of furniture beyond his guitar and notebook. But he was on a creative roll: by early summer 1969, he had completed another album's worth of songs, possibly even enough for a double set. Most of these were débuted on the road, usually at the perennial Tea Party, but also in Canada and Texas, two venues where the band were taped at gigs which eventually provided the raw material for 'Live 1969'.

This double album, like the existing bootleg tapes from the same era, demonstrate that the band were infinitely stronger in person than in the studio. 'What Goes On' held the most dramatic transformation: laboured and clipped on the third album, it became an extravaganza onstage, building into a repetitious instrumental section which could have lasted forever, as powerful as anything the band ever recorded. 'Sweet Jane' was written in the spring of 1969, as were 'Rock & Roll', 'Over You', 'Coney Island Steeplechase' and a dozen more. Some were throwaways; the medley of 'Sweet Bonnie Brown and 'It's Just Too Much' on the 'Live 1969' album was simply a Chuck Berry soundalike. Others formed the backbone of Reed's recorded repertoire for the next four years.

Receiving neither royalty cheques nor any further advances from MGM, and convinced that the company had lost interest in them, the Velvets faced the prospect of completing their four-album contract with little enthusiasm. "We weren't that interested in giving them another one to just let die," Maureen Tucker recalled. In between their constant treks up and down the East Coast, the band made a series of visits to the MGM Studios in New York during the summer of 1969, recording at least thirteen songs. None of these was copyrighted at the time, suggesting the Velvets knew they weren't going to be released. The story goes that the band deliberately taped sub-standard renditions of these songs in order to encourage MGM to break their contract, so that the Velvets could then look for a more lucrative deal elsewhere. The tale is almost believable, until you hear the tracks, many of which are far more commercial than anything the band had submitted to MGM in the past. It's hard to credit, for instance, that a label which had issued 'The Gift, 'Heroin' and 'Murder Mystery' would suddenly have considered 'Rock & Roll', 'Lisa Says' and 'We're Gonna Have A Real Good Time Together' too *recherché*. Yet at the same time, it's interesting that the band chose not to record 'Sweet Jane' at MGM, unquestionably the strongest of their new material.

The truth may be that MGM dropped the Velvets not because their songs weren't good enough, but because the label's hierarchy - now dominated by easy-listening king Mike Curb - had elected to drop all bands with drug references in their lyrics from their roster (all, that is, except for Eric Burdon and The Animals, who were too successful to sacrifice). The Velvet Underground were the epitome of what Curb disliked about the rock business: given that their display of gold records was decidedly bare, they would have been prime contenders for the guillotine.

What the Velvets left, voluntarily or not, in MGM's vaults was sufficient for two albums of 'archive' recordings in the 1980s - 'VU' and 'Another View', both of which boasted crisper, brighter sound than anything the Velvets issued during their lifetime. Besides an early version of Reed's paean to the liberating arrival of 'Rock & Roll', the albums included a jaunty 'We're Gonna Have A Real Good Time Together', a one-verse set-opener that lived up to every promise in its title; an obscure rocker called 'Foggy Notion', which was as imprecise as its title suggested, and chugged along quite happily for several minutes; 'I'm Sticking With You', a *faux naïve* successor to Maureen's showcase on 'Afterhours'; and 'Ocean'.

'Ocean' is proof that Lou Reed intended more than contract breaking when he approached the final MGM sessions. A brooding, complex song, it evokes the mysterious power of the waves - at once threatening and calming, capable of drowning a man in the fluid which comprises most of the human form: water. "A guy goes mad on the track, and obviously goes mad," Lou explained. "The ocean engulfs him. It gets very eerie." And so it does, though the madness Lou found so explicit isn't overt in the song. "I am a lazy son/I never get things done" Reed sings, filial guilt a subject with which he had been made very with familiar over the previous decade. And behind him Maureen Tucker's cymbals echo the hiss and fall of the waves, portending approaching doom. The lure of the sea, and the shame of the son: psychodrama was not far away in the latter days of 1969.

"It was a process of elimination from the start. First no more Andy, then no more Nico, then no more John, then no more Velvet Underground." (Lou Reed)

Maureen Tucker remembers that in 1969, Lou Reed stopped taking drugs. At the same time, The Velvet Underground dropped 'Heroin' from their live shows. "That track tears me apart and I don't want to know about it anymore," he explained later. So when The Velvet Underground settled in for a New Year season at the Philadelphia Second Fret in late December 1969, 'Heroin' was gone - and in its place was another set of new songs, including early versions of 'Goodnight Ladies', 'Oh Jim' and 'Sad Song', the last of which was also apparently taped in a studio session. Most bizarre of the additions was 'Oh Sweet Nothing', a hymn to non-awareness which comprised countless repeated verses about fictional nonentities, the lead character named after the archetypal American newsboy, Jimmy Brown. The song was incidental, however, beside its arrangement, with Reed's guitar pulsing distorted, yet fiercely controlled notes, four to the bar, a valediction to LaMonte Young's ideas of repetition and continuity, and a weird prediction of the unchanging tones which were to dominate 'serious' music in the early 1980s.

After the Philadelphia gig, Steve Sesnick was able to arrange a new record deal - with Atlantic, the label which had rejected Reed's "drug songs" four years earlier. Label chief Ahmet Ertegun, writer or producer of many of the classic Fifties R&B records that had fuelled Lou's teenage dreams, championed the band; in return, they began to rehearse the pick of their new material, cutting demo versions of songs like 'New Age', 'I Found A Reason' and 'Countess From Hong Kong'.

In March, Maureen Tucker took a sabbatical to prepare for the birth of her first child. She was replaced on drums by Doug Yule's brother Billy, and the new line-up took a week or so to rehearse before retreading familiar paths through Philadelphia and Boston. Then, in mid-June 1970, they returned to New York for their first hometown gigs in three years.

They were booked for a ten-week season at Max's Kansas City, unofficial clubhouse for the Warhol entourage, and second home to Velvets Reed and Morrison during New York stopovers. The contract required they should play twice nightly from Wednesday through Sunday; on Mondays and Tuesdays they could begin work on their first record for Atlantic.

The internal chemistry of The Velvet Underground had now altered almost beyond recognition. Sterling Morrison was immersed in the college courses he'd been forced to interrupt to join Reed's band in the first place; he showed up for the Max's gigs, but played only a minimal role in the recording studio. That left Lou, and the two Yule brothers, with the group's avant-garde strain long since submerged beneath Doug and Billy's orthodox rock credentials. The Velvets who played at Max's, and recorded 'Loaded', weren't the same band who'd made 'Heroin' or 'Sister Ray': they sounded more like a cross between The Flamin' Groovies and the early Mothers Of Invention, revivalists of ancient rock styles with a cynical edge. "I was giving out interviews saying, yes, I wanted the group to be a dance band," Reed recalled. "But there was a large part of me that wanted to do something else. That part of me wasn't allowed to express itself, in fact was being cancelled out."

'Loaded' tells its own story. With Reed having sung himself out on stage, he turned over many of the lead vocal chores to Doug Yule. Either way, there's precious little of the real Lou Reed on the record. Like The Mothers Of Invention's 'Ruben And The Jets', most of 'Loaded' is an affectionate pastiche of the music that turned Reed on as a kid - like the straight doo-wop of 'I Found A Reason', sung in hallowed tones by the band, and debunked only by Reed's clever-clever monologue; or 'Head Held High', which could have turned out like 'White Light/White Heat', but instead came over as a forced parody of early Sixties garage-band punk.

Parody, in fact, laces the album - 'Train Comin' Round The Bend' satirising the trend for rock bands to "get their heads together in the country", 'Oh Sweet Nuthin' capturing the lazy country-folk vibe of The Grateful Dead's latest move. Even 'Rock & Roll' is a muted celebration, with the propulsive solo Lou unleashes midway through sounding like an unwelcome visitor from the past.

Only two tracks carry any real resonance, 'Sweet Jane' and 'New Age'; and both were fatally wounded during the recording process. 'Sweet Jane' became Reed's standard set-opener for more than a decade: he described it as "a salute to nostalgia", which was at least one stage removed from the unashamed nostalgia of the rest of the album. Ironic in the extreme, it poked scorn at the comfortable middle-class existence he'd left behind on Long Island, took a sideswipe at social comment and "protest kids", and adopted a pose of supreme indifference and innocence. But it was the riff that counted - a simple three-chord progression which locked into the rock bloodstream and became an instant standard, fodder for aspiring guitarists ever since.

'New Age' was more subtle in its charms. In the studio, with Yule impersonating Reed, the song adapts Andy Warhol's worship of Hollywood movie stars to its own ends, as the singer approaches an ageing actress with a chat-up line that concentrates entirely on her bygone fame. "It's the beginning of a new age," he promises, in a voice devoid of any passion. In concert, Reed aimed the lyric at two of New York's icons: "It seems to be my fancy/to make it with Frank and Nancy". But in Yule's hands the humour was lost.

The album began with a straightforward piece of Sixties summer pop, 'Who Loves The Sun', and tailed away into the laborious ending of 'Oh Sweet Nuthin'. Between was merely emptiness: a Velvet Underground album on which it is difficult to find Lou Reed, even when he is the vocalist. The album title was apparently an ironic comment on its hit-making potential; but 'Loaded' is less a commercial move than an abandonment of responsibility on the part of its creator.

The album was completed in July, mixed, and sent in to Atlantic. It was released three months later, having - according to Reed - been butchered en route: "The songs are out of order... they don't form a cohesive unit, they just leap about. They don't make sense thematically. The end of 'Sweet Jane' was cut off, the end of 'New Age' was cut off, the guitar solo on 'Train Coming Round The Bend' was fucked around with and inserted." 'Sweet Jane' was indeed missing a middle section that Reed usually performed in concert at this time, though its omission merely strengthened the song's musical structure, and Reed dropped it from his live renditions after 1973. As for the rest - well, you could shuffle the songs until doomsday without coming close to the 'thematic sense' of 'The Velvet Underground'. Reed was more honest when he admitted: "I just gave up on it. I wasn't there when it was done."

That presumably explains the way in which the album was packaged and presented. The album cover had none of the conceptual unity with the music that had marked previous releases - well, maybe it did, because it was cheap and nasty. On the back, all Lou's songs were credited to The Velvet Underground, who were listed individually - Doug first, his name followed by the claim that he'd been responsible for "lead guitar, vocals, lyrics and song compositions". Then followed Sterling, "lead & rhythm guitars & song composition"; and then, at last, Lou, credited with "rhythm guitar, piano, vocals, lyrics & song composition". Maureen Tucker was listed as the album's drummer, though she took no part in the sessions; Billy Yule, 'Tommy' and Adrian Barber were given thanks for their "percussion assistance". (Barber was the man who taped the infamous Star-Club tape of The Beatles live in Hamburg in December 1962, incidentally, now graduated from the Liverpool beat scene to become a studio engineer in New York.)

Even though Reed had relinquished vocals on several tracks to Doug Yule, the billing order was, to say the least, ungracious. Even more unseemly was the secret battle that erupted over the songwriting copyrights. With the exception of 'Who Loves The Sun', which was admitted as a Reed/Yule collaboration from the start, Reed copyrighted all the 'Loaded' songs in his own name in late October 1970. Four days later,

Yule retaliated, copyrighting his arrangements of 'Head Held High', 'Sweet Jane' and 'Rock & Roll', as heard on 'Loaded', for the Velvets' joint publishing company, Virpi Music. And in December, 'Cool It Down', 'I Found A Reason', 'Lonesome Cowboy Bill' and 'Oh Sweet Nuthin'' were also claimed by Virpi, who credited all four songs to Reed/Yule/Morrison.

With his songs apparently mutilated in the studio, his track order ignored, his name reduced to third billing and his songwriting royalties set to be divided three ways, it's no wonder that Reed regarded the making of 'Loaded' with some misgivings. Yet the fact that so many strokes were pulled is an indication of how little interest Reed was taking in his career by August 1970. The record was completed while he was still a member of the band, but somehow he never noticed that his songs had been tampered with - or if he did, he simply didn't care. Later he cared passionately, and lawsuits began to be assembled. But for the moment Reed was the leader of The Velvet Underground only in theory.

The season at Max's was his final fling. As tapes of the period show, the Velvets had now become little more than a bar band, background music for the Warhol clique to discuss Factory gossip. Lou was still toying with new songs - 'I'm Free' and 'Walk And Talk It' were two that surfaced during rehearsals - but the actual performances were shambolic, almost devoid of life. Lou had become little more than a parody himself - his butch haircut and Jaggeresque stage movements were decidedly camp, and between sets he sat alone in the Max's bar and worked his way through one beer after another.

Steve Sesnick had steered the Velvets through the previous two years, finding them work at his own club when no-one else would employ them, and convincing Atlantic Records that the band was a commercial proposition. When Lou began to close himself off from the rest of the world, Sesnick must have felt betrayed. One night at Max's, he told Reed he wasn't prepared to make the effort any longer. He continued to manage the Velvets, in name at least, but his personal relationship with Lou was fractured.

Lou had accepted Sesnick as a substitute for Andy Warhol - not just as a manager, but as an adviser, straight man, cheerleader, all the psychological props required to keep the team on the road. When Sesnick pulled back, Reed had no back-up; and he felt lost. A couple of days later, the Velvets were astonished to find Lou's parents backstage at Max's. And shortly after that, on August 23, 1970, Lou announced that he was leaving the band, and returning to Freeport, Long Island - to live with the man and woman who had been the butt of his conspiracy theories for the previous decade.

Despite being cast as the villains in Reed's pubescent melodramas, there is nothing to suggest that his mother and father were anything other than concerned middle-class parents, convinced that their son would be best-served by a career in business. They were distraught when he confessed to being a homosexual, wrote songs about illegal drugs, and caught hepatitis at regular intervals. Depressed and undermined by the

Velvets' internal politics, Reed was in need of moral and physical sustenance, which his parents provided to the extent that by 1972, when he
re-emerged on the rock scene, he had noticeably gained weight, and his
constitution was strong enough to consider going back on the road.

Touring was one of the pressures that weighed on Lou in August 1970.
Sesnick was in the process of negotiating another enervating series of
shows in California and down the East Coast; Lou found himself unable
to write outside of New York, and saw little point in continuing to force
himself into promoting a band that no-one wanted to support. So the
Max's show on August 23 was the end of the road - and, fortuitously, in
the audience that night was Brigid Polk, as ever accompanied by her tape
recorder. When Atlantic demanded one last album from the band in 1972
to complete their contract, Polk's tape was exhumed, doctored, and
issued as 'Live At Max's Kansas City'. No mention was made of the fact
that this was Reed's last night with the band; at that stage Atlantic had
the remaining Velvets still under contract, and were hopeful that Doug
Yule might yet pull out a hit record. The album is as amateurish as the
rest of the Max's recordings, but the fact that Reed knew it was his last
VU show allowed him to mix the band's dance songs with some of their
stranger ballads, and the record ends with Reed piping his way happily
through 'Afterhours', a suitably bizarre conclusion to his career with The
Velvet Underground.

That should decently have been the end, but having carried the weight
through the last few months, Doug Yule simply assumed the leadership
that had been his by default, and carried on. Willie Alexander replaced
Lou; then, when Maureen Tucker returned in place of Billy Yule, and
Sterling Morrison left for a career in academia, Walter Powers completed
the line-up. Tucker soon left again, with Billy Yule stepping in once
more, and as late as November 1973 The Velvet Underground were still
valiantly touring East Coast colleges, playing a country-rock hybrid that
owed more to The Grateful Dead than the disciples of LaMonte Young
and Andy Warhol. There was even one more VU album, 'Squeeze',
which was effectively a Doug Yule solo project (he played almost all the
instruments, wrote and sang all the songs, and even managed to turn in a
fair pastiche of Reed's style on 'Little Jack' and 'Caroline'). In concert,
the group performed selected highlights from 'their' back catalogue, plus
an unlikely selection of covers including Bobby Bland's 'Turn On Your
Love Light' and the Dixie Cups' 'Chapel Of Love'.

Lou would have loved it.

SEVEN

BETWEEN AUGUST 1970 AND JANUARY 1972, Lou Reed retired from the rock business - not that the rock business noticed. The demise of The Velvet Underground and Reed's departure from the group weren't news stories in the States outside the pages of *Creem* magazine, perennial champions of Reed's art. The original band never toured Europe, and Reed remained virtually unknown in Britain until David Bowie began to drop his name during 1971.

The rock scene that Lou abandoned had shed most of its allegiance to the spontaneity and ambition which had been the Velvets' original hallmarks. What began as a means of enfranchising growing numbers of adolescents during the mid-Fifties had become an industry in its own right, basking in the self-consciousness of the artists and the vast revenues they generated. As the original rock audience grew into adulthood, so they demanded music which both reflected their own changed circumstances, and at the same time offered the taste of nostalgia for a less complicated age. This manifesto - making adult music for an adult audience, using the conventions of teenage rock'n'roll - was shared by Lou Reed, though his individual path to maturity was somewhat different.

Though rock began as the commercial folk music of a land named puberty, rooted in the twin traditions of country and rhythm & blues, its promise of liberation from conventional existence attracted a wider audience than teenagers. When British musicians discovered the 'ethnic' simplicity and emotional power of blues and rockabilly, they attempted to strike the same seam in their own music. Imported back into a nation where the founding fathers of rock had been emasculated or driven from the radio, the British Invasion of beat and R&B sparked a fresh budding of American talent - much of it college kids already educated in the social awareness of the folk tradition.

Through the lyrical perception and playfulness of Bob Dylan and the unceasing musical curiosity of The Beatles, rock music became ever more experimental and ambitious during 1965 and 1966. Recording technology improved to cope with the demand, and by the start of 1967

many of the best-selling records in Britain and America were incorporat-
ing collage techniques borrowed from the avant-garde. Inspired by the
kaleidoscopic plains which unfolded before them under the influence of
hallucinogenic drugs, and convinced that they were growing ever closer
to some vital spiritual truth, the rock aristocracy slowly turned away
from mass acceptance. Their drug escapades automatically erected barriers between themselves and much of their audience: for every fan who
followed The Beatles towards the nirvana of acid and dope, several more
dismissed them as fools. But the solidarity of what began to be known as
the 'counter culture' compensated for this increasing polarity of attitudes.
While teen-orientated idols like The Monkees and Bobby Sherman
revived the adulation that had once greeted Elvis Presley and The
Beatles, the class of '65 were headed for the furthest borders available,
certain that their followers would join the trip.

The strict division between 'rock' and 'pop' that emerged after 1967
was only bridged by a handful of artists, foremost among them The
Beatles and The Rolling Stones. Rock controlled the 'intelligent' music
media, leaving the teen magazines to fight over the 13-year-olds. The
new rock barons imposed their own definitions of culture, which
involved a vague commitment to political revolution, a stand against the
Vietnam War, and the certainty that the use of illegal drugs was a haven
of sanity in an increasingly neurotic world.

Few of the rock idols of the late Sixties survived untouched into the
new decade. The Beatles fell apart, the Stones developed into fashion
icons, Bob Dylan moved into semi-retirement, Janis Joplin, Jim Morrison
and Jimi Hendrix all overdosed on the drugs that were supposed to set
them free. While many of their younger successors skipped the politics
lesson and set their controls for musical sophistication or, at the other
extreme, lowest-common-denominator macho posing, the folk tradition
reasserted itself. In the Sixties, you made a personal statement by exploring the boundaries of recorded sound, or of the unconscious mind. In the
Seventies, the tradition of the artist was turned back towards songwriting
- in particular, confessional writing.

For the remainder of the decade, mainstream American rock was dominated by the generation of 1970, or their reservists. For every Neil Young
or Joni Mitchell, able to catch some transcendent lyrical insight, there
were twenty soft-rockers mixing their own self-pitying and forlorn tales
of love with gentle covers of 'classic' soul tunes or Hank Williams ballads. James Taylor set the mould: he was briefly greeted as 'the Messiah
of Rock', and then just as quickly vilified as a self-indulgent wimp by the
same people, who chose to ignore the fact that - unlike most of his contemporaries - he was a singer and writer of rare wit and self-deprecation.
Taylor came from the East Coast, Mitchell and Young from Canada, but
the sound of the Seventies was the sound of California, where the diet of
sun, sea and sniffing cocaine became the accepted backdrop to the indulgences of the record industry.

While California's soft-rock rebels captured the American adult market, and Britain spawned a generation of 'progressive' groups creating

ever more tenuous and tedious concept albums in the tradition of Tolkien's *The Lord Of The Rings,* the teenage market in Europe and the USA demanded new sensations of its own. America found TheJackson 5, precocious musical sophisticates who miraculously revived the innocence and charm of the girl group era; and Britain discovered glam-rock.

Though glam quickly became a fashion statement rather than a musical credo, its original motivation was to put the fun back into pop. In the person of Marc Bolan, and then Gary Glitter, Slade and a host of others, glam became one giant party game, with a soundtrack that updated the music of Chuck Berry, Eddie Cochran and Gary U. S. Bonds. But the movement's theoretician, and its only significant songwriter, was David Bowie. Through the early Seventies, Bowie rode a switchback of career moves and artistic volte-faces which established him as the key icon of the era; and for the remainder of the decade he continued to explore a riveting combination of musical risktaking and lyrical nihilism - only to cast the lot aside in the 1980s and re-emerge as a soft-headed fashion victim, desperately searching for sanctuary in the middle of the road.

Late in 1970, however, he made one of rock's most significant statements when he appeared on the cover of his third album, 'The Man Who Sold The World', in a flowing dress. In September of 1971, shortly after recording the follow-up 'Hunky Dory', Bowie visited New York with his manager, Tony De Fries, his wife, Angie, and his guitarist, Mick Ronson. Bowie met Warhol at The Factory, and RCA Records, to which Bowie had recently signed, held a reception for their new protégé at Max's. Lou Reed, encountering Bowie for the first time, was amongst the guests and is reported to have been impressed by what he heard of 'Hunky Dory', especially the song 'Queen Bitch'. "I knew there was someone else living in the same area I was," he said later.

Bowie mixed freely with others from the Warhol crowd at the reception. Never a man to ignore someone else's good ideas, he took careful note of the Warhol/Factory style - the frank sexuality, the decadent glamour, the 'instant superstar' philosophy, the legacy of The Velvet Underground - and adapted many of these ideas into the image he would soon create for himself in the UK. 'Hunky Dory', released in December of 1971, contained the track 'Andy Warhol', his tribute to the artist, and a month later he confessed - with a cynical eye towards the consequent publicity - to being bisexual. By mid 1972, having reinvented himself again as a visitor from space and ultimate rock hero Ziggy Stardust, he had taken to prostrating himself on his knees before his guitarist, flicking his tongue out towards Mick Ronson's crotch.

By daring to confess in public to longings and acts which had been illegal in Britain just four years earlier, and by wearing sexually ambiguous clothes and make-up, Bowie neatly defused the claustrophobic moral strictures of the entertainment industry. Adolescents traditionally experience the ambivalent pull of their hormones between one sex and another: here was someone giving that confusion a voice. For females attracted by a man who didn't assert his manhood, or males tantalised by the hint of forbidden fruit, David Bowie was a godsend; and after him, bisexuality could never be a taboo again.

On Long Island, rock's original poet of sexual ambiguity took no immediate part in this revolution. But unwittingly David Bowie had set the agenda for Reed's return. Bowie's dabbling with sexual identity had none of the obsessive force of The Velvet Underground's airing of sado-masochism and poly-perversity. But it brought it into the mainstream, and when Reed finally chose to return to his music, it was Bowie whom he picked as his new mentor. By this time Bowie, who owed a debt of honour if not hard cash to Reed, was well on the way to becoming a global superstar.

In the autumn of 1970, Reed had no thoughts of making a comeback. As with Bob Dylan after his legendary motorbike crash in 1966, rumours abound about Lou's activities and condition during the eighteen-month caesura in his career.

Some observers have speculated, as they did with Dylan, that Reed was being cleansed of drug contamination, though we have Maureen Tucker's testimony that he was no longer using drugs in 1970; others suggested that he had suffered some form of breakdown. Reed's own testimony was quite explicit: "I was a typist for two years, in the family business. My mother always told me in high school, 'You should take typing. It gives you something to fall back on.' She was right." 'Two years' is, as ever from Lou, an exaggeration; but for several months in 1971, Reed was apparently willing to clock in at the tax lawyers' office which he had ridiculed since he had moved to Syracuse.

Maybe Reed needed the security; maybe he just needed legal advice. During 1971, Reed fought and won a courtroom battle to gain sole copyright to the songs on 'The Velvet Underground' and 'Loaded'. Sterling Morrison commented a decade later: "Lou really did want to have a whole lot of credit for the songs, so on nearly all the albums we gave it to him. It kept him happy. He got the rights to all the songs on 'Loaded', so now he's credited with being the absolute and singular genius of the Underground, which is not true." Morrison, you should note, didn't dispute Reed's right to the 'Loaded' credits, merely to his status as sole inheritor of the VU mantle. Lou found moral justification in the decision of the court, and soon afterwards was also able to free himself from his management contract with Steve Sesnick.

Privately, Reed told friends he met in New York that he would never sing in public again. His artistic urges were now being channelled into verse, where he was free from the pressure to translate his thoughts and words into fodder for a bar band. In the early months of 1971, he completed a substantial body of work, some of which appeared sporadically in the rock/counter-culture magazine *Fusion* over the next few years. Feeling his way back towards the outside world, Reed showed up at a poetry reading at St. Mark's Church in the Village in March 1971, just down the street from the Dom where the Exploding Plastic Inevitable had been born.

Around the same time, he began a relationship with Betty Kronstadt, a waitress and aspiring actress whom he apparently met in a supermarket.

Everyone who met Betty - or Krista, as she styled herself for professional purposes - remembers her as a haven of sanity and common sense, just the kind of woman whom Reed's parents must have dreamed he would one day marry. With her neat, conventionally-cut blonde hair, a string of pearls around her neck, dressed trimly and smartly, she was worlds away from the sexual adventure playground of the Factory scene, and the violence and horror of much of Reed's writing. Lou seems to have relished her purity, and no doubt found her a dramatic antidote to the denizens of Max's Kansas City. Tentatively, he began to celebrate their union in verse, and then in song.

"I think I am now in love," Reed confessed in a poem openly named *Betty.* "I seem to have all of the symptoms/(ignore past failure in human relations/I think of Betty all the time)". In another piece, *He Couldn't Find A Voice To Speak With,* Reed began: "I am sorry princess I'm so slow in loving./Believe me, it is inexperience,/this inability to show affection,/the long minutes without words/and then a clumsy pinch perhaps". He described himself as "a sad and moody self... spellbound by possibilities and amazed at my own dullness," but concluded: "In my head are a thousand words for each and every love song."

Naked emotion of this kind rarely surfaces in Reed's work; it is usually cloaked in irony or distanced by being placed in the mouth of a fictional character. But none of Reed's creations ever spoke in such a direct tongue. At times, these poems are so open that they veer into self-pity, the adolescent ramblings of a man simply setting feelings on the page with no thought of translating them into art. A poem called 'Waste' offers Lou's darkest piece of self-analysis: "An education gone to waste/talent left ignored/imagination rent with drugs/someone who's always bored". That's a stunning confession, but the lameness of the ignored/bored rhyme removes it far from what Reed, in another context, described as "the spirit of pure poetry".

Reed's verse crept out unpublicised through the early Seventies, before there was a pause, and a second wave, which Lou intended to publish as a book. From this first era, there are vignettes of family life, like *This Is Not The Age Of Curtsy, Barely Civil Strangers Passing,* with "my sister" complaining when Lou wants to try on female wigs in a store: "No, I'll not have my brother acting the transvestite". In *His Friends Were So Surprised,* the central character "flipped out one icy day/his mind, not an ankle to be set in fracture" and requires "calming drugs to soothe it", while his friends rush to explain his behaviour to his father.

The best of these poems address Reed's own art. *Playing Music Is Not Like Athletics* is an assurance that "Talent carries its own weight/the intellect it weds determines greatness". And in *Thoughts Turn To Murder Late At Night,* Reed confronts his own demons of violence, noting wryly that karate raises "violence to the level of an art, which, unlike ballet, does not require the total man".

One poem cast a shadow over the paeans of love and trust. *He Thought Of Love In The Lazy Darkness* begins conventionally enough with the unworthy narrator speaking to the angelic lover - and ends with the thought "of dissolving you like a mint/or crushing you like a ladybug". It's the sole admission in these poems that romance involved a balance of power that Reed might not be able to pull off. Given the ambiguity of Lou's sexuality from adolescence onwards, the balancing act was always likely to prove too arduous.

Around May 1971, soon after Reed began seeing Betty, he ended up in a Village bar with rock producer Richard Robinson, and his rock critic wife Lisa. Robinson had been a stalwart champion of the Velvets, and began encouraging Reed to consider a solo career. Lou eventually gave in, and during the final months of the year he sat Richard and Lisa down in a room and reeled off a succession of new songs. Coy and miraculously self-confident, Lou exhibited intense pride in his creations - though many of them were actually leftovers from The Velvet Underground era. 'She's My Best Friend', the aptly titled 'Lisa Says' (which Reed performed as if he had written it as a thank-you note to Mrs Robinson), and 'Walk And Talk It' were all more than a year old, while other songs like 'New York Telephone Conversation', 'Hangin' Round' and 'Walk On The Wild Side' were no more than sketches of work in progress. More substantial were 'The Kids', full of Dylanesque internal rhymes, in which Lou announced himself as "the waterman"; 'Wild Child', a series of snappy vignettes of Village life, with Betty making an appearance in one verse after an acting audition; and 'I Love You', a delightfully one-dimensional lesson in romance which shared the wide-eyed innocence of his recent poems.

Having convinced both the Robinsons and himself that a comeback was a viable option, Reed prepared himself for the recording sessions, to be held in London in January 1972. During the latter half of 1971, meanwhile, he summarised his views on the rock circus in prose, as if to steady himself for a return to the fray. His essay, *Fallen Knights And Fallen Ladies,* was to form part of a book called *No One Waved Goodbye* - a sober reflection on the self-destructive urges that had robbed rock of a generation of leaders from Brian Epstein to Jimi Hendrix. While other writers focused their attention on one victim, Reed's analysis was more general. In a slightly mischievous hint at autobiography, he offered selected highlights of his time as a budding musician at Syracuse, and his initiation into the drug scene.

Against this humble background he traced the meteoric rise and decline of Epstein, Brian Jones and Jimi Hendrix - taking on the persona of the late Rolling Stones' guitarist to examine the nature of fame and its conflict with art, against the backdrop of the otherworldliness of the musician's life. Totally lacking in illusions, he dramatised the pull between audience expectations and the artist's own needs; and, in an eerie prophecy of the way he would spend the next few years, he painted a devastating picture of the gap between reality and image: "Who can you talk to on the road? Long-haired dirty drug people wherever you look. The boy passes over a bag of green powder... and passes out. Don't take that, it has horse tranquiliser in it. Oh, I shot up to your song. I got busted to your song. Oh please bless me and touch me and make it all go away. Who can you talk to when you're famous and alone and all the people idolize you and want to get high with you? Perhaps I should die, after all, they all (the great blues singers) *did* die, didn't they? But life is getting better now, I don't want to die. Do I?"

Lou was talking for Janis Joplin, last of the rock casualties he recalls in *Fallen Knights And Fallen Ladies*. But he might as well have been speaking for himself. The Lou Reed of summer 1971 was clean, confident, slightly chubby (all that home cooking) and in love. Over the next four years, Reed was made to live out the implications of his own valediction on Joplin: "She realised too late the habits of years are not undone in days... all of us are fallen knights". Reed's fall would be more spectacular, more public and eventually more deliberate than most.

EIGHT

"I'm not going to do things that complicated any more, because I realised people just don't catch it, and now I'm not that excited by the idea." (Lou Reed, 1972)

"I'm very good at the glib remark that may not mean something if you examine it too closely, but it still sounds great." (Lou Reed, 1979)

BESIDES PIONEERING A VOYAGE ACROSS the genders, David Bowie inspired the creation of The Velvet Underground cult. Bowie had followed the Velvets' career with enthusiasm since 1967, when his then-manager Kenneth Pitt had introduced him to their début album. At a time when no-one in Britain listened to the band, Bowie was performing their songs onstage, even borrowing a line or two from 'Venus In Furs' for his own 'Little Toy Soldier'. 'Waiting For The Man' was a frequent inclusion in his live shows. And on his commercial breakthrough, 1971's 'Hunky Dory', Bowie concocted a fair pastiche of the Velvets' style in 'Queen Bitch', crediting it on the album sleeve as "some VU White Light returned with thanks". By early 1972, he was playing 'White Light/White Heat' on BBC radio, altering the first line so it ran: "White light makes me feel like Lou Reed".

Such hero-worship could hardly go unnoticed. No sooner had Reed arrived in London in mid-January 1972 than he engineered another meeting with Bowie, and phone numbers were exchanged for the future. Reed, meanwhile, was set to begin work on his first solo album, tentatively titled 'Park Avenue', in a bid to assert his status as a New York icon.

Producer Richard Robinson had decided to capitalise on Reed's increased notoriety in Britain by locating the sessions there; it was Reed who hit upon Morgan Studios in Willesden, because he'd read that was where Rod Stewart had recorded 'Every Picture Tells A Story'. Reed's tastes in rock were now utterly conventional. Besides Rod Stewart, he admitted to a taste for The Rolling Stones and Chuck Berry, the familiar prophets of every bar-room band.

The musicians assembled to aid the recording of what became 'Lou Reed' were equally unadventurous, ranging from two keyboard players from the progressive rock band Yes, Rick Wakeman and Tony Kaye, to hardened sessionmen like drummer Clem Cattini and guitarist Caleb Quaye. Robinson also recruited two 'chick singers' to provide the vague hint of soul that the era required.

'Lou Reed' was, in its creator's words, "all love songs". "All easy options" might have been a fairer account, as the album followed the example of 'Loaded' by steering clear of any of the awkward questions posed by the first three Velvets' records. The moral complexity of the third album, the belief that "no kinds of love are better than others", vanished without trace. In their place was a jumbled set of Velvets rejects and one-dimensional throwaways, all wrapped in melodies as strong and lingering as anything Reed ever recorded. 'I Love You' highlighted Reed's mood: here were no metaphors or imagery, merely a gentle confession of love that would have suited any teen idol. "I figured that if I could take a phrase like that and turn it into something then that would be something of an accomplishment," Reed boasted.

'Love Makes You Feel' captured the same mood, with an effortless grasp of rock dynamics that proved Lou's innate ease with the form. 'Wild Child' was one of the strongest efforts, matching Reed's Dylanesque words to a 'Bringing It All Back Home' style backing. And 'Going Down' rationalised his indulgence in a conventional, heterosexual relationship, diminishing his mental anguish of late 1970 at the same time as he presented a girl in the arms as the cure for all evils.

'Berlin' repeated the joke of 'Afterhours' by spotlighting Reed the relaxed cabaret singer, using the divided German capital - a city he'd never visited - as a predictable home of romantic decadence. Reed attempted to lace the song with hidden meaning, claiming "You don't know the sex of the person I was singing to - it's ambiguous." Well, his companion was five feet ten inches tall: Lou tells us that in the first line. But otherwise the only ambiguity on display was the clash between the recollections of tranquility, and the failed humour of including an American government slogan - "Don't forget/hire a vet" - in the final verse. 'Vets', in this instance, were Vietnam veterans, not animal doctors.

Reed's work had always been determinedly apolitical: save for a throwaway reference to "soldiers fighting with the Cong" on 'I'm Sticking With You' and a blanket condemnation of all politicians in 'Heroin', he had conspicuously ignored the central political issue of the age. After basing their libertarian principles around drug use in the late Sixties, the rock mainstream had by 1972 begun to coalesce around the Vietnam issue, knowing that the bulk of the American public was on their side. Reed, like Andy Warhol, treated politics as an unnecessary nuisance. *Warhol's Diaries*, for instance, show him arriving at receptions for the Empress of Iran, unable to comprehend why demonstrators should be massed outside the hotel to protest against human rights abuses. Closeted within a self-elected élite, Warhol and - at this stage - Reed felt immune from wider social issues. It meant that Lou's work escaped the naïve sloganeering of, for instance, John Lennon's 'Power To The People'; but it also gave a song like 'Berlin' an unreality that sabotaged its pretensions towards the poetry of decadence.

What poetry there was on 'Lou Reed' was carried on 'Ocean', one of the record's few gestures towards real life. Like the rest of the album, it suffered from the heavy-handed, workmanlike musicianship of the band, but Reed's strangled vocal, veering between an uneasy stability and a manic gasp, gave the track an unexpected note of drama. And by choosing to end the album with the song, Reed admitted that he had written nothing better since 1968.

Constructed to capitalise on Reed's notoriety and to sell records, 'Lou Reed' was contrived from start to finish, but at least it was carefully contrived, which after the mechanical writing and playing on 'Loaded' was something of an improvement. Reed was as conscious as anyone that he had removed his own personality from the project.

"I'm always studying people that I know, and when I think I've got them worked, then I go away and write a song about them," he confessed in a rare moment of self-analysis. "When I sing that song, I become them. It's for that reason that I'm kind of empty when I'm not doing anything. I don't have a personality of my own, I just pick up on other people's." Next in line was David Bowie.

First, Reed had a heritage to mould. During the January 1972 album sessions, he flew to Paris for a couple of days to perform at the Bataclan Club, alongside VU cohorts John Cale and Nico. It was his first appearance with either for almost three years, and the trio instantly ignited the delicate fires of old. Reed picked at an acoustic guitar or, during 'Berlin', sat cross-legged on a stool with a cigarette posed carefully in his hand. Cale hammered at his electric viola; Nico intoned ominously. Together and alone, they offered a selection of songs from 'The Velvet Underground And Nico', among them a dramatically sparse 'Heroin'; Nico ended the performance with the eerie 'Janitor Of Lunacy'. Before the show, she and Lou had rehearsed almost her entire Velvets' repertoire, a throwback to the days of the Dom in early 1967. Afterwards, the three dispersed, leaving behind vague promises to repeat the experience .

With the album completed, Lou returned to the States, and auditioned touring groups. He eventually picked on The Tots, an unregarded bar band featuring twin guitarists, Eddie Reynolds and Winnie Latorta, bassist Bobby Reseigno, and drummer Scott Clark. Lester Bangs suggested that The Tots were "the ugliest cretins ever assembled on one stage... an intentionally asexual band"; elsewhere Lou had to endure criticism that he was being upstaged by Reseigno's flamboyant stage movements. The ensemble made a nervous début at the Millard Fillmore Room of the University of Buffalo, offering a mixture of songs from the upcoming album, and rocked-up, smoothed-out renditions of Velvets' songs like 'Heroin' (which Lou introduced night after night as "a junkie's dream") and 'Sister Ray'. Reed rarely played guitar onstage: instead he waved his hands above his head like a parody of Mick Jagger, and then recited polite introductions to each song like a trained showman.

The release of his album coincided with his first U.S. tour. Critical response was encouraging, though newfound Velvets devotees bemoaned the lack of electric viola and feedback guitar. Diehards went further, one outraged fan translating his anger into a privately printed pamphlet which suggested that Lou Reed had been made by a stand-in. The ironic twist was that in the great American outback, Lou let his road manager, Ernie Thormahlen, do his interviews for him, and no-one noticed the difference.

To help RCA promote the album, Lou scrawled out a brief biography, which was sent out with a simultaneous translation for those unable to decipher his half-formed penmanship. The Velvets had never needed to send out bios: no-one would have printed them. Unwittingly, RCA had given Reed his first shot at creating and maintaining the image of his choice:

"1. Played in Long Island hoodlum bands where there were fights.
2. Attended many schools - always had bands i.e. Pasha & the Prophets, L.A. & the Eldorados.
3. Expelled from R.O.T.C. for threatening to shoot officer.
4. Rejected from army - deemed mentally unfit - X5. Worked as song writer and met rejection.
6. Worked with Warhol and Velvet Underground through various permutations & helped create earlier "mixed media environment" also known in happy Sixties as "psychedelic".
7. Left Warhol, realigned band & ultimately realigned self.
8. Exile & great pondering.
9. Lawsuits & depression.
10. R.C.A., solo album, satisfaction."

Fleshed out and interpreted, this selective account of his first thirty years served as the landscape for most pen-portraits of Reed over the next two years. Reed's history dwelt on fights, hoodlums, the ROTC shooting incident, mental instability, and countered them with the myth of the artist rejected by his peers. It ignored his comfortable upbringing, college, Delmore Schwartz, poetry, homosexuality, LaMonte Young and the desire to be greater than Dostoevsky. And the media, for the most part, ignored them too. Between them, Reed and his supporters in the media extended this chosen image, and lo and behold, Reed began to live up - or down - to it.

First, Reed had another design to wear. Back in England in June 1972, he was adopted by David Bowie and his entourage. Reed had begun his solo career under the management of one Fred Heller - motto: "Lewis is going to be big in this business". Within weeks, Heller had been replaced by one of the RCA A&R men who'd recommended signing Reed, Dennis Katz. But Katz's supremacy was soon challenged by Bowie's manager, the irrepressible Tony DeFries, whose overwhelming enthusiasm gathered him a sheaf of admirers from Bowie to Iggy Pop. Reed was less impressed - "He was always running around telling people he was my manager, which he wasn't, although he tried," he reflected in 1973. But he was more than willing to accept the instant respect due anyone from the Warhol milieu, then at the height of its chic value in Britain.

Bowie was as impressed as anyone, and his own rise to fame since the beginning of the year allowed him the chance to repay the compliment. With his guitarist and stage foil, Mick Ronson, Bowie offered to produce Reed's next album. As proof of his devotion, he invited Reed to guest at his headlining show at the Royal Festival Hall, a benefit concert for the 'Save The Whales' charity - not a cause Reed had espoused in the past. Reed duly appeared to mass adulation, walked through three of his most famous songs, and the bond was sealed.

A week later, Lou and The Tots set out on their first British tour with a show at the Kings Cross Sound. Reed, the leather-clad symbol of the New York underground, remade himself in the image of David Bowie - a little glitter sprinkled across his face, two broad swathes of eyeliner, and a costume covered in spangles. "I did three or four shows like that, and then it was back to leather," Lou admitted after the tour. "We were just kidding around - I'm not into make-up." These tentative forays into the glam scene were merely the beginning, however. Reed relished the fact that he was being grabbed onstage by both girls and boys, and he accentuated the campness that had been stealthily creeping into his performances since 1968.

The tour had its more comic moments, such as the night when Reed and The Tots invited support act Philip Goodhand-Tait, a sensitive pianist-singer-songwriter, onstage to jam on 'Sister Ray'. For a country which had never seen The Velvet Underground, however, The Tots shows were the real thing; and the Bowie imprint merely added to the legend.

During the summer, Andy Warhol had approached Reed with the offer of writing songs for a Broadway musical he was planning with fashion designer Yves St. Laurent. This wasn't Warhol's first venture into the theatre: *Andy Warhol's Pork,* staged off Broadway and then in London in 1971 and much admired by Bowie who wound up employing most of the cast, had offered satirical snapshots of the Factory community in the person of Amanda Pork and her friends, who indulged in lengthy conversations about masturbation, watched all the while by a Warholian voyeur. The Warhol/St. Laurent commission was vaguer, and never reached fruition; but it gave Reed the excuse to write openly about the experience of cross-dressing and homosexuality.

These songs were among those on display when Bowie, Ronson and Reed went into Trident Studios in August 1972 to record 'Transformer'. This time the recipe was, Reed announced, "all hate songs", no more accurate than his opposite description of the début. "There's a lot of sexual ambiguity in the album, and two outright gay songs - from me to them, but carefully worded so the straights can miss out on the implications and enjoy them without being offended."

The entire concoction set Reed at the heart of the glam scene. The cover picture was tame enough - Reed eye-shadowed and faintly lost in a bleached-out picture by New York based Englishman Mick Rock, who became Reed's court photographer for the rest of the decade. It was the back which set tongues wagging - on the left a lingerie-clad transvestite posed against black velvet, on the right a New York gay clone, with bulging pectorals, one arm posed coyly on his waist, the other tugging playfully at a leather cap, and what looked like several pounds of sausage meat forced down his skin-tight jeans. Some people assumed Reed was the TV, others the clone; Ernie Thormahlen took the honours both times. But the inference was clear: sexual barriers had been removed.

The carefully juxtaposed cover photos were no more contrived than the music inside. Over eleven immaculately coiffeured songs, Reed dropped glimpses of the New York gay scene, the Factory, cross-dressing, oral sex, Andy Warhol's philosophy, sexual guilt and drugs. Stirred with a hint of irony and more than a little humour, 'Transformer' emerged as a primer for the new gay/glam crossover. It also provided Reed with a genuine hit record, in the shape of 'Walk On The Wild Side'. "The people I was around at the time thought Bowie would be the perfect producer for me to make a record that would sell," Reed commented rather ingenuously in 1982. "And it turned out to be totally true, didn't it?"

'Transformer's' strengths were all on the surface, which is what made it the ideal record for 1972/73. Bowie and Ronson produced it with all the sparkle they'd given Bowie's own Ziggy Stardust, a character whose appearance was as important as his message. In their hands, Reed became another Ziggy, reeling off attitudes and anecdotes like a walking Warhol doll. The doll's pose was slightly jaded humour born out of experience - tossing off glib asides with a knowing smile. 'Wagon Wheel', one of several nondescript rockers on the album, epitomised its lyrical softness. "If you get kicks from flirting with danger/Just kick her in the head and rearrange her," ran one couplet, neatly summarising the album's pose of callous, carefree amusement. In 'I'm So Free', Reed claimed: "I do what I want and I want what I see" - the wet dream of the spoiled child. And on 'Hangin' Round', Reed sharpened the knife: "You're still doing things that I gave up years ago."

This pose of studied superiority ran through the album. Only once did Reed let the mask slip - on 'Perfect Day', which followed the romantic scenario of 'Berlin' until Reed confessed: "You made me forget myself/I thought I was someone else, someone good". The rest was in the classic Warhol tradition, exotic but finally empty - even the lilting 'Satellite Of Love', a natural hit single which somehow failed to chart.

Warhol's pale visage hung silently over the album. He had suggested the coy opening line to 'Vicious' - "You hit me with a flower" - and Lou simply maintained the attitude for another three minutes. His proposed musical spawned at least two of the songs - 'Make Up' and 'New York Telephone Conversation', while another, 'Andy's Chest', was a Velvets' leftover inspired by Warhol's shooting. And then there was 'Walk On The Wild Side'.

As Reed told the story during his remarkable Bottom Line shows in 1978, his most famous song was inspired by Nelson Algren's novel of the same name. Working for his father's company in 1971, he'd been approached by theatrical entrepreneurs who wanted to turn the book into a musical, and figured that - after Ray Davies - Lou was the ideal adaptor. So Lou reads the book - "It's about cripples in the ghetto, are you kidding? I'm the best qualified person to write a book about cripples in music?" - steals the title, gets fired from the project, and then plays with a song to fit the concept.

By late 1971, he had enough of a song to play to Richard Robinson. But the lyric was unfocused, full of vague references to New York landmarks like the Empire State Building and 42nd Street, but with no voice or direction. Perhaps inspired by Warhol's commission, Reed eventually hit on the idea of peopling the song with Warhol's second wave of superstars - Holly Woodlawn, Candy Darling, Little Joe Dallesandro, the Sugar Plum Fairy (Joseph Campbell) - each portrayed for posterity, and at the same time gently teased by the ironic title line.

'Walk On The Wild Side' ended up no more than caricature, but it had a stunning musical setting, underpinned by Herbie Flowers' two-note bass slide, and decorated by the vocal doodlings of the "coloured girls". What gave the song its legend, though, was the fact it became successful - and was played on the radio by DJs too stupid to realise that Reed's novelty was full of people "giving head" and becoming transvestites.

As for the subjects of the song, they basked in the dubious notoriety it brought them. Candy Darling, before his/her death from cancer in 1974, suggested to Lou that they record a 'Candy Darling Sings Lou Reed' album, and it might even have happened - stranger things did in the mid-Seventies.

With 'Make Up', Reed made his most overt statement of homosexual sympathies to date, without involving himself in any way. "The gay life at the moment isn't that great," he explained when the album was released. "I wanted to write a song which made it terrific, something that you'd enjoy." So he pictured a morning-in-the-life-of a transvestite, which begins as she raises her sleepy head from the pillow, and then follows her through the routine of applying lip gloss, eyeliner and perfume, before slipping into "gowns, lovely, made out of lace". Isn't she "a slick little girl"?"Just because you're gay doesn't mean you have to camp around in make-up," Lou admitted the following year. "The make-up thing is just a style thing now. If people have homosexuality in them, it won't necessarily involve make-up in the first place." But by linking the two strands of sexual ambiguity, Reed simply confirmed the prejudices of the majority.

Yet at the same time, he lent support to the mainstream of the gay liberation movement, so styled since the cause of homosexuals had become a slightly unwelcome part of the revolutionary Left coalition in America after 1968. At anti-Vietnam demos, gays paraded with placards that read

"Bring the beautiful boys home", or "Suck cock and beat the draft". The Left was having enough difficulty assimilating the Black Panthers, and was already under siege by the women's movement, who found that they were still being cast in the role of sex slaves and housewives by men who said they wanted to rip society's straitjackets apart. The radical machos who were the standard bearers of the Left wanted nothing less than identification with the camp followers of the gay movement.

The American cultural mainstream lacked the example of a David Bowie, a public figure willing to declare himself homosexual - though a couple of leading women tennis players came close to the edge. When the Left splintered in the early Seventies, fragmenting into single-issue campaigns that lacked an overall perspective, the gay movement emerged stronger than most: like the women's movement, it had never trusted the motives of the heterosexual male Left in the first place. But the stereotypes of limp-wristed, cross-dressing faggots lived on.

Valiantly, the gay crusade adopted the motto "We're coming out of our closets", in the vain hope that enough people would declare themselves to break down the wall of hatred and disgust that surrounded them. It proved to be a tortuous, erratic progress, which was set back a decade or so by the discovery of AIDS.

Reed's contribution to the march of freedom was, at best, double-edged: it's uncertain that the Gay Liberation Front would have chosen him as a public representative. But in 'Make Up', he used their slogan as his chorus: "We're coming out/out of our closets/out on the streets". For that, he could be forgiven any manner of notoriety.

Andy Warhol might have missed the significance of the wording, but 'Make Up' would have suited his theatrical purposes perfectly. So too would 'New York Telephone Conversation', set to a finger-knotting guitar riff which Reed showed off to friends months before he'd written the song. Sung as a jesting duet with David Bowie, it summed up all the exuberance and triviality of the Warhol crowd, endlessly self-obsessed and gossiping. As a gentle satire on all Warhol's uses of taped conversation, from *a* to *Pork*, it did exactly what it was supposed to do.

Just one song on 'Transformer' offered the lyrical ambiguity of old - perhaps because it had been written in 1968. "If you didn't know it was about Andy's shooting, you'd never understand it," Reed explained helpfully, without helping at all. If the opening lines sounded like a grim threat towards Andy's would-be assassin, Valerie Solanas, the rest took a leap towards fantasy, directed partly at Andy, partly at Solanas, and partly at the pure joy of playing with words: "And kingdom's Christian soldiers dear for you/And melting icecap mountain tops for you/And knights in flaming silver robes for you".

Typically, the 1968 Reed was betrayed by his four-years-older counterpart, who added a cheap, jokey verse about Daisy Mae and Biff, and then admitted: "All that stuff about her nose going down to her feet - I don't know what it means either. I just put it in so that people would hear it when they were stoned and could laugh at it." Poetry made into jokes for potheads; sexual stereotyping and liberation confused as one and the same; Reed's ideas subjugated by Andy Warhol's: these were the roots of 'Transformer'. Add the spice of David Bowie and Mick Ronson's music, and the chic, glamorous ambience of the age, and you have artistic candy-floss - pink, fluffy and overflowing, but leaving you with a small piece of wood, and a stale taste in the mouth. Glam-rock was never intended as anything more than momentary pleasure but 'Transformer' has nevertheless survived the intervening decades better than any of its contemporaries.

For a few weeks, Bowie and Reed became inseparable companions. "I had a lot of fun," Reed recalled in 1973, "and I think David did." But as soon as Reed returned to the States, he began to have doubts about their relationship. "I don't know what he was up to," he admitted plaintively. "I honestly don't know." Though he and David rubbed noses for Mick Rock's camera at the swish party that followed the climax to the final UK Ziggy Stardust tour in July 1973, there were no more collaborations. "There's only one person who has a viler temper than mine, and that's David Bowie," Reed teased in 1973. At the end of the decade, the two men put their tempers to the test - in public. Until then, they paid each other lip service, and moved on.

"I think I am now in love.
I seem to have all of the symptoms." (Lou Reed, *Betty*)

"She was a secretary when one was needed at the time."
(Lou Reed, 1975)

"You can't fake being gay. If they claim they're gay, they're going to have to make love in a gay style, and most people aren't capable of making that commitment. That line that everyone's bisexual - I think that's just meaningless." (Lou Reed, 1973)

After 'Transformer' and an American tour, Lou Reed married Betty Kronstadt. Lou's manager, Dennis Katz, used the occasion to announce that Betty was taking great care of Lou's health, keeping him from drinking or trifling with drugs. After his first New York solo show at Alice Tully Hall in January 1973, however, journalists noted that Reed was maintaining a terrifying alcoholic intake, mixed (he said) with Valium. Three months later, still out on tour, still being advertised as a moderate man, Lou was trading double Scotches with the writer Lester Bangs. As he was helped to his room at the end of the night, Lou turned to the assembled company and slurred: "I know why you're all here. You just want to get a headline story, 'Lou Reed ODs in Holiday Inn', don't you?" "I drink constantly", he confessed to Bangs. "It destroys the nervous system. I'm getting tired of liquor because there's just nothing strong enough."

Strong enough for what? Lou Reed in early 1973 was plump and pale, his lazy eye accentuated by exhaustion, his hands trembling as he reached for the glass. Onstage, during a 30-date American tour which culminated in a bizarre 'battle of the bands' with Genesis in Canada, Reed had reasserted himself as the 'Transformer', complete with lipstick and eye shadow, flowery flares and a glittered jacket, signalling songs with hand movements like a camp traffic cop.

About his drug habits, Reed was more coy. "I still do shoot speed," he said that Spring. "My doctor gives it to me. Well, no, actually they're just shots of meth mixed with vitamins. Well, no, actually they're just Vitamin C injections." Whatever the substances, they cut across the effects of the alcohol, leaving Reed constantly wired, constantly on the edge of collapse. By his side, Betty watched sympathetically, anxious to preserve Lou from himself.

What had happened since late 1972, when Reed had been in command of himself and his addictive tendencies? Success. 'Walk On The Wild Side' had been a hit single in America, and 'Transformer' was on the stereo of every slightly confused adolescent from Los Angeles to London. Success had been the dream of the young rock'n'roller, but - as Delmore Schwartz had said - "In Dreams Begin Responsibilities". Reed was being torn between his own artistic conscience, which told him that most of what he had written and recorded since 1969 was escapism from his calling as a writer, and the "starmaking machinery behind the popular song", in Joni Mitchell's immortal phrase, which demanded more meat for the grinder. "When I get bored, funny things happen," Lou told Nick Kent in 1974, and in the midst of feverish activity, Lou Reed was bored.

The irony that he had married a conventional blonde at the moment when he was crowned as the Prince of Rock Decadence cannot have escaped him. Their relationship was fated from the moment when Reed began to trash himself in public. The chasm between 'real' life and his public mask loomed too wide; if someone was going to fall in, then everyone on the team would follow.

In the midst of the chaos, Lou met John Cale to discuss a possible reunion of the original Velvet Underground. "People don't know what we can really do," Reed commented. Cale was by now a flourishing solo artist, heading a smaller cult following than Lou's, but one which allowed him to mix semi-classical endeavours like 'The Church Of Anthrax' and 'The Academy In Peril' with softer concoctions like 'Vintage Violence' and 'Paris 1919'. Confident of his abilities as a writer, Cale was no longer prepared to play second fiddle - or second electric viola. The project would depend, he explained... "on how many of my ideas could be used. If we're just playing songs then there's no point. It would have to be on the same basis as before with the same realism about performing." Reed, for his part, was reluctant to relive the past: "Cale wants me to play the kind of feedback guitar I used to do, and I don't do that anymore." The encounter bore no fruit, and an attempt by Cale the following year to persuade Reed to play on his 'Fear' album proved equally unsuccessful.

A British tour was scheduled for April and May to coincide with the belated entry of 'Walk On The Wild Side' into the UK charts, but Reed put it back two months to allow himself time to finish writing his next album. Obsessed with the effects of amphetamines on the human body; puzzled by the demands of marriage; searching for a project which would rekindle his creativity, Reed enlisted the aid of Bob Ezrin, producer of two well-received albums by Alice Cooper. Reviewing the material Lou had already completed, Ezrin suggested that Reed weave them into a story, "a film for the ear" (as the album was eventually marketed). As he had done with The Velvet Underground, Reed responded to the challenge.

'Berlin' was chosen as the album's title; it allowed Reed to reprise part of his 'Transformer' song. The setting was purely arbitrary, despite Lou's protestations: "Berlin is a divided city and a lot of potentially violent things go on there. And it's not America, although some of the characters appear to be American. It just seemed better than calling it 'Omaha'. Berlin was just suggestive to me. It makes it tackier that it's in Berlin - it reminds me of Von Stroheim and Dietrich." And, to confirm that he knew no more about Berlin than he did about Omaha, Reed added: "The more sophisticated you are, the more Berlin represents."

Thankfully the album itself, recorded once again in Willesden with the help of British musicians, did not operate on such a shallow level. Though Lou's manager Dennis Katz reckoned that "it was intended as a black comedy", shedding some doubt on his own awareness of the project, Lou had darker motives. When he had assembled his songs into some sort of order, he designed the framework to hold them - a gloomy tale in which an expatriate American (this is all happening in Berlin, remember) plays out the final stages of a doomed relationship with a German speed freak and hooker (ditto). "It's involved with violence, both mental and physical," Reed explained. "It takes place for real in Berlin in 1973. The really important thing is the relationship between the two major characters. The narrator is filling you in from his point of view, and his point of view is not particularly pleasant."

Consciously or not, Reed also used 'Berlin' like a latter-day Delmore Schwartz, as a testing ground for possible courses of action in his own life. What would happen if he took speed for weeks, months, years? Was there a way out from his relationship with his wife? Was violence a justifiable response to frustration? These were the questions Lou faced; and Caroline and the unnamed narrator gave him answers, not always the ones he wanted to hear.

The September 1972 suicide of Andrea Feldman - alias Andrea Whips, star of Andy Warhol's film *Heat* - had sent a shudder through the Warhol community. Self-destructiveness was nothing new at the Factory, but Andrea had died convinced both that she was Warhol, and that Warhol was controlling her movements. Now the rest of the crew watched each other nervously for signs of the same disorder.

Andrea's death left its mark on Lou Reed, along with the rest of Andy's friends. So when it came to solving the tragedy of the fictional Caroline, suicide came to seem a suitable method. Strangely, ironically,

TOP LEFT: Lou Reed as a student at Syracuse University, 1963. TOP RIGHT: The Velvet Underground, 1967; left to right: Reed, Sterling Morrison, and Maureen Tucker.

ABOVE: The Velvets, 1970; left to right: Morrison, Tucker, Reed and Doug Yule. *(Jim Cummins/Starfile)*

Influenced by David Bowie's brand of glam rock, Reed dons make-up and black nail varnish, 1974.
(Mick Rock/Starfile)

ABOVE: David Bowie prepares for a Ziggy Stardust concert in 1973.

ABOVE: Reed performing at the Charlton Football Ground, London, May 18, 1974.
(Barry Plummer)

ABOVE: Reed with Nico in 1973 *(Mick Rock/Starfile)* and (BELOW) with Andy Warhol in 1976. *(Chuck Pulin/Starfile)*

ABOVE: Reed with 'Rachel'. *(LFI)*

ABOVE: Reed appearing at the New York Palladium, November 1976, with his TV screen stage set. *(Bob Gruen/Starfile)*

ABOVE: Reed's regular band from the late seventies, who appeared on the 'Take No Prisoners' live album. *(Bob Gruen/Starfile)*

Above: Reed at the Nelson Mandela Benefit Concert at Wembley Stadium, London. *(LFI)*

ABOVE: Reed with his wife Sylvia and the 'New York' band being presented with gold discs by WEA executives Paul Conroy (far left) and Roy Stills (third left). *(Barry Plummer)*

Reed and John Cale promoting 'Songs For Drella'. *(LFI)*

The Velvet Underground re-form for the Andy Warhol Exposition at Jouey-en-Josas, France, 1990. Left to right (BOTTOM): Reed, Cale, Tucker and Morrison. *(Renaud Monfourny)*

inevitably - choose your own adverb - the theme of 'Berlin' crept into real life. A few months after the album was released, Lou recalled someone in his immediate circle "standing there holding a razor blade up, and she looks like she might kill you, but instead she starts cutting away at her wrists and there's blood everywhere." Five years later, talking to Allan Jones, he filled in the details: "During the recording sessions, my old lady - who was an asshole but I needed a female asshole around to bolster me up, I needed a sycophant who could bounce around and she fit the bill, but she called it love, ha! - she tried to commit suicide in the bathtub at the hotel. Cut her wrists - she lived. But we had to have a roadie there with her from then on."

Reed's total contempt for his wife was simply another pose; to the king of the street punks, it was just another slashed wrist in just another bathroom. But this horrific gesture marked a point of no return for their marriage. When the album was completed and Reed moved on to play in Paris, he kicked her out. "Sometimes you're better off without anything," he explained a few weeks later, "make a fresh start."

Mr and Mrs Reed were not the only casualties during the Berlin sessions. When they were completed, as Lou recalled, "Bobby (Ezrin) turned to me and said, 'Lou, I think the best idea is that we put it in a box, put the box in a closet, leave it there and don't listen again'. And I think he was right." Ezrin returned to the States, and suffered some form of breakdown which required a brief period of hospitalisation. Small wonder that Lou recalled in 1976: "We killed ourselves psychologically on that album. We went so far into it that it was kinda hard to get out."

So what was this record that inspired suicide bids and nervous breakdowns? Simply a work of art to set alongside the finest achievements of Lou Reed's career. For the first time in five years, Lou allowed himself to explore issues that were not already settled. Almost every song cuts away at an open wound, demanding immediate attention. And the whole dramatic ensemble is set against a magnificent instrumental backdrop, at one minute lush like a Stravinski tone poem, at another sliced to the bone so there is nowhere to hide from the reality of love and death.

Bob Ezrin masterminded the music, establishing a star-studded session crew (with players like Jack Bruce, Steve Winwood and the Brecker Brothers), to which he added the dual guitar thrust of Steve Hunter and Dick Wagner, who'd worked with him on the Alice Cooper albums. Among the musicians on the album was keyboardist Blue Weaver, who was dubious about Reed's involvement: "We went in and laid down all the instrumental tracks, the whole thing was done and sounded great. Then they brought Lou in. He can't do it straight, he's got to go down to the bar and then have a snort of this and that, and then they'd prop him up in a chair and let him start singing. It was supposed to be great, but something went wrong." Reed's response to this was an incoherent, apoplectic series of threats and curses, but Weaver's testimony is undermined a little by the album credits, which list him as having only performed on one song.

'Berlin' was undoubtedly a collaborative effort, however, and for the first time since 1968 Reed was bouncing ideas off someone he could regard as an artistic equal. The validity of the claim that he and Ezrin constructed an entire concept album is open to question. The second side of the record definitely comprises a suite, a numbing series of songs which sink inexorably from depression to despair and ultimately to the death of feeling. The first half of the record is less structured; there's no obvious storyline at work. But apart from 'Berlin' itself, which is there purely to establish the location, and to allow Ezrin a little pleasure with his sound effects tapes, every song on the album is relevant to the investigation.

In 'Fallen Knights And Fallen Ladies', Reed had imagined himself into the psyches of rock idols in decline. 'Lady Day' is the name given the jazz singer Billie Holiday, who drugged and drank herself to death in 1959. The song of that title may be a picture of Caroline, the heroine of Berlin; but more likely it's a portrait of the real-life obsessive. Like a master storyteller, Reed never gives us the whole picture at once: 'Lady Day' is two episodes from a documentary, the first showing the singer entering the bar, the second following her empty progress 'home' to her green-walled hotel. The rest - the alcohol, the heroin - is left to the imagination, while Reed sends out a brief message of sympathy and regret.

The narrator of 'Men Of Good Fortune' says "I don't care at all", which is pretty much how he reacts to Caroline's death at the end of the record. But the real statement here comes from Lou Reed, and was directed at Long Island, and his own particular man of good fortune. Faced with a choice between wealth and poverty, Reed can see only paradox: rich men have opportunities denied to the poor, who have "no rich daddy to fall back on"; but "men of good fortune often wish they could die/While men of poor beginnings want what they have and to get it they'll die". Reed makes no moral judgements at all.

The first of two songs titled 'Caroline Says' not only continues Reed's tradition of giving voice to his female heroines, like Candy, Lisa and Stephanie in the past; it also offers an irresistible challenge to the amateur psychologist, who might be tempted to identify the song's "Germanic queen", manipulating and hurting men, as Nico. That aside, it's a damning portrait, both of the subject and the narrator who sits there and takes it when "Caroline says that I'm not a man".

The problem here is interpretation - the temptation to ignore Reed's protestations that his work is fiction, and read autobiography into every lyric. It's an issue which surfaces even more strongly with 'How Do You Think It Feels', a question that is both direct and rhetorical. "How do you think it feels," Lou sings, "When you're speeding and lonely... When you've been up for five days... Cause you're afraid of sleeping". And his voice, utterly devoid of the coy innuendo of his earlier solo work, has the dull, desperate creak of experience, asking himself the ultimate question: "When do you think it stops?"

'Oh Jim' demonstrates the difficulties of trying to force these ambivalent songs into a neat plotline. The narrator this time is talking to a man who has been enticed into drug addiction by his "two-bit friends", and is "filled up to here with hate". His advice? "Beat her black and blue and get it straight." It's one of several songs on this album that offer male violence as a comment on male-female relations, a sobering statement from a man whose recent marriage was already on the verge of collapse. So was Reed singing to himself - "They asked you for your autograph/They put you on the stage, they thought it'd be good for a laugh" - or to a character in the opera? Ultimately, it doesn't matter. The words carry their own weight.

The second half of 'Berlin' is more transparent - a 15-minute journey through pessimism, pain and emotional decay. The second 'Caroline Says' actually uses the tune, and a few of the lyrical ideas, from the Velvets' out-take 'Stephanie Says': this time, Caroline says "Why is it that you beat me, it isn't any fun". She finds refuge in speed, her friends laugh, and "it's so cold in Alaska". Finally, she shoves her hand through a window, just to find out if she can still feel.

'The Kids' is as melodramatic a piece of music as any rock musician has recorded. On one level, it's a piece of gross emotional manipulation, a callous and pathetic exploitation of pain. On another, it's an almost unbearable voyage to the bottom of the slough of despond, which drags down anyone who hears it.

His voice deathly pale, devoid of any emotion beyond acceptance, Reed recites another chapter of Caroline's tale - how her children are taken away from her "because they said she was not a good mother". Poor parenting, in this context, involves sexual promiscuity and drug use: Caroline is either a whore, a junkie, or both. But the role of the narrator is equally shady: he is "a tired man, no words to say", who is also "much happier this way", and who sees Caroline as "a miserable rotten slut" who "couldn't turn anyone away". Then Reed's voice trails away, to be replaced by the agonising cries of small children - legend has it they were Ezrin's, told that their mother wasn't coming home any more. By using girls too young to act the extremes of emotion, 'Berlin' cuts right to the bone, and exploits them at the same time - a double bond of love and prostitution that mirrors the album's central relationship.

After 'The Kids', we see 'The Bed' - scene of Caroline's suicide. Reed's voice expresses shocked, innocent wonder at this turn of events, while his words tell another story: "Funny thing, I'm not at all sad/That it stopped this way". And finally, there's 'Sad Song' - a production extravaganza with a cast of thousands, which helps to distance us from the emotional void of its narrator. He looks back through photos of Caroline with faint regret, before concluding: "I'm gonna stop wastin' my time/Somebody else would have broken both of her arms." And back comes the chorus, with the final verdict: "Sad song, sad song".

It's difficult to recall another rock album that explores such emotional terrain - and which deals so uncompromisingly with tragedy unaccompanied by remorse or guilt. 'Berlin' stands as a savage counterpoint to the collapse of Reed's marriage; sometimes, as Lou sings, "It has to be that way".

Betty won her divorce in the autumn of 1973, while Lou prepared for another tour, his first as a major star. "Everyone should have a divorce once, I can recommend it," Lou crowed a few months later; but the settlement forced him to abandon his Upper East Side home and spend several weeks based in hotels, besides paying substantial alimony. "All the money I make, she gets," he commented. "Now I don't get headaches any more and I'm poorer."

After the glitzy surface gloss of 'Loaded', 'Lou Reed' and 'Transformer', the realism and depression of 'Berlin' jarred with many people's preconceptions about Reed's pose and purpose. Orchestrated beyond the narrow restrictions of New York rock, the album scandalised as many as it intrigued; and those who didn't dismiss it as wilful image-plundering saw it as a sidetrack from Reed's role as poet of the Warhol underground.

For Lou, the album had a more immediate purpose. After several years of work which pandered to his image rather than stretching it, 'Berlin' represented an engagement with real life. And it hurt. "I had to do 'Berlin'," Lou explained early in 1974. "If I hadn't done it, I'd have gone crazy. If I hadn't got it out of my hair, I would have exploded. It was a very painful album to make. I don't wanna go through it again, having to say those words over and over and over." In the same interview with rock journalist Nick Kent, Reed came clean about the vacuity of his solo career to date: "I wasn't exactly exhilarated or thrilled by the whole thing, 'Lou Reed' and 'Transformer'. Boredom isn't the proper word - I knew things weren't right and I was waiting. Like my marriage, it was kind of a pessimistic act - nothing else to do at the time. Then one day it dawned on me that if you don't like it you can always walk out. And as soon as that becomes clear, it was all very simple."

Simplicity, in Reed's religion, always equalled directness - which is how Lou engineered the break-up of his marriage, and confronted the demons head-on in a masterpiece of decay and emotional removal. 'Berlin' portrayed both those states, but could not have been written under the influence of either. They were there as an escape route, however, already laid out as a path if circumstances should press too close to the bone. When the marriage failed, its emotional turmoil tolled out a message to the manipulator of the scene. When the album was misunderstood, it simply confirmed Lou's suspicion that involvement entailed pain. And to avoid pain, you had to remove yourself, and your work, from anything too real. "The way that album was overlooked was probably the biggest disappointment I ever faced," Lou told Allan Jones in 1977. "I pulled the blinds SHUT at that point. And they've remained closed."

So was born the 'Rock & Roll Animal' - a parody of rock excess which fitted Reed so well that it became impossible to distinguish from his actual personality. Lou had coined the phrase a year or so earlier, and had confidentially predicted that it would be the title of his album after 'Transformer'. Instead, he used it for a live album taped at the end of 1973 at the Academy Of Music in New York City and issued just a few months after 'Berlin'. For his European tour in September, he had assembled a new band, capitalising on his recording work with guitarists Steve Hunter and Dick Wagner, and also enticing Ray Colcord, Pentii Glan and Pete Walsh into the line-up.

Reed submerged his face beneath a topsoil of white powder, and accentuated his lips and eyes in black, emerging onstage like a panda in a braided suit. Ignoring his guitar, he exhibited a catalogue of rock clichés, pouting and thrusting out his pelvis like Mick Jagger, mincing like Bowie and Ronson, pointing at the audience with the command of Iggy Pop, coyly mimicking Monroe or Mansfield for the audience - even, horror of horrors, tossing his microphone into the air with the shamelessness of Roger Daltrey. Behind him, the twin guitar thrust of Hunter and Wagner robbed his songs of their subtleties. Everything from 'Sad Song' to 'Heroin' was transformed into a riff, ripe for guitar sparring and copious pyrotechnics, little of which had anything to do with Reed's original conception. Brutal and unfeeling, the Hunter/Wagner band recorded magnificent hard rock, and the bare material for heavy metal bands to come was laid out on Reed songs like 'Sweet Jane', 'Rock And Roll' and 'Waiting For The Man'.

Both in style and execution, though, the band's metallic rasp sacrificed the notion that art was the sum of possibilities. In the hands of Hunter and Wagner, the songs were means to an end, and nothing more. Their creator let his band loose, and watched impassively as they trampled his favourite children into the dirt.

Not that Reed admitted it at the time. "It's the way those things should be done and hadn't been done correctly," he smirked when the 'Rock And Roll Animal' set was released. Only later would he start to make excuses, claiming that without his live album, no-one would have issued the Velvets' 'Live 1969' set; and that the new arrangement of 'Heroin' was "desecrated" and "blasphemous". He said he'd promised RCA two commercial albums in return for being allowed to make 'Berlin', and 'Rock And Roll Animal' was the first.

Along with the pose and the metal, Lou Reed began to take on the lifestyle of the carbon-copied hard rocker. The early weeks of 1974 took a harrowing toll on his health, and when he was seen in public again in March, he was unrecognisable from the manic figure who had toured America three months earlier. Apparently living on endless speed runs, interrupted by occasional collapses when the system was wired one twist too far, Reed scarcely ate; weight slid off his bones, and the grim mask of his skull began to cut close to the pallid wrap of his face.

Accentuating his deathly visage, Reed's hair had been shaved down to a thin, moss-like coating, and then bleached white; Maltese crosses were cut into what remained. Though the designs originated, as their name suggests, from Malta, they were indelibly associated with the German Reich, having decorated the wings of Von Richtofen's airplanes in the First World War. Many people confused them with the hated Nazi swastikas, and pondered Reed's sanity aloud.

Management aide Barbara Falk noted that Reed and Dennis Katz "did have a fall-out when Lewis appeared with those Nazi crosses in his hair": this wasn't the way to reach Las Vegas. A week or so later, the crosses had gone; but the image remained, and with his hair still cropped to the bone, Reed invited comparisons with the fearsome caricatures of Nazi stormtroopers that littered American war comics.

Onstage, Reed clung pathetically to his microphone for support, dressed in shades and leather jacket that accentuated his stick insect pose. Along with Rolling Stones guitarist Keith Richard, Reed began to be fingered as an imminent rock'n'roll victim. Six months after issuing an album that traced the dissolution of a body and a personality, Lou seemed determined to run the experiment again - this time for real.

The 'Rock & Roll Animal' was such a successful media-play that, even at this distance, it is impossible to judge whether Reed was aware of the fine line he was treading. Like a true Warhol disciple, however, all he knew how to do was work. The spring of 1974 saw Reed attempt to restore three ancient relationships. He once again contacted John Cale about reviving The Velvet Underground; negotiations toppled for a second time. He joined Nico's sessions for 'The End', but the two fell out: "He wants to be black", Nico explained helpfully. And in a gesture of reconciliation, he recruited Andy Warhol to devise a visual presentation for his live shows. Warhol wasn't up to the task, however. His artistic work now amounted to little more than painting celebrity portraits to expensive commission, and lending his name to increasingly vacuous and trivial 'underground' films. Both activities mocked his work of the early Sixties. "It was very sad," Lou explained, "because he said while we were doing it, 'You know, it can never happen again'. And he was right. Andy's situation is kind of harsh. All that Sixties energy and now we're in the Seventies and there's nothing there." That was exactly the pose which Reed was trying to create for himself, of course, only the analogy failed to hit home.

Writing songs for Iggy Pop, rehearsing an acoustic set with Steve Katz, planning a new album, recruiting a fresh band: Reed was busy throughout the early summer of 1974, while the adrenalin raced continuously through his body. Before setting out on another European tour, he arranged a series of sessions at Jimi Hendrix's Electric Lady Studios in New York. These were his first solo sessions outside Britain and what emerged was a record with a very American sound. Katz, brother of Dennis and former member of The Blues Project, was co-opted as producer. As it turned out, he had to take complete control of the project from start to finish. "I slept through 'Sally Can't Dance'," Reed admitted in 1976. "They'd make a suggestion and I'd say, 'Oh, alright'. I'd do the vocals in one take, in twenty minutes, and then it was goodbye." That was exactly the process which Blue Weaver had described on 'Berlin', when Reed angrily denied it. For 'Sally Can't Dance', however, no confession was low enough. "It's cheap and nasty," Reed announced when it was released. "It was produced the slimiest way possible." At the time that was a compliment.

Three years later, talking to Allan Jones, Reed made no excuses: "I

HATE that album. I just CAN'T write songs you can dance to." And another year later: "I sound terrible, but I was singing about the worst shit in the world. That WASN'T a parody, that was what was happening."

Irony being the secret god of Lou's career, "the worst shit in the world" brought Reed his first - and only - Top 10 album. 'Rock And Roll Animal' was the killer punch: 'Sally Can't Dance' was the sucker that crept through the unexpected opening. It was not the guitar extravaganza that fans of the Hunter/Wagner band might have expected: the two duelling guitarists were not present at the sessions.

Instead, Katz gave Reed the ersatz black music feel that was rapidly becoming *de rigueur* among the rock élite - vaguely exotic rhythms borrowed from 'ethnic' cultures added a taste of spice to the customary white rock pudding. Katz's dessert was better produced than most, and Reed and RCA reaped the benefits. Katz never worked with Reed again. For devotees of his career, 'Sally Can't Dance' was - probably still is - the bottom of the pit. Reed had been muddle-headed before, but never had he turned his music into a cynical contrivance. The album felt vapid, lukewarm and false: the consensus was that Reed had jettisoned his last ounces of credibility.

'Sally Can't Dance' was no more blatant a career move than 'Transformer'; but while his collaboration with Bowie had followed the acceptable route of pastiching Andy Warhol, Reed's latest concoction was mixed with black music, and couldn't be trusted. Though he'd scarcely mentioned the subject in public, Reed had been a passionate black music fan since the Fifties. What else were the earthy harmonies of the doo-wop kings, or the torrential currents of Ornette Coleman? "I just have to watch myself that I don't get into jazz," Reed had blustered in 1972. "Jazz I just can't bear." This was just another pose, however: Reed had followed the zigzag progression of modern jazz since the late Fifties.

More to the point, Lou idolised Al Green. True successor of the Southern soul tradition of the Sixties, caught midway between religious fervour and self-parody, Green was a perfect soul icon for the new decade; and he could outsing anyone since Solomon Burke. When Lou heard his 'Belle' album, he proclaimed: "That record is for KEEPS. It is no accident. And the stuff he's singing about!" Green's record documented the battle between religious and secular love, a contest worthy of a Norman Mailer - or a Lou Reed.

In 1974, Reed's debt to Al Green was less serious. In conversation, Lou was apt to drop into unpleasant euphemisms, to shock more than anything: "our coloured friends" was a favourite expression, while he explained the growth in popularity of soul music thus: "When nothing's happening, nigger music - pardon me - soul brothers and their turbulent rhythm kinda takes over. It gets called disco."

So did 'Sally Can't Dance' - an album which pitted Reed's wavering monotone against a bank of horns and female singers, and then started off with a track called 'Ride Sally Ride', a phrase first heard in Wilson Pickett's 'Mustang Sally', and then used as the title for a song by - who else? - Al Green. The 'Sally' motif recurred on the title track, set to a shambling dance rhythm; while 'New York Stars' not only began with the guitar riff that later inspired David Bowie's 'Stay', but also jerked to a rhythm that approximated funk.

Like Al Green, Reed used the medium of dance to stir up more complicated issues. 'Ride Sally Ride' set the tone for the album, with its elegiac French horn and piano introducing Reed's unassuming, distant voice. The album's secret theme soon arrived: "Isn't it nice," Reed sang in a voice devoid of passion, "when your heart is made out of ice". Even when inviting a man or woman to undress, he slipped the words out as if they had no meaning at all.

The same tranquilised persona was draped across 'Baby Face', a cool and undramatic account of the collapse of a homosexual affair. Ennui summed it up perfectly - the voice sober, accepting, totally matter-of-fact, giving the track the same glacial feel as the denouement of 'Berlin'.

For all its pose of disinterest, however, 'Sally Can't Dance' unveiled more of Lou Reed than any of his previous solo albums. Back to Ennui again: "Pick up the pieces that make up your life," Reed whispered, "Maybe some day you'll have a wife, and then alimony." And through the song, after each admission of an omen come home to roost, ran the line: "It's the truth".

'Sally Can't Dance' was also the album on which Reed chose to record 'Kill Your Sons' - the decade-old description of electro-shock treatment that was nothing if not autobiographical. Like the victim of a lobotomy, Reed droned out the lyrics beneath a distant buzz of guitars: this is what you've reduced me to, he seemed to say, as he catalogued the mental vacuity caused by his treatment, or sideswiped his sister and her middle-class Long Island lifestyle.

'Billy' took another perspective on Reed's past. It set him up as a schoolboy rebel, whose copybook path into non-conformity is viewed against the academic and social success of his friend Billy. Then, at last in Lou's work, comes the Vietnam War: "He had to go, but not me, I was mentally unfit, or so they say". Bob Dylan approached a similar subject in 'John Brown', an early Sixties folk ballad which ended with its hero collected in pieces off the plane from Saigon. Billy's fate is less dramatic: as Reed puts it with a stab of wit, "His nerves were shot, but not me". And in conventional folk ballad tradition, the song ends with Reed pondering "which one of us was the fool".

'New York Stars' pointed the same question in another direction. It's difficult to recall another song that has such contempt for its audience, an irony (that word again) compounded by the enormous sales of the album. Over four minutes of designer funk, 1974 style, Reed tore down the masks which separated artist from consumers, and revealed that both halves of the relationship were rotting from the inside. Anyone who had seen Reed onstage since the end of 1973 should have recognised his early reference to "the faggot mimic machine"; later in the same song they could find themselves counted as "ghouls". In the album's only naked show of emotion, Reed switched briefly out of his dull monotone to sneer his contempt for those who watched him perform: "They say, 'I'm so empty, no surface, no depth. Oh please, can't I be you, your personality is so great'." It's a stunningly arrogant piece of writing, a desperate bid to topple the castle and himself with it; and it was Reed's biggest selling record.

While the title track offered light relief - was Reed sniping at Nico, Edie Sedgwick or another Warhol acolyte when he recalled the way 'Sally' "used to ball folksingers"? - 'Animal Language' confirmed that hatred and derision were the fuel that powered the album. Originally titled 'Mrs O'Riley's Dog', it was a cheap piece of rock bubblegum that used miaows and bow-wows as its chorus lines. The verses told a story, of sorts, hinged around cruelty and callous indifference - quite funny, too, if you kick cats around for pleasure.

Consciously or not, the song evoked one of the most horrifying scenes in modern literature - the fantasy sequence in a novel that Reed loved, Hubert Selby Jnr's *The Room*. Trapped within a police cell for nameless crimes, awaiting implacable judgement, the book's hero twists the certainty of his fate into perverse wish-fulfilment. In his head, he captures the policemen who had brought him in, and trains them to act as dogs - placing them through a sickening cycle of assault and degradation, tieing their balls round with wire which he can yank to elicit a response, slicing their arms and legs on the stony ground they are forced to walk on all fours, finally exhibiting them before their families, and inflicting round after round of torture, humiliation and anguish until he can demonstrate that he has reduced them to, at best, the blind obedience and fear of the captured animal.

'Animal Language' has none of that bile or fury; but in its description of animals used as objects of perverted enjoyment, it hints at Selby's desperate vision. That it does so within the confines of the novelty song, and the album's most commercial arrangement, is one final nod of disgust from its author.

"The worst shit in the world": it's an apt description of the record, after all. While Reed played at indifference, he unleashed a statement of utter contempt for his career, his public and ultimately himself. Small wonder that Lou should attempt to salvage his pose by a protestation of innocence: "I'm passive and people just don't understand that. They talk and I just sit and I don't react and that makes them uncomfortable. I just empty myself out so what people see is a projection of their own needs."

Lou Reed as wastepaper bin for the worries of the world: it was a tempting image. But Lou let something else slip in the same interview: "I collect people - just certain special ones." And there, on the back cover of his album, behind the jaded, bleached image of the 'Rock & Roll Animal', was part of his collection. By 1976, Reed was willing to admit that he had taken to picking up street queens on 10th Avenue, bringing them home, photographing them, and capturing their voices on tape. On the 'Sally Can't Dance' cover, reflected in Lou's shades, is the jaded, asexual face of a street hustler. The design is based, say the credits, on a photograph by Lou Reed.

By the time that the 'Sally' cover documented the death's head Reed persona, the man himself had graduated to tight blond curls. Onstage in Europe that summer, Reed vamped his way through a powerful, though less bombastic than before, hard rock show, which ended with the ensemble gathered round stage-front mikes for a chorus of 'Goodnight Ladies'. The show's highlight, as it had been the previous year, was 'Heroin': as Reed chronicled the heady rush of blood through the brain, he rubbed his wrists nostalgically.

Reed's ambivalent attitude towards drugs was neatly summarised when he followed a great rock tradition by teasing the Australian press at the start of his August 1974 tour. "I don't take drugs," he smirked, before announcing, "I want people to take drugs." In Australia, his junkie role-playing continued - but that was just a rehearsal for the fall 1974 tour of the States.

This memorable jaunt began with an ill-conceived RCA promotional push for the 'Sally Can't Dance' album. September 13 was proclaimed Lou Reed Day in Cleveland: Lou celebrated by claiming free records from every radio station he visited, and encouraging his hosts to play banned records over the air. A couple of weeks later it was Lou Reed Impact Day in New York. The 'Sally' album reached the shops, and Lou played shows at the Felt Forum arena. His hair now jet black, soaked in Biba polish, Reed stumbled around the stage. The band played 'Heroin': Reed stared out into the spotlights, reached into his back pocket and pulled out a rubber hose, which he tied round his arm. Then he pumped up a vein, and let it shine in the glare of the lights, before giving a gesture of disgust and continuing the song.

By the end of the tour, the pantomime had reached its climax. Reed forgot the rubber hose, and used the microphone cord as a ligature, tightening it with his teeth. Then out came a syringe - and Reed proceeded to inject a mysterious substance into his vein. Was it heroin? Was it, as some speculated, water? Was the entire thing a fake? It didn't matter; and at an arena gig, no-one could be certain what had happened. But the image lingered on, and added fuel to the talk that these were Reed's final shows, that he would be unlikely to live beyond Christmas.

Accompanying Reed on this leg of the tour was someone, or something, noticed by Lester Bangs: "long dark hair, bearded, tits... grotesque, abject, like something that might have grovellingly scampered in when Lou opened the door to get the milk and papers in the morning". This was officially "Lou's babysitter" - a role she played for the next three years. And his name was Rachel.

NINE

"Rachel knows how to do it for me. No-one else ever did before. Rachel's something else." (Lou Reed, 1976)

"IT WAS IN A LATE NIGHT CLUB IN Greenwich Village," Lou told his friend and photographer Mick Rock. "I'd been up for days as usual, and everything was at that super-real, glowing stage. I walked in and there was this amazing person, this incredible head, kind of vibrating out of it all. Rachel was wearing this amazing make-up and dress, and was obviously in a different world to anyone else in the place. Eventually I spoke and she came home with me. I rapped for hours and hours, while Rachel just sat there looking at me, saying nothing. At the time I was living with a girl, a crazy blonde lady, and I kind of wanted us all three to live together, but somehow it was too heavy for her. Rachel just stayed on and the girl moved out. Rachel was completely disinterested in who I was and what I did. Nothing could impress her. He'd hardly hear my music and didn't like it all that much when he did."

To his collection of street queens, Lou had added his most exotic specimen - only this time the exhibit stayed on to run the museum. Note the quick switch of pronouns in Lou's explanation: just as in 'Walk On The Wild Side', he became a she.

Taking Rachel on the road was Lou's most overt statement of, at least, bisexuality. Maybe she was originally intended as amusement, to shock as much as to fulfil any emotional role. But she occupied a central place in Reed's work and emotions until 1978, and her arrival signalled a timely step away from the abyss which Reed had failed to see from behind his thick black shades.

The rest of the world greeted his relationship as final proof of his decline. Lester Bangs' jumble of adjectives and insults set the tone: those who met Rachel thereafter were amazed to find a very tall, elegant and striking (wo)man, embodying a compelling mix of traditional male and female qualities. Mick Rock took a beautiful photograph for *Penthouse* that captured their relationship: clad in matching black leather, supported by pencil-thin legs, the couple embrace - Lou in front, facing the camera with a dazed smile on his face, while Rachel supports him from behind, her hands clasped possessively over his crotch, a look of serene composure in her eyes.

Rachel sparked an immediate creative rush, after a year in which Lou had composed little new material. By January 1975, he was in the studio, taping songs meant for an album to be called 'Coney Island Baby'. The sessions were interrupted by further demands for a tour, however - Reed was never so popular a concert draw as when his fans feared his every appearance might be his last. Reed set 'Coney Island Baby' aside; dug out his working tapes of the electronic music project he'd been toying with since the late Sixties; and stood aside while RCA dragged a second live album from the legendary Hunter/Wagner tour.

This album was called 'Lou Reed Live', though its cover belied it. Once again, Reed decorated the record with a shot that neither reflected the time it had been recorded, nor when it was being released. Frozen like a corpse across the front cover, this Lou Reed looked like a harbinger of personal destruction. Coming weeks after the reports that he was now shooting up onstage, 'Lou Reed Live' twisted the 'Rock & Roll Animal' myth into hypertension.

Just as Reed continued to use old photographs to sell new product, the media reviewed his past exploits, not his contemporary ones. His February 1975 European tour marked a decisive step away from the guitar sparring of recent times; most remarkably, the star of Reed's band was one Doug Yule, whom he'd not worked with (bar one recording session for 'Sally Can't Dance') since Reed left the Velvets amidst claims and counter-claims about the true author of the band's final songs. Reed and Yule announced that they'd settled their differences, which they blamed on Steve Sesnick, anyway. And in a rare moment of democracy, Reed let Yule take centre-stage. When he'd allowed Doug to sing on 'The Velvet Underground', he'd set him up as an unwitting fall guy for his most ambiguous lyrical conceits. Second time around, the gesture seemed genuine, and Yule relished the opportunity to repair the critical damage left by his hapless continuation of the Reed-less Velvet Underground.

Backed by woodwind, guitars and (briefly) violin, Reed reasserted his control over his music during this European visit, even essaying some rare rhythm guitar himself. But he was fated to attract drama: a political riot in Rome on February 13 spilled over into the concert arena, and Reed was struck on the head with a brick while playing his first song, 'Sweet Jane'. The show was abandoned, while the next concert in Frankfurt was also aborted, with the promoter claiming Reed had suffered a "nervous collapse". Once again, a riot ensued, though Lou wasn't there to act as short-stop for the bricks.

But the rest of the tour continued without incident. When it was over, Reed and Rachel returned to New York, where they shared Lou's Upper East Side apartment - now tastefully furnished in velvet, with gold records on the wall accompanied by a pair of antelope horns and a zebra-skin rug. Sat on the mantel was a windscreen sign reading 'Clergy' - very useful for those lightning stops at the drug store - and by it a well-thumbed copy of *The Physicians' Drug Reference.*

It was here that Lou continued work on 'Metal Machine Music', before moving the entire enterprise into more professional surroundings. By late spring it was finished, and delivered to a disconcerted record company - complete with its jabbering sleeve-notes, written as if during a temporary seizure, and a sleeve design that used two uncompromising exhibitions of Reed's physical decline, both more than a year old alongside the message: "Terminal 75".

'Metal Machine Music' was meant to provoke, and it did. Lou's manager, Dennis Katz, was among those who raised siren voices against releasing the record; and he was on Reed's hitlist. So too was the hierarchy at RCA, the rock press, anyone who had less than total faith in Reed's ability to survive and maintain his faculties intact under storm and stress.

By July 1975, with Reed sent round the world on the first leg of a multi-artist package named, crassly, 'Startruckin', he found himself in New Zealand, ten thousand miles from Rachel (who'd been unable to get a passport for the trip), and refused to go any further. He spent hours on the phone to her, sleeping at night with the receiver off the hook and the call connected to New York, so he could resume his conversation immediately he awoke. The promoters were convinced that his nervous system had finally collapsed; and to anyone who had watched his relentless trail towards self-destruction, New Zealand looked like the setting for the climactic crisis of Reed's career.

Having succeeded in winning his way off the tour, however, Reed sprang his counter-attack. He returned to New York and launched into an energetic proselytising campaign on behalf of 'Metal Machine Music', each explanation supported by an array of classical music references and scientific jargon. Far from being emotionally incapable, Reed seemed more ebullient than ever; and his thick dark hair and fleshy face were pointedly at odds with the deathly, wired figure on the cover of his devilish electronic creation.

Into his interviews, Reed dropped baffling remarks about "that kike" Dennis Katz. A few weeks later, Katz was no longer Lou's manager, and Lou had begun a process of minute investigation into the status of his financial affairs. Meanwhile, he went back to the 'Coney Island Baby' project, dismissing the January 1975 tapes and starting afresh with producer Geoffrey Diamond. When that was completed, he began work on a series of songs for a musical adaptation of Andy Warhol's *Philosophy* - a charmingly shallow series of bon-mots and style tips which reflected the distance the artist had shuffled from his avant-garde theories of the previous decade. "I was so surprised," Andy admitted in his practised tone of naïvety. "He just came over and said, 'Can I do it?', and I said yeah, and he came over the next day and had it all done." Even allowing for Warhol's customary exaggeration, Reed's enthusiasm for the venture was real enough. But Reed had grown sufficiently distant from the Warhol crowd to see it through spectacles more clear than rosy. He looked beyond the surface glitz of Warhol's book, and began to dig at what Andy's philosophy really entailed.

Then he returned to Warhol: "I played them for Andy. He was fascinated but horrified. I think they kind of scared him. But I'm thinking of doing them as my next album." In his own gentle way, Lou let the world know that he had moved beyond Warhol's guidance: "I see him all the time. I've talked to him more than probably anyone I've ever talked to. He showed me how to save a lot of time." And I'm sure Lou found that very useful. A decade earlier Andy had taught him how to live out his art in his life. Now all Warhol could offer Lou was short-cuts in a busy schedule.

Late in 1975, Lou appointed a new manager - or rather a booking agent, as he distrusted the idea of anyone else seeking to control his career. The new man was Johnny Podell, who'd booked some of the biggest tours of the mid-seventies, notably the CSNY and George Harrison concert series of 1974. Podell, fast-talking, all skin and bone and at that time in his life very fond of cocaine, was a man of the streets, and Lou adopted him as the latest in a succession of bosom buddies-cum-mentors, just as he had done Katz, Heller, Sesnick and Warhol before him. At Ashley's, the music biz bar and restaurant on 5th Avenue at 13th Street where Lou and Podell hung out with their friends, the regulars quipped that their business relationship was "a marriage made in the emergency ward"!

Meanwhile, Lou had a team of lawyers on his side, delving through the financial reports and tax returns filed by Dennis Katz since 1972. Reed was convinced serious malfeasance had taken place: "I went over things with a microscope and found it so interesting I've got three lawsuits going. I'd like to have the affidavits published - everything from misrepresentation to fraud and back again. The management I had then had me in a cocoon of paranoia: when you're ripping somebody off that much, you don't want them outside talking to people." This placed an intriguing new slant on Reed's behaviour in recent years: was he really suggesting his lifestyle had been determined by paranoia inculcated by his management?

The recording sessions for 'Coney Island Baby' were caught up in the legal battle. Injunctions were taken out by Katz's lawyers to prevent the album being released; Reed regularly arrived at the studios to have subpoenas placed in his hands.

Somehow, the album rose above its surroundings. 'Coney Island Baby' was Reed's most tender and evocative album to date - a bouquet of roses hiding an occasional razor-sharp thorn. From its album cover onwards, it heralded the birth of a new man: this time, the Reed persona was a cross between a choirboy and a clown, staring coyly and impassively from behind a bowler hat. The back cover shot even suggested Reed saw himself as Charlie Chaplin, perhaps, or Tadzio, Gustave von Aschenbach's fatal attraction in Thomas Mann's *Death In Venice*.

The record was equally disarming. Reed had always signalled his love for Fifties doo-wop, but no album made his passion as clear as 'Coney

Island Baby'. Almost every track was soaked in a lush bed of harmonies, while the simple chord changes and rich melodic shifts had the emotional resonance of the classic Fifties ballads from 'I Only Have Eyes For You' to 'Earth Angel'.

Most of the album simply said 'I Love Rachel' - from 'Crazy Feeling', with its admiring "You're a queen, such a queen" to the timely revival of 'She's My Best Friend', a 1968 Velvets song into which Lou now sprinkled a little current gay slang. But Rachel's finest inspiration was the title track, a shockingly bare glimpse into the soft heart of one of rock's most feared hardmen. Over a simple, elegiac guitar figure, Lou recited a litany of high school dreams, from the time when he "wanted to play football for the coach". The rest of the piece, originally titled 'Glory Of Love' after The Harptones' song which inspired it, caught the mood and stretched it out, evoking the unexpected, disconcerting and utterly transforming power of love which had rescued Lou from his decline. In one verse Reed looked back over his shoulder at those who had doubted his ability to survive; in another he reflected what it was like "to find that your soul is been up billed for sale". And through it all, in a cathartic wave of emotion, shone the glory of love, waiting to see you through.

As Reed's serenade to his own 'Coney Island Baby' came to a close, he stepped closer to the mike and dissolved years of image-mongering in a single sentence from the heart: "I'd like to send this one out to Lou and Rachel, and all the kids out at PS 192 - man I swear I'd give the whole thing up for you." There's nothing like it in rock, nothing as bare or as open to the moment. It was a stunning rebuttal to years of mockery and derision - an affirmation of a creative instinct returned to life.

The rest of the album paled alongside such heartplay, though the self-parody of 'A Gift (to the women of this world)' was a beautiful illustration of Reed's sly and unpredictable humour. Then there was 'Kicks' - a track which in six minutes came close to debunking every hint of salvation and rebirth on the record. Set against a backdrop of casual New York conversation, 'Kicks' was a vicious, callous invocation to the addictive power of violence, with the narrator compelled to admiration by the skill with which his counterpart has committed murder. "I need kicks", ran the repeated refrain, before Reed showed a horrific ability to grasp the psyche of the casual killer: "When the blood came down his chest/It was way better than sex/It was way better than getting in/It was the final thing to do/Get somebody to come on to you/Then kill him now". And while the tension of the vocal grew, the blabber of conversation continued unabated.

As ever when dealing with violence, Reed's stance was ambiguous: it was impossible to tell whether the narrator, alias Lou Reed, was supposed to be identified with the Lou who was taking part in the background conversation; and whether, if so, the song was meant as a chilling portrait of a man who could disguise murderous impulses behind a soft social veneer.

'Kicks', with its amoral spotlight on sexual obsession and murder, was more real than anything Reed had written in years - suggesting perhaps that his relationship with Rachel had unlocked a muddy stream of emotions. During 1975, Reed worked up a series of poems in similar style, all part of a proposed verse collection to be called *All The Pretty People,* due for publication from Stonehill in 1976. One of the poems was *Kicks,* a reworking of the song lyric, or perhaps an early draft, as this version dealt too many cards with an open hand: "I know you'd like to try a law to break in/Anything that they're for/You're against and for taking". Nothing that obvious reached the song - and nor did one of the most intriguing couplets from the poem: "When you stabbed that man/I finally knew it must be me".

"They have a certain progression," Lou explained about his collected poems. "From the start they get rougher and harder and tougher until it's just out and out vicious, doesn't rhyme, has no punctuation, it's just vicious and vulgar." The progression is certainly there from Reed's first love poems to Betty in *Fusion,* to the gallery of vignettes unveiled in the pages of the *Coldspring Journal* in January 1976. Not since the first Velvet Underground album had Reed touched so close to the street, recreating the thoughtless violence and sickening amorality of the denizens of Times Square after dark. The 'Coney Island Baby' album had been fashioned in the style of casual conversation, full of the slips and mishaps that trip from the tongue when you talk faster than you speak - the wrong usages of tense or pronoun that you only recognise after they've splurted out of your mouth, by which time you're headlong into another phrase and the mistake doesn't matter.

The *Coldspring Journal* poems, collected under the title *Attitudes By Lou Reed,* had the same urgency, twisted into a callous indifference towards human flesh. *Street Hassling,* for example, opens with a graphic account of a fight that luxuriates in the blood and broken teeth, and then shifts the camera to reveal the sado-masochistic rituals of uniforms and beatings that fuel Reed's sexually ambiguous characters. Likewise *The Man* - who could be the doctor in the city ("they had to tie him to a chair/and beat the living shit out of him") or the famous folk singer ("he likes to have razors scrape down his back/he's got this old Jewish thing 'bout Negroes") or the narrator ("I'm the man who's really got some"). *Games* retraces the steps of 'Waiting For The Man', only with added realism, through the eyes of a man caught between obsession and indifference, and spurred by need. At *The Movies,* "The dude who was on my left/Just got up and he was leaking/On the dude that was next to him". And *The Slide* looks at the nervous organisation of the New York scene - "Now they got their own baths, yay,/With entertainers and shit" - from the gnarled viewpoint of someone who says "I've got nothing about gay guys" but then boasts "It's guys like me... Who hate them, beat them."

Like Hubert Selby's *Last Exit To Brooklyn, Reed's Attitudes* dealt with extreme situations which have become the everyday currency of the New York streets - examined in the words of the players, rather than of some outsider plastering morals or ideas over a scene he doesn't understand. Reed's authenticity was deflected through a poetic vision that turned the incoherence of the street into an artistic method, dropping words off the end of thoughts, and leaving his intention misted in a flurry of activity and anger.

But while Selby's book suggested that his characters were merely pinballs being thrown around a slot machine on some uneven club floor, Reed's poems had a terrifying lack of perspective. In a stunning show of bravado and artistic daring, Reed left us with no comment on his characters. They exist, and Reed understood them perfectly; maybe he even *was* some of them. There was no genteel distancing of the poem from the real world, no breath of light to suggest that this was merely a poet's fantasy. Reed's *Attitudes* had the greasy stain of truth; he wasn't about to tell you how close they were to home.

Compare 'Coney Island Baby' and the *Attitudes* poems, and - *Kicks* aside - you have two starkly contrasting visions of life. The record celebrates hope and the birth of love; the poems luxuriate in violence and the threat of death. "The test of a first-rate intelligence," wrote Scott Fitzgerald, "is the ability to hold two opposed ideas in the mind at the same time; and still retain the ability to function." In late 1975, Lou Reed qualified with ease.

"All the albums I put out after this are going to be things I want to put out. No more bullshit, no more dyed hair, faggot junkie trip. I mimic me better than anyone else, so if everybody else is making money ripping me off, I figure maybe I better get in on it. Why not? I created Lou Reed. I have nothing even faintly in common with that guy, but I can play him well - really well." (Lou Reed, 1976)

The combination punches of 'Metal Machine Music' and 'Coney Island Baby' - extreme noise terror followed by the glory of love - shattered Lou Reed's "faggot junkie trip". With it went his manager, Dennis Katz; then his record company, RCA. With his solo contract up for grabs, Reed chose not to re-sign with the label by whom he'd felt betrayed over his electronic masterpiece: instead he went to Arista Records, headed by Clive Davis, the ex-president of Columbia Records who was renowned as a champion of the artist over the corporate man.

The approach from Davis came at the height of Reed's legal wrangles with Katz. "There was just Rachel and me living at the Gramercy Park Hotel on $15 a day," Lou recalled, "while the lawyers were trying to figure out what to do with me. Then I got a call from Clive Davis. I felt like saying, 'You mean you want to be seen with me in public?' I knew then I'd won."

Reed joined an Arista roster which also contained Patti Smith, most vocal representative of the so-called New Wave scene that had sprung up in New York during 1975. Unlike its slightly later British counterpart, which it both inspired and infuriated, the American New Wave was literate, geared towards concept art, aware that the complacency of the rock élite had eroded the artistic energy and experimentation opened up by the first wave of singer-songwriters, and their psychedelic forebears. While London resounded to the urban working-class, disenfranchised and disinterested by a culture that equated adulthood with middle-age, New York took a more angular approach - as evidenced by the complex guitar duels of Television's Tom Verlaine and Richard Lloyd, the disarmingly basic philosophical truths of David Byrne, and the rich farrago of imagery, conceit and manic energy that Patti Smith poured out in her poetry.

Of all the American New Wave, Smith must have intrigued Reed the most. Here was a frighteningly literate mistress of words who was prepared to sacrifice meaning on the altar of rhythm. She broke as many images as she saved, but the sheer thrust of her delivery, in person or on the page, slapped down any opposition. When she combined her heady poetic bursts with the stripped-down raunch of the Sixties garage bands, Patti Smith opened, in her own phrase, a sea of possibilities. Her début single, 'Piss Factory', was as much the voice of the street as anything Lou Reed ever wrote, and like his own *Attitudes,* it combined the effect of spontaneity with the craft of the poet. When she extended over a whole album, 'Horses', Patti Smith created a record as startling as anything heard since - it was the constant comparison - the first Velvet Underground LP. The producer of this masterpiece? John Cale.

Immersed in legal problems, Reed must have greeted the New Wave as a dubious relief. Speaking on the record, he kept his distance: "I'm too literate to be into punk rock. The new bands are cute, but I don't really know anything about punk at all." And he furiously denied any idea that he had inadvertently spawned the new movement himself.

For the best part of a year, however, Reed stalked the opposition at Max's Kansas City and CBGBs. He watched The Ramones, Richard Hell, Pere Ubu; advised Television's Tom Verlaine about his choice of début single (and was overruled); and put on an air of insouciance as John Cale joined the Patti Smith Group to butcher Lou's 'Waiting For The Man' at the Bottom Line.

Reed wasn't averse to making club appearances himself. Late in 1975 he'd joined former Turtles Flo and Eddie - friends of his arch enemy Frank Zappa, though perhaps he didn't realise that - to perform a parody of 'Walk On The Wild Side'. Then a few weeks after the Cale/Smith show, he ventured onstage with his former partner at St. Mark's Church in the Bowery - just along the street from the site of the Dom. Lou débuted 'Coney Island Baby', joined Talking Heads leader David Byrne in supporting Cale's 'A Close Watch', and then combined with Cale for the ritual 'Waiting For The Man', which was rapidly becoming a sine qua non at New York punk shows. Cale and Reed attacked a similar repertoire at another New York club show a few months later.

Both inspired and dampened by the energy of the New Wave, Reed went into the studio in the summer of 1976 to record his first Arista album - tentatively titled 'Nomad', with Andy Warhol set to provide the cover art. Neither the title nor the concept survived: the album emerged under the title 'Rock And Roll Heart', packaged within Mick Rock photographs of TV screens, which in turn showed a Mick Rock film of Lou.

To inaugurate a new record deal, which he had greeted as some kind of salvation, Reed might have been expected to deliver a knockout punch. Instead, 'Rock And Roll Heart' was a lacklustre, bizarrely underwritten effort, which became an event only by virtue of Arista's punitively expensive promotional campaign. The record took just 27 days to record and mix; much of that time was devoted to writing and arranging the songs, as Reed arrived in the studio with only a couple of tunes complete. Ideas came from anywhere. "This waiter came up to me in a restaurant and said, 'Listen, I write songs, what do you suggest I do?' I said, 'Let me hear them so I can steal them off you if there's anything good'. "

Lou was only kidding, but earlier that year a teenage member of his British Fan Club sent him a poem called *Vicious Circle,* and was then amazed to buy 'Rock And Roll Heart' and find that Lou had turned his title and lyrical thrust into a new song. 'Follow The Leader' was a two-chord chant that Lou had been busking around since 1971; anxious to get maximum mileage, he'd also recycled it as a poem, simply titled 'The Leader'. 'Banging On My Drum' was another two-liner, variously interpreted as an ode to masturbation and a parody of the New Wave: "Three chords is three chords," Reed explained, "but there is a finesse to it." 'Claim To Fame' had the smart-ass wordplay of 'Transformer'; 'Rock And Roll Heart' and 'I Believe In Love' repeated the pop melodicism of 'Coney Island Baby', but were simply filled with mildly self-mocking jokes. 'Sheltered Life' took the same route and offered more fun on the way: a rewritten Velvet Underground song from 1966, it became a hilarious piece of image puncturing, as Lou coyly announced that "I've never taken dope and I've never taken drugs" while the band concocted a cocktail jazz accompaniment. Strangest of all, 'Chooser And The Chosen One' was a slightly funky instrumental. Even among such minimalist company, the fact that Reed chose to say nothing was a story in itself.

Much of the music jerked along at a frenetic pace - another hint that Lou felt threatened by the effortless energy of Patti Smith and The Ramones. By delivering the style but not the message of New Wave, however, Reed put himself up as a pretender rather than a monarch, fighting desperately to be considered for a crown that had once been his by right.

The album was most convincing when Reed forgot the competition and concentrated on mood. 'Ladies Pay' and 'You Wear It Well' were lyrically simple to the verge of obscurity, but they had an emotional core that harked back to the last album. "It's almost evil the way it goes past - it's like a sound wave," Reed offered as a clue to 'Ladies Pay'. Stranger and more gripping still was 'Temporary Thing', a dirge-like monologue delivered in a tone of unseemly passion. "I thought, 'Oh no Lou, you're right on the edge'," Reed explained, and it sounds like it. But the words - a ragged anti-apology from a post-coital seducer - were somehow less than the feeling, which was a failing of the whole album.

'Rock And Roll Heart' sold enough to keep Reed's career afloat, but it was scarcely the great return that artist or label boss had predicted. Lou went immediately into another project, his sole effort at producing another artist - one Nelson Slater, a survivor of one of Lou's Syracuse bands who was now living in California.

Slater's album was entitled 'Wild Angel', and although its gentle, slightly funk-tinged production was unremarkable, it set out to shock in other ways. Its cover paraded a picture of a woman, apparently naked, hair shaved from her head, manacled in a pose half agonised, half ecstatic, with a black metallic chain pulled tight across her rouged mouth. For further delectation, the back cover juxtaposed the elegantly coiffeured Slater with a close-up of the desecrated face.

Packaged like a skin mag, with song titles like 'Dominating Force' and 'Things Have Happened Strange', 'Wild Angel' might have been 'Venus In Furs' revisited. But the tone of the record was gentler than that, and Lou Reed - credited with piano, guitar, backing vocals and production - made his presence felt on just one track, 'We', where the band came close to recreating a hint of the atmospherics of 'Heroin'. Otherwise, 'Wild Angel' was a record more notable for the identity of its producer than for any musical value.

Meanwhile, RCA sought to capitalise on the publicity around Lou's move to Arista by issuing 'Walk On The Wild Side' - a 'greatest hits' package notable for its cover polaroids of Lou and Rachel, and its inclusion of 'Nowhere At All'. This was an out-take from the 'Coney Island Baby' sessions, a gritty rocker which sounded the way the Hunter/Wagner band would if they'd ever been let loose in the studio.

The constant thread of irony that holds Lou Reed's career together surfaced after the release of 'Rock And Roll Heart', when he took the same songs and musicians on tour. The lazy purveyor of half-formed ideas was supplanted by an artist at the peak of his powers, and even the new songs found a purpose in the vibrant R&B settings of the live shows.

The secret was trumpeter Don Cherry - collaborator with the pick of the jazz avant-garde since the late Fifties, sideman to Ornette Coleman and Archie Shepp, and one of Reed's inspirations when he first mastered the possibilities of the electric guitar. Onstage, at the Palladium in New York and the Roxy in Los Angeles, Don gave Reed's music a rich taste of the black music heritage, opening up his garage-rock to the delights of blues, free-form jazz and soul.

Everything in the set was transformed, from 'Sweet Jane' to the slightest of the new songs, and Reed responded like a speed freak injected with methedrin. Rolling proudly through the rockers, squeezing new layers of tenderness out of his voice on the ballads, Reed for the first time began to sound like a torch singer, scat singing at the mike while the band roared behind him.

Behind the band, meanwhile, lay the stage set: a bank of 48 black and white television sets bought from a New York hospital, showing a video prepared by Mick Rock from film taken at Lou's house, some of it centring on his face, the rest purely abstract. Like a satirical comment on Marshall McLuhan's theories of the media, Reed presented the TV as a mere backdrop to life and art, simultaneously invoking the power of the small screen to create haunting images, and its transient, ephemeral nature. The audio-visual ensemble was Reed's first venture of that kind since the days of the Exploding Plastic Inevitable: where Warhol's troupe had wanted to overwhelm the senses, Reed showed that the mind could control and diminish the mythical force of the broadcast image.

Sadly, this triumphant tour made little impression on the rock world, merely by virtue of the fact that the staging demanded intimate settings. When Lou requested permission to transfer the set-up, TVs included, to the London Palladium, bastion of traditional showbusiness virtues, the management took fright, assuming that their precious theatre would be overrun by drug-crazed punks.

The tour also ended in personal trauma. Reed was accompanied throughout by Rachel, who acted as a minder-cum-manager. "Rachel has looked after the money and kept me in shape and watched over the road crew," Lou announced proudly. "At last there's someone hustling round for me that I can trust." By the end of the tour, though, Rachel was suffering from an infected lung; then he/she was mugged in LA. "He got kicked in the chest and stomach and had some internal bleeding. That really had me strung out. This guy jumped him. But Rachel gave him back more than he got. You see, Rachel's a street kid and very tough underneath it all." He was a tough street kid; she was a tender, caring lover. He/she kept Reed sane and relatively sober throughout the legal and personal trials of 1976.

When the Reed package eventually reached Europe in March 1977, minus the 48 televisions which Reed offered for sale to everyone he came across, Lou and Rachel celebrated three years of friendship with a party, cutting a three-tier wedding cake emblazoned with a Valentine heart. Onstage, Reed was no longer accompanied by Don Cherry, whose schedule wouldn't allow for a lengthy European visit. Marty Fogel did his best to cover, but the shows lost a little of their lustre. Both here and back in New York in May, Reed débuted several new songs - stridently unmelodic R&B tunes for the most part, like 'Leave Me Alone' and 'Pretty Face', with one chord pounded over and over again, while Fogel's saxophone wailed in a parody of the freedom of be-bop, and Reed growled out uncompromising messages of rejection and contempt.

Revealing plans to score Terry Southern's script for a movie adaptation of William Burroughs' *Junkie,* or produce an album for his college friend Garland Jeffreys, Reed tackled the rock press with arrogant self-confidence. He began encounters with journalists by quizzing them about their sexual preferences and religion; "You're here to be annoyed", he snarled at one interviewer who dared to question the ritual. Whereas Lou had once given days to Lester Bangs, in the knowledge that he would be portrayed in print as a slobbering junkie, incapable of controlling his body let alone his mind, he now treated each encounter as a test of strength. Some writers kept pace with his ferocious alcohol intake and won grudging respect.

Others were chewed up and spat out or - much worse, to the working journalist - simply ignored, fed one-word answers or assaulted with two questions for every one they asked. "Journalists mean nothing," Reed shouted at a reporter from *Punk* magazine. "They don't mean shit. They do not sell records. I do interviews just to find out what people like you are up to, what you think I'm supposed to be doing."

Less than a year after the soft-centred exhibitionism of 'Coney Island Baby', and before that the uncontrolled and purely instinctive behaviour of the 'Rock & Roll Animal', Reed substituted a new and utterly threatening image. Clad in black, emotions masked behind his ever-present shades, he acted like a wall to unwelcome enquiries. He commanded a furious tongue, with a host of deflating insults primed for action. As a public relations exercise, it was unusual; but it guaranteed a break from the compulsive honesty and pathetic self-abuse of the 'Sally Can't Dance' era.

This fresh demeanour extended beyond the interview situation. Back in Europe in August 1977 to headline the Mont De Marsan Punk Festival, and then perform several shows in Germany, Reed threatened one promoter with a can opener, then sacked his sound man on the spot and "kicked his monitors offstage". And these were the shows which he chose to tape for his next album, tentatively titled 'I Wanna Be Black'.

Lou had written a song of that title in 1974, and capitalised on its shock value ever since. Scabrously funny, it assaulted white liberal culture's hipper-than-thou reverence of black ethnicity - Norman Mailer's vision of the teenage hipster as a White Negro, the unquestioning respect paid to the Black Panther movement, and closer to home, the apparent wish of every white rock star to perform black soul music. "I don't wanna be a fucked-up middle-class college student any more," Lou wrote. "I just wanna have a stable of foxy little whores". Any racial stereotypes that were around, this song fingered them: Lou wanted to "have natural rhythm... and have a big prick too". He even dared touch unassailable spiritual leaders: "Wanna be like Martin Luther King/get myself shot in the spring".

Coming from Lou Reed in 1974, the irony was obvious. By 1977, with Reed playing variations on jazz and R&B with a mixed-race band, that irony was double-edged. Now you could take the song straight, or almost: the Lou Reed who pulled Don Cherry into his band and added the blues to 'Sweet Jane' might very conceivably want to be black.

'I Wanna Be Black' was performed like a disco song, all chopping rhythm guitar and a shuffle beat. "Nobody wants to be a rhythm guitarist any more except niggers," Reed told Creem with his customary tact in 1978. "You know that Marvin Gaye song, 'Gotta Give It Up', the album version? When Marvin says, Here comes the good part, it's the truth. That rhythm guitarist, his throwaways are riffs that people would give their left ball for. I tried to do that kind of guitar on 'I Wanna Be Black'; naturally, I fucked it up, but that's my attempt to do Ed Brown."

By late 1977, Reed had grown so fond of his little jest that he announced his 'I Wanna Be Black' album would feature a cover photo of a black-faced Lou munching on a watermelon. But these were cheap shots, and Lou knew it. By the time of the German gigs in August 1977, he was working on a more significant centre-piece for his new album.

He taped the European shows in stereo binaural sound - a technique developed by the German engineer Manfred Schunke, whereby 50% more information was stored on the tape than before. "It gives you the chance for studio perfection while retaining the live sound," Lou explained, though that wasn't really it. The true attraction of the binaural system was that it came close to reproducing the rabbit-punch impact of live sound - the overwhelming roar and pulse that is rapidly diminished across 24-track tape in the studio. Reed was thrilled by the results, and seems to have submitted an entirely live album to Clive Davis for release. Arista turned it down, and sent Reed back to the studio. There he pulled in Richard Robinson, veteran of Lou's first solo effort, and together they began to use the German tapes as a blank canvas over which Lou could add texture and colour.

"I was being betrayed by all the evil people around me," Lou recalled in 1982. "The original producer had walked out, I'd had to change studios because we had a fight there - and then Clive Davis came in and told me I should make a new record and throw this one away. But the record came out, and I wasn't crazy. They were just stupid. The head of Arista was stupid."

So stupid was Clive Davis, in fact, that it was he who persuaded Lou Reed to turn 'Street Hassle' from a two-minute snapshot into an epic masterpiece. Realising that the live material wasn't strong enough to support the whole album, even with studio tailoring, Reed worked up a lyric fragment, a chilling monologue about a hit-and-run drug overdose.

"When Clive heard the original, which is 2' 11" long, he said that it was great, and I should make it longer," Reed explained. "So I did. 'Street Hassle' is basically a two-minute-odd tape loop. The basic track's all the same, but with different overdubs put over it. It shows how many ways you can look at the same thing. What I did was record a whole string section but I only used part of it - the cello. I only brought in the whole string section for one part, so it kind of sweeps in real panoramic. I had three vignettes, so I thought the perfect thing here was to dissolve, like in a movie - shift one set of music past another set, sort of pan them and BOOM! you're into the second world."

Like the second half of 'Berlin', 'Street Hassle' had all the ingredients of fiction - a sharply drawn set of characters, a dramatic situation, and a perspective that shifted to switch its shadow, and our sympathy, from one face to another. More than any other Reed song, it showed his ability to paint on the grand scale - to keep one theme in mind across a wide canvas, to pull off a miniature version of the fragmented landscape of the New York album.

The song turns around an insistent musical phrase, introduced on cello in an overture section which lasts for some two minutes, bringing in keyboards and guitar, and then - having established the theme - falling silent. Waltzing Matilda was Reed's title for this first movement: Matilda meets the "sexy boy", $80 changes hands, and the couple make love - manufacture it, create a fantasy out of a financial transaction. In a poignant, breathtaking series of images, broken by Reed's monotone scat singing, we watch the lovers lifted "wholly and boldly out of this world"; and in the morning, "Neither one regretted a thing".

After a moment's silence, the voice of Genya Ravan appears, gently keening a wordless chant of regret and foreboding. As the cellos appear behind her, so Ravan gives way to Reed in classic pose - the unmoved, cynical observer, the indifferent observer of the dark side of the New York streets. "Hey that cunt's not breathing, I think she's had too much," he begins, lecturing his listener about the responsibilities you face when it's your old lady who turns blue and ODs at a party. "When someone turns that blue it's a universal truth, and you just know that bitch will never fuck again . . . So why don't you grab your old lady by the feet and just lay her out in the darkest street and in the morning she's just another hit and run". As the cellos fade away, all that's left is Lou Reed, jaded voice of experience and despair, reciting the mantra of the streets: "You know some people got no choice and they can never find a voice to talk with that they can even call their own. So the first thing that they see that allows them the right to be, why they follow it, you know it's called - bad luck".

That section was the original 'Street Hassle'; but Reed had another camera angle to show us. As the riff tugs us back into the song, the voice of Bruce Springsteen emerges from the speakers, reciting a sad mono- logue, half home truth, half nursery rhyme, about "a real song, a song she won't admit to herself". Its payoff is a cunning parody of Springsteen's own most famous lyric: "Tramps like us, we were born to pay".

Then, finally, we hear Lou Reed - not the studied outsider, profession- ally distant, but the flesh, blood and tears human who sang 'Coney Island Baby'. In a voice closer to defeat than anything he'd ever exposed on record before, Lou makes his own farewell to romance and dreams: "Love has gone away/Took the rings off my fingers/And there's nothing left to say/But oh how I need him baby". "They're not heterosexual con- cerns in that song," Lou hinted when the album was released. "I don't make a deal of it, but when I mention a pronoun, its gender is all impor- tant." And in the same interview, he stated that the *raison d'être* of the album was Rachel. "At the end of Street Hassle," he commented else- where, "that person really exists. He did take the rings right off my fingers, and I do miss him."

Rachel and Lou did have a partial separation in late 1977 or early 1978: later that summer, Andy Warhol noted that "He's sort of separated from Rachel the drag queen but not completely, they have separate apart- ments." And the desperation in Reed's voice in the final minutes of 'Street Hassle' is testament to how the separation affected him. But he didn't allow his own pain to disturb the balance of the song; in fact, he seems to have been quite aware that he could slip his confessional piece past the listener as simply another scene in the movie. "Take the person who's singing in the second part of 'Street Hassle'," he noted early in 1978, "the one who's saying, 'Hey, that's some bad shit'. Now he may come off as a little cruel, but let's say he's also the guy who's singing the last part about losing love. He's not unaware of those feelings, he's just handling the situation, that's all." And handling the situation was what 'Street Hassle' allowed Reed himself to do.

The appearance of Bruce Springsteen on the record attracted much comment: Reed had, after all, told *Punk* magazine in 1976 that Bruce was "a shit... a has-been. He certainly looks Jewish." By 1978, Reed's opinions had changed: "Bruce was mixing in the studio below us, and I thought, 'How fortuitous'. People expect me to badmouth him because he's from New Jersey, but I think he's really fabulous. He did the part so well that I had to bury him in the mix. I knew Bruce would do that recitation seriously, because he really is of the street, you know" - unlike, presumably, anyone else singing on the record.

While Reed completed work on 'Street Hassle', he received unexpected news: he had been awarded a prize as one of the year's five best new poets from the American Literary Council of Little Magazines. Given primarily for his *Attitudes* selection of the previous year, the award attracted little attention in rock or literary circles; ironically it also marked the end of his public life as a poet. Reed himself asked for the publication of *All The Pretty People,* his first verse collection, to be postponed, then cancelled; after having a sketch published in the magazine *Art Direction,* he drew back from working outside the rock field, at least for public consumption.

The concentration on music was aptly timed, as Street Hassle was about to reclaim much of his critical reputation. In the build-up to the album, Lou was asked to host the prestigious rock TV show *Midnight Special,* but then withdrew when the producer demanded that certain words in four of Reed's songs - 'Heroin', 'I Wanna Be Black', 'Street Hassle' and 'Walk On The Wild Side' - would have to be bleeped before transmission. It didn't matter: Lou was convinced that his new album would clean up by itself. "I'm right in step with the market," he told *Creem* the week the album came out. "This album is enormously commercial."

'Street Hassle' emerged at the commercial height of the New Wave, especially in Britain, where The Velvet Underground's heritage was being widely acclaimed as the true spark of punk. While 'Rock And Roll Heart' had been a lukewarm response to rock's fresh input of energy, 'Street Hassle' was marketed from the first as a grand statement from the man who had invented punk. In Britain, the title track was issued as a 12" single, backed by two classics from the Velvets' catalogue; for once, the juxtaposition didn't embarrass Reed's new work, and reviewers on both sides of the Atlantic competed to raise 'Street Hassle' to the skies.

Strip away the ten-minute title track, though, and it's easy to see why Clive Davis must have viewed the original live album with such trepidation. The rest of 'Street Hassle' is loud, uncompromising and defiantly unmelodic - and it introduced a new Lou Reed persona, who interrupted the familiar half-spoken monotone with a quavering, tremulous baritone that sounded half distraught, half disturbingly hilarious.

This was as naked an exhibition as any of Reed's lyrical self-analyses.

LOU REED

By divesting himself of his most recognisable characteristic, the Lou
Reed voice, he exposed himself to ridicule. For the next two years, Reed
persevered with this new style, dragging out notes in a parody of vocal
flexibility, forcing sound from his chest rather than the side of his mouth,
unveiling something vulnerable and uncomfortable. 'Gimme Gimme
Good Times' set the theme for the album. While the old Lou droned out
the first verse of 'Sweet Jane', Reed spat out a series of sarcastic asides:
"Hey, if it ain't the rock and roll animal himself . . . fucking faggot
junkie". And then came the song, a reworking of the 'Sweet Jane' riff
which announced that to Reed, good times and pain were once more just
one and the same.

A psychoanalyst would have had a field day with the record. Back in
1976, Lou had determined that there would be "no more bullshit, dyed
hair, faggot junkie trip". The confrontational opening to 'Gimme Gimme
Good Times' forced the point home. And with the faggot junkie trip, Lou
was also jettisoning the faggot junkie voice - the familiar tones which
had seen him from 'Waiting For The Man' to 'Rock And Roll Heart'. On
'Street Hassle', only the title track allowed the old Reed any house room.

Gone too was the tight, professional attitude to the three-chord rock
song. Over the five minutes of 'Dirt', the band continually sparked into
life and then expired in a series of throaty coughs, like an engine on an
icy morning. Off key, playing across the rhythm, they set an ironic comment on Reed's vicious lyrics, a character assassination of someone
who'd betrayed him. Lou had used the same title for one of his *Attitudes*
poems, only there his diatribe was turned inwards: "It's psychologically
better/That I think - dirt/They can think I'm dirt/Let them think that I'm
dirt". Second time around, Reed blasted those who'd "eat shit they'd say
it tasted good/If there was some money in it for 'em". He veered in and
out of a quote from Bobby Fuller's 'I Fought The Law', a belated throwback to the rock and roll era issued in 1966, which taught Lou everything
he needed to know about rhythm guitar playing. And while the band
lurched along behind him, he flung the accusation at anyone who was listening - his audience, Rachel, the press - "The only word for you is dirt".

'Shooting Star' repeated the dose - the same lumbering music, the
vocal quavering like the words of a dying man, totally alienated from any
concept of melody or scale. 'Leave Me Alone' said it straight: a nagging
R&B sax riff behind a tuneless dirge, with Reed roaring like a wounded
animal, lashing out at anyone and everyone in range: "Leave me leave
me leave me leave me alone". It was as painful to listen to as it was
to sing.

In the late Sixties, Reed had introduced several Velvet Underground
gigs with 'We're Gonna Have A Real Good Time Together', a two-line
promise of rock and roll solidarity that had since been adopted by the
Patti Smith Group. Lou wanted the song back, but he wasn't offering
anyone a good time, together or separately. He stripped it down to a quavering voice backed by an echoed guitar that seemed to satirise his new
persona; only after several minutes of deliberately unsatisfactory music
did Reed allow the band to take up the riff, while his backing vocalists

threw in some tags that sounded like refugees from a Beach Boys album.

One side of the album opened with the ironic 'Gimme Gimme Good Times', and delivered only 'Dirt' and 'Street Hassle'. The other began with 'I Wanna Be Black' and ended with 'Wait', another almost incoherent lyric set to a laboured parody of the early Sixties girl group sound. First Lou wanted to be black; then he wanted to be eighteen again, with the radio blasting The Shirelles' 'I Met Him On A Sunday' and Jan & Dean's 'New Kid In School', vocal riffs from both of which ended up in Lou's arrangement.

Against the clarity and tight cutting of 'Street Hassle', the remainder of the album was wilfully indulgent: "For every dark mood, I also have a euphoric opposite", Lou recognised that summer, and this album suggested that even euphoria had its darker side. When he boasted that 'Street Hassle' was "not disposable, like most records: the situations are real and human, and I wouldn't change a hair on it," it was obvious he was only talking about one song: the rest was a gesture of disgust, with the past, with Reed's own image, with the expectations of the rock circus. To mark the release of 'Street Hassle', Lou played a week of shows at the Bottom Line, which had become his favoured venue in New York. It was small enough to be intimate, familiar enough to be friendly, and its acoustics were perfect. So Reed brought in the Record Plant Mobile recording truck, and taped the entire week. He took the results to Manfred Schunke's studios in Wilster, Germany, and emerged by the end of the year with 'Take No Prisoners' - a double live album that was as shocking and brilliant as any concert recording in rock and roll.

At the Bottom Line, Reed had taken the 'Street Hassle' songs, a cross-section of Velvets classics, and some solo landmarks like 'Walk On The Wild Side' and 'Coney Island Baby', and then used them as the raw material for a set that mixed rock with stand-up comedy. This was the personification of the Lou Reed who attacked critics and told autograph hunters to fuck off. The songs became mere background to Reed's monologues - slapping down members of the audience, reeling off a succession of slick one-liners, throwing darts at Patti Smith or Andy Warhol, playing out every lyric for its full sexual innuendo. Reed saved his most acidic bile for rock critics - notably John Rockwell of the *New York Times* and Robert Christgau of the *Village Voice*. "Who needs them to tell you what to think?" he complained, before telling his audience exactly what to think. Christgau, described onstage as a "toefucker", took the assault in good grace: in his *Voice* column he simply thanked Lou for pronouncing his name right.

On 'Walk On The Wild Side', Lou updated the story of Warhol's associates, joking about Candy Darling's silicon implants which had given her cancer, ripping Joe Dallesandro to shreds for his lack of intelligence. And for the first time he told the story of how he'd written the song - the commission to write music for an adaptation of Nelson Algren's book, and then the decision to take the title and run.

"We're a fucking orchestra," Lou said of his band - whom he now wanted to call New York - after the Bottom Line shows. And the 'Take

No Prisoners' album sounded like it. From the initial adrenalin rush of 'Sweet Jane', which hits harder than any live material ever captured on record thanks to Schunke's Stereo Binaural Sound, to the final atonal thrash of 'Leave Me Alone', Reed and his band celebrated their own power, and Reed's blood-rush of confidence and bravado. "I wanted to make a record that wouldn't give an inch," Reed explained. "I think of it as a contemporary urban blues record. That's what I write - tales of the city. And if I dropped dead tomorrow, this is the record I'd choose for posterity."

"I believe in all things in moderation - including moderation. I did more than abuse my body in the past. I very often wounded it. I enjoy age. I was miserable when I was younger." (Lou Reed, 1979)

When Delmore Schwartz needed an escape from the encroaching gloom of poor reviews, professional disappointments and personal paranoia, he moved into the hinterland of New Jersey, and played at being the gentleman-poet-farmer. Away from the judging eyes of the city, he could meditate or disintegrate at will: he maintained privacy in which to rebuild his soul and concoct his conspiracy theories. In New Jersey, he could survive: his mania took hold only when he returned to the city.

In the summer of 1978, Lou Reed lived on Christopher Street in the heart of the West Village. The street is the focus of New York's gay neighbourhood, home to stereotypes of every variety, and stores which cater for an exclusively homosexual clientèle. Reed lived over a bagel store with his two dachshunds, Duke and Baron, in a six-room apartment stuffed full of electronic gadgetry - videos, TVs, cameras, guitars. Neatly furnished and maintained, it provided Lou with a *pied-à-terre* in the midst of the community which had been his lifeblood for the previous fourteen years.

Yet by 1978, Reed hankered after more. His relationship with Rachel now all but over, he had no direct ties to the city; having survived years of perilous living, he needed - at the age of 36 - to adapt to the passage of time. So between making 'Street Hassle' and 'The Bells', Lou bought a sizeable property in Blairstown, New Jersey, where he could fish on a man-made lake, shoot hoops in his backyard, and follow his latest diet of fresh fruit juice and nuts.

Spending long weekends out of the city, for the first time since he had been at Syracuse, Reed had plenty of time to think. "I really love it," he beamed. "It smells great. Even if you wanted to do something, there's nothing there. It's appalling how much sleep I get."

His three-year-long tryst with Rachel had been the most significant romantic engagement of his life; and its demise left Reed contemplating the future with some cynicism. At the end of the year, he gave a remarkable confessional interview to *Creem*, unveiling for the first time the extent of his involvement in the homosexual lifestyle, and tracing the sorry history of his secret desires back to the electro-shock therapy of the late Fifties. The conversation was triggered by his disgust at the failure of a Gay Rights Bill to make it through Congress. "I have such a heavy resentment thing because of all the prejudices against me being gay," he complained. "How can anybody gay keep their sanity?" Whereas in the past he'd been coy about his preferences, now he came out in style: "I just wouldn't want listeners to be under a false impression. I want them to know, if they're liking a man, that it's a gay one - from top to bottom." And in another interview early in 1979, he took a cheap shot in the same direction: "You want to know the real Lou Reed? Turn around. Now bend over."

Even when they live on Christopher Street, gays have to live with the guilt and anxiety ignited when they subvert the expectations of their families. Guilt quickly breeds self-loathing, and there had been plenty of that in Reed's behaviour since the early Seventies. It also spawns aggression - which in Reed's case was often turned against women, and what they represented to straight men. Talking in *Creem*, Reed unveiled a distressingly chauvinistic line on sexual relations: "You know, a lot of women get very tired of being needed. They think, 'I want you to pick me up and throw me through the window and say, "Ah fuck you".' I'm a chauvinist down to my toes. I think women admire force all the more for not having it - it's axiomatic that a woman is all the more impressed that you could kill her. A woman can get turned off if you're appreciative of her, when what she really wants is to be smacked across the mouth. My attitude often gets to be, 'Screw you too - and I'll screw your girlfriends just for spite'. Which is a terrible way to do things, because it's not like I would enjoy it. Of course, they would, it goes without saying."

Of course. With men as opponents to be defeated, women merely meaningless prizes you pick up along the way, Reed's part in the sex war was combative rather than caring. Again and again in his songs and poems, sexual desire had been linked with the exercise of power - from the blatantly obvious example of 'Venus In Furs' to the obsessive physical violence of the 'Berlin' suite, or the grim couplings and savage assaults of the *Attitudes* poems.

Ironically, in the light of his words above, Reed's salvation came in female form. The commentator on matters of S/M and transvestism, Angel Stern, remembers visiting a gay men's club in New York with Anya Phillips, a Chinese-American impresario famed for her rubber catsuits. The club was the Eulenspiegel, which was focused towards S/M, though as Angel Stern recalls, "It was just conversation. It was mostly gay men. We went there one time together and they were really hostile, but Anya didn't care, she went back there again with another girlfriend of hers and they met Lou Reed that night and the rest is history. Her girlfriend became Lou Reed's wife." The woman in question? Sylvia Morales, born in Britain to a Latin American family in the late Fifties, and by 1979 working as an artist and designer.

Unlike his relationship with Rachel, or before that with his first wife, Lou kept the growth of his affair with Sylvia out of the public gaze. The transformation from "chauvinist down to my toes" to the happily married husband of 1980 was conducted in secret - though the strains showed on the album issued shortly after the marriage.

Though Sylvia seems to have accompanied Lou on his Spring 1979 tour of Europe, there is little sign of her presence on the album which he was promoting then: 'The Bells'. This strange, weighty and often startlingly honest work is perhaps the least popular Lou Reed album of all: even 'Metal Machine Music' has its aficionados, but almost no-one - save for Lester Bangs, who wrote a brilliant justification of the album in *Rolling Stone* - has a word to say for 'The Bells'.

From the start, the album was a self-conscious step into the unknown. Through the auspices of Bob Ezrin, producer of 'Berlin', Lou was put in contact with Nils Lofgren, a singer-songwriter and former sideman to Neil Young whose own career was just sliding away from its peak. "He had some tunes but no words," Reed recalled, "so he'd send me cassettes and I'd write lyrics." This long-distance collaboration provided enough songs for three to appear on 'The Bells', and three more on Lofgren's contemporaneous 'Nils' album.

Otherwise, as Lou was quick to point out, "Most of the other songs were co-written with the band, which is something I haven't done since the Velvets". Over the previous couple of years, Reed had assembled the most durable band of his career, led by keyboard player Michael Fonfara and saxist Marty Fogel. With Ellard Boles on bass and Michael Suchorsky on drums, this core of musicians had seen Reed through 'Street Hassle' and 'Take No Prisoners'; Fonfara was actually a survivor of the band which had cut 'Sally Can't Dance' back in 1974.

To this line-up, Reed reintroduced Don Cherry, for their first collaboration in the studio. Though Cherry could play R&B riffs to order, his presence automatically tipped the balance of the album towards avant-garde jazz, leading Lester Bangs to pronounce it "the only true jazz-rock fusion anybody's come up with since Miles Davis' 'On The Corner' period". More importantly than that, Cherry allowed Reed to make 'The Bells' as much an exploration in sound as an exercise in lyrical composition.

Until you grasped the significance of production, 'The Bells' was difficult to assimilate. Reed had promised: "It's gonna be a big sound, with various machines making the guitar sound like a symphony". That was vague enough to mean anything, and it didn't explain the saxophones bleating off-key in the mix of the title track, or the tinkling percussion of 'City Streets'. Like David Bowie on his trilogy of albums recorded (like 'The Bells') in West Germany around the same time, Reed was exploring the meaning of musical noise, and the way in which he could influence moods by the juxtaposition of sounds. 'Disco Mystic' is the obvious clue, in retrospect: for the first time in a Reed song, the sound said it all, a swirling, vaguely oriental wave of rhythm which was topped with a meaningless, monkish chant of the title. This was disco dub music, years before the event, with Don Cherry repeating the same hungry sax riff over and again in an effort to convey the mindless repetition of the dance.

On 'I Want To Boogie With You', Reed had another sound in mind. He'd been exhilarated by 'Born To Be With You', the album which errant producer genius Phil Spector had produced for Dion DiMucci in 1977. "It's a piece of genius," Lou remarked at the time, "and Dion doesn't know how good it is." Lou set about to show him, creating the same languorous, deadening rhythm as Spector, and coating it with saxophones that sounded like clarion calls for the dead. Once again, the lyrics were incidental, despite their humorous subversion of Reed's anti-romantic stance.

Bruce Springsteen was the apparent model for 'Looking For Love', lyrically a rather arrogant piece of blustering, though the words were hidden beneath the E Street raunch of Reed's band. Completing the first side were the three Lofgren/Reed collaborations. 'City Lights' introduced another new Reed voice, a breathy bass tone with all the streetwise swagger taken out, to deliver the sorry tale of how Charlie Chaplin had been banished from America and then given a belated, hypocritical tickertape return. 'With You' had Reed returning to his quavering voice from 'Street Hassle', with a hint of London twang thrown in. Could the lyrics possibly have been a sideswipe at David Bowie? They were vague enough to serve any purpose. Of the Lofgren/Reed songs, 'Stupid Man' had the longest resonance, especially in the light of the songs on the album's second side. The title suggested another of Lou's ritual character assassinations; but the scenario was more touching, with a father racing home to see his baby daughter in an apparent mood of reconciliation.

Reconciliation - the attempt to put right the sins of the past - was the core of the latter half of 'The Bells'. With music as disturbing and oppressive as anything he'd produced to date, Reed explored the age-old dilemmas of blood and guilt, salvation and repentance, freedom and death. With 'Kicks' on 'Coney Island Baby', he set an unsettling account of violence against the banal chatter of party conversation. The buzz of voices reappeared on 'All Through The Night', with Reed instantly recognisable among the revellers, confident and humorous as ever. Almost hidden beneath this ambient tape and the deadening rhythm of Don Cherry's saxophone was the cry of the private man - his new-found quaver accentuating the desperation of the moment, leaving him somewhere out on a limb, midway between laughter and tears. The words told their own story - despair, fear, sickness of the soul: "With a daytime of sin and a night time of hell, everybody's gonna look for a bell to ring all through the night... I'm feeling mighty ill myself, it happens all the time... It ain't so much when a man's gotta cry to get a little loving and some peace of mind". And the final plea from the heart: "Why can't someone shed a tear for things that don't happen?"

The next song suggested a reason. 'Families' marked a final coming to terms with his blood inheritance, only to admit that there could be no reconciliation, merely good intentions. A mournful chorus repeated over and over, "How's the family", while the band played a tuneless funeral dirge, and Lou Reed told them exactly how the family were, in a voice tipped beyond emotion into despair: "And mama I know how disappointed you are/And papa I know that you feel the same way too/And no no no I still haven't got married/And no no no there's no grandson planned here for you". Each verse raised the temperature; by the end, Reed was pleading with his parents, "Let's not start this business again/I know how much you resent the life that I lead". Then there were the references to the family law firm, to the way in which every attempt at bridging the gap had merely widened it, to the sad fact that "we make each other cry". With strangled cries of "mama" or "papa" at the end of each litany of woe, 'Families' was Lou Reed's equivalent of John Lennon's 'Mother' - a song which Lou had recognised as a masterpiece when it first appeared in 1970. Like Lennon, Reed chose to play out his anguish in public, as if his admission of guilt would in itself begin the process of healing.

After two uncompromising essays in flagellation, Reed introduced the title track - an eerie, stultifying voyage into sound, which was finally broken by an ambiguous epiphany. The track consisted of a series of lengthy, monotone drones, produced on the electronic keyboard - each supported by the plaintive bleating of saxophones, in an overt tribute to Don Cherry's former bandleader, Ornette Coleman (Cherry even began the track with a quote from Coleman's 'Romany Woman'). Occasionally the tone shifted; in the distance could be heard the faint echo of voices, like monks whispering a humble incantation of prayer. For a moment, synthesised gongs shattered the atmosphere; then the deadening noise returned. Finally, Reed's voice struggled out of the mix, reciting a fragile, beautiful tale of despair which ended in suicide, as the hero hears the tolling of the bells over Broadway, and steps out from his ledge to walk into the air.

It was a breathtaking moment - a gasp of poetry amidst a storm of pain and oppression. And it concludes twenty minutes of music as difficult to take as the second half of 'Berlin', or the ear-piercing squeal of feedback guitar on 'I Heard Her Call My Name'. Part Hollywood Gothic, part Germanic gloom, part exploration of the claustrophobia of personal relationships, the second side of 'The Bells' is a masterpiece that is harrowing to listen to. Small wonder that it was greeted with such distaste by almost everyone - bar Lester Bangs, who had himself been forced to learn something of the pathos of Reed's vision.

'The Bells' was issued in the spring of 1979, to coincide with Reed's tour of Europe, where 'Take No Prisoners' had also just been released. Reed was a victim of record company contractual wrangles that meant that the live set had to be given to his old label, RCA. When it came to the tour, it was the Reed of 'Take No Prisoners' who triumphed. Lou visited the Berlin Wall for the first time; to celebrate the occasion, he restored several songs from the 'Berlin' album to his set, playing them with an energy and power that belied the emotionless landscape of the original. His fire carried beyond his singing, however. At another German gig, he took a dislike to a member of the audience early in the show, and refused to go on until he had been removed from the auditorium. Interrupting 'The Kids', Reed bellowed from the stage at the bouncers like a rabid headmaster, and when the audience reacted with booing, he led the band back to the dressing room. Chairs and glasses were thrown angrily round the arena by the disgruntled audience, $17,000 of damages were caused, and Reed was arrested and charged with inciting a riot.

"They took me to jail alone," Reed complained. "How would you like to get into a van with twelve goose steppers saying they're going to test your blood?" And he denied any responsibility for the violence: "The problem was a bunch of drunken American soldiers. They wanted to have a riot, and they had one."

Elsewhere, Lou managed to complete the shows, which extended the black music slant of his 1978 concerts. He rearranged 'Heroin' into a soul ballad; adopted an Isley Brothers-style falsetto vocal for 'Perfect Day'; and for the finale, he allowed bassist Ellard Boles to sing The Supremes' 'You Keep Me Hanging On' while he watched from the side of the stage.

At the last night of the British leg of his tour, at Hammersmith Odeon on April 10, David Bowie watched from the side of the stage, while Lou unnerved his audience by leaving the houselights on throughout the show. Later, Lou took his evening meal with Bowie and their respective entourages, in the genteel surroundings of the Chelsea Rendezvous restaurant. They began the meal in a spirit of friendship and mutual respect, offering each other elaborate toasts across the table. Then Reed erupted, lunging out at Bowie and striking him several times around the head, screaming "Don't you ever say that to me". He was restrained, and within seconds the pair had kissed and made up. Minutes later, Bowie obviously repeated the offending remark; Lou grabbed him by the shirt, and hit him, and cried out again: "I told you NEVER to say that". Lou then left the restaurant; after a shocked silence, Bowie followed him, tears in his eyes, kicking chairs out of his way, and smashing the plant pots arranged by the door of the restaurant. In the morning, Reed cancelled all his engagements, and flew to Dublin for the next concerts.

All this might have passed without notice had not two British music journalists, Allan Jones and Giovanni Dadomo, witnessed the incident. The fracas was front page news in the following week's *Melody Maker*. Speculation mounted about what Bowie might have said, with the consensus being that he had offered to produce Lou's next album - if Lou cleaned up his act.

Back in the States, Lou admitted, "Yes, I hit him - more than once. It was a private dispute." And he launched into another vague denial of culpability, claiming: "It had nothing to do with sex, politics or rock and roll. I have a New York code of ethics. Speak unto others as you would have them speak unto you. In other words, watch your mouth."

On June 3 and 4, Reed's New York ethics were on display at the Bottom Line. The first night, he raged around the stage in a temper, smashing microphones against each other. Beginning the revamped 'Heroin', he greeted the audience applause by calling out, "How do you think it feels, when I hear you calling for a pop song called 'Heroin'? The evil of that drug - you don't know. When I say it's my wife and it's my life, do you think I'm kidding?" A year earlier, during a one-off gig in Amsterdam, Lou had performed the same song with tears streaming down his face.

Twenty-four hours later, Reed spotted the face of his record company boss, Clive Davis, in the crowd. Giving him the finger, he called out, "Here, this is for you, Clive. Where's the money, Clive? How come I don't hear my album on the radio?" Davis watched impassively, as Reed renewed his assault on the rock critics he'd vilified on 'Take No Prisoners', then left the audience waiting twenty minutes or more for an encore. Later that week, Reed issued a statement to the press - through Davis's company, Arista: "I've always loved Clive, and he happens to be one of my best friends. I just felt like having a business discussion from the stage. Sometimes, out of frustration, you yell at those you love the most. I have a mouth that never sleeps, and I suppose that's why I make rock and roll records. Trying to read anything deeper into all of this is pointless."

Frustration and despair - two reactions to extreme psychological pressure. In the past, Reed had used drugs as his crutch; "I'm into drug masturbation", he had boasted in 1977. Now he banned them from the dressing-room. But he continued to drink, and the alcohol, which had helped to unlock the searing emotions of 'The Bells', also uncaged violence.

Using up so much of his psychological turmoil in song and on stage, Reed no longer needed the outlet of poetry. Instead, he returned to prose, and began work on a humorous parody of detective novels, called either 'A Fifth Of Fong' or 'Fong's Fifth', Reed wasn't sure which. "If you're going to talk about the greats," Lou had noted in the mid-Seventies, "there is no-one greater than Raymond Chandler". But his hero was no Philip Marlowe walking those mean streets; Octavian Fong was a Chinese Puerto Rican, adrift in Manhattan. "'Trash begets trash', said Fong" was, Reed announced, the novel's first line; and that was the last the public ever heard of Octavian.

1979 was the year when Reed revealed his secret dream of being Shakespeare or Dostoevsky; it was when he unveiled the extent of his homosexuality, and the depth of his dispute with his family. It was also his last year as a single man. After another brief European visit late in the year, Reed returned to New York, and began work on a new collection of songs, which would dig deeper into his complex feelings about love, filial guilt and the power of redemption. When they were completed, he married Sylvia Morales.

TEN

ON VALENTINE'S DAY 1980, LOU REED and Sylvia Morales were joined in matrimony, upstairs in Lou's apartment on Christopher Street. It made a strange kind of sense for rock's most consistent ambassador of sexual ambiguity to stage his wedding at the heart of New York's gay community. After the short ceremony, attended by a handful of friends, Mr and Mrs Reed celebrated in the Village.

"I now know that certain things will get taken care of and looked out for on the home front, where you can get hurt a lot," Reed revealed a couple of months into the marriage. "It's nice to have a trustworthy situation at home, a security situation. It's good to know that you're covered, and beyond just friendship, I'm a great one for commitment. I like to look at centuries passed, when knighthood was in flower - I'm still a great one for that. I think I've found my flower, so it makes me feel more like a knight."

"Finally, all of us are fallen knights," Reed had written in 1971. His marriage to Sylvia suggested that Adam and Eve might finally be forgiven for the Fall. Reed certainly approached his new status as a husband very seriously: "The last thing in the world I would be interested in doing is blowing it, on a personal health level. I think drugs are the single most terrible thing, and if I thought there was anything I could do which I thought might be effective in stopping people dealing in drugs and taking them, I would do it. I just think it's the worst conceivable thing in the world. Before, I didn't care.

"I'm not interested in any morality plays. I just wanted to make it clear to you. I'm not proselytising, but as far as my early demise goes, I've made a lot of efforts in the other direction. Such as things you might consider dull - working out, playing basketball, keeping my head together and all that. I find destructive people very, very boring, and I'd like to think that I'm not one of them."

The break in the steady, wave-like graph of Reed's personal life was more dramatic than that. His marriage to Sylvia ended eight years in which he had laid himself absolutely bare in public. Even such masters of professional truthtelling as John Lennon had barely approached

Reed's capacity for exhibitionism. Lennon carried out most of his orgies and indulgences behind closed doors. There were times when Reed didn't seem able to contemplate his own destruction without an audience.

February 14, 1980, marks the end of Lou Reed as a public figure. There were to be no more masks, paraded and then stripped away in a flight of daring or self-disgust. There were no more confessional sparring matches with drunken or drugged journalists, no more displaying of grudges in front of spellbound concert audiences, no more luxuriating in dissolution and despair. Instead, the entire span of Lou Reed, man and musician, would be controlled by Lou Reed, and only bared for the public in predetermined doses. The man, in all his baffling and thrilling complexity, vanished beneath the consistent image of the loving husband, committed writer and level-headed performer. Where Reed had once been buffeted by storms of emotion and chemical stimulation, his every move would now be planned and plotted in advance. No media access would be allowed without Reed's control. Press conferences would be manipulated, each journalist made to feel privileged to meet the maestro, and only afterwards would they realise that they had all been fed identical anecdotes and epigrams.

At first, the closing of the doors merely roused speculation. Pundits remembered the short and shocking coupling between Lou and Betty, and took silent bets about the possibility of Sylvia surviving until Christmas. Instead, Sylvia stayed, and Lou stayed, and at the time of writing they are still together, sharing the farm in New Jersey and the flat in Manhattan, and collaborating on the ways in which Lou's visual image is presented to the public.

Just one aspect of Lou Reed escaped the new régime: his music. That changed, along with the rest of his life, but he could not keep himself entirely out of his songs. And the first album he issued after his marriage, 'Growing Up In Public', was as intriguingly confessional as anything in his entire career.

"There are seven million stories in the city," ran Arista's rather ambitious trailer for the album. "'Growing Up In Public' is all of them." Nonsense, of course: 'Growing Up In Public' was the story of Lou Reed - fictionalised in some places, told straight in others; at times sentimental, at others harsh and cold; but always related to the strange tangle of events which had brought Lou intact through the Seventies, and left him in 1980 with a young wife and a functioning career. The album songs, said Lou, "are a composite picture of a certain kind of personality, not necessarily mine".

Reviewers hurried to connect the writer with the characters, given the basic similarities of their lives - falling in love, rejecting the family, drinking. But there is no way that all the songs on the album can be directly autobiographical. For a start, the three tunes that deal with the relations between parents and sons, 'How Do You Speak To An Angel', 'My Old Man' and 'Standing On Ceremony', have wildly differing scenarios. The father of the album's opening song, for instance, is "weak and simpering at best"; on the next track, he is a bully, who "beat my mother". In 'Standing On Ceremony', the mother dies; Lou's parents, as he was quick to point out, "are both alive, and they both like the album". Well, I wonder.

Like Delmore Schwartz, Reed used 'Growing Up In Public' to turn real life into art; and to use art as a playground for theories about real life. Laid over musical accompaniment, mostly composed by Michael Fonfara, that was so unsuitable it threw all the attention back on the words, his lyrics exposed all the uncertainty of the professed homosexual beginning a marriage, and the mixture of guilt and resentment towards his parents which had already been laid bare on 'The Bells'.

More than any previous Lou Reed album, however, 'Growing Up In Public' read like the work of a professional writer. In numerical terms alone, there were more words on this album than anything Lou had written to date. What's more, they gave every sign of having been honed and crafted to perfection, as they sparkled with puns and wordplay, tripping off the tongue with the effortless wit of Oscar Wilde at his most arch. Not that Reed was joking over the issues: he merely used humour, directed most often at himself, as a way of getting closer to the truth.

The album's slightest song was 'The Power Of Positive Drinking', a title which Lou may have borrowed from a 1978 country hit by Mickey Gilley, but was more likely just a perversion of Norman Vincent Peale's legendary self-help manual. The lyric is mostly an extended joke, with Lou as the hardened barfly forced to endure "mixers, sippers and sob sisters", as Dorothy Parker might also have put it, to get his Scotch. But the final line suggested that Lou realised the alcohol habit was there for life: "When I exit, I'll go out gracefully, shot in my hand".

On this album, every joke had a point. In 'Smiles', a playful and self-mocking tune about Reed's impassive public demeanour, he blamed his mother for teaching him never to show enjoyment, and ran off a list of crocodile smilers whose hypocrisy had robbed this most natural facial expression of its meaning. The link between his family and the suppression of emotion doesn't only feature here, however. 'How Do You Speak To An Angel' may present the narrator's parents as caricatures - the simpering father we've already met, and the "harridan mother" - but together they leave him with a "classically neurotic style", unable to approach the mythical creature of beauty who has arisen before him.

'My Old Man' and 'Standing On Ceremony' paint an even darker portrait of the relationship. 'Standing On Ceremony' is a devastating snapshot of emotional inhibition; even as his mother is dying, his father (played by Reed in a gruff, fierce voice he'd never raised on record before) nags him to "remember your manners/will you please take your hat off". "We were always standing on ceremony", Reed calls plaintively, before hiding from responsibility in a bar during the song's final verse.

But it's 'My Old Man' which was Reed's most overt family portrait, one which - even if it's totally untrue - makes it unlikely that 'Growing Up In Public' was his parents' favourite album. Lou admitted that some of the details in the first verse about his days at public school in

Brooklyn were real - remember PS 192 from the final lines of 'Coney Island Baby'? But the rest he denied - the father who forced Lou into "bullying and having to hide under a desk on the floor/and when he beat my mother it made me so mad that I could choke". Set to a propulsive rock rhythm that drove Reed restlessly from line to line, 'My Old Man' was performed with an urgency that reeked of sincerity, even if the details weren't strictly accurate. "And you know what he said to me?", Reed cried out in utter disbelief as the song faded away, "he said, Lou, why don't you act like a man".

Acting like a man was exactly what Lou was doing as the album was being recorded, via his marriage to Sylvia. And that's the other great theme of this album - the tortuous progress of a new relationship from initial attraction, through the minefield of mutual discovery, to the eventual embodiment of hope in the marital vows.

'How Do You Speak To An Angel' set the scene - with Reed overawed by the beauty of the creature he had met in the most unlikely surroundings. 'So Alone' took up the story, with her phone call asking for company, nothing more, and the relationship crawling forward and back towards some kind of resolution. The jerky rhythm of the song reflected the course of the affair - it was all loose nerve ends and potential misunderstanding, like anxious couplings in a Woody Allen movie, with Lou's voice raised in self-defence as he explained some ambiguous remarks, and then taking the attack himself when he accused 'her' of "asking one man about another man's vice". "Can't you understand that it's frightening when you hear women talking about castrating and hating men", was Lou's first public response to the feminist movement; in the song, he reacted by taking 'her' to a disco, and telling her to "shake your booty mama". "You said you liked me for my mind," Lou swaggered in a menacing, arrogant voice, "Well I really like your behind". And then he dropped back into the conciliatory tone of the earlier verses, as the couple agree to disagree, and eventually fall into an exhausted sleep - anything to avoid being alone.

Treat the album as a fairytale, and you move into 'Think It Over', the most poignant song about love in Reed's catalogue. It began with a beatific vision of Sylvia, "black hair framing her perfect face/with her wonderful mind and her incredible grace", which prompts the hero "to offer her his heart, once and for all, forever to keep". She responds with a glimpse of paradise, and then she sighs, and suggests caution, and time to think it over. The music supported the delicacy of the moment, and Lou bent his voice into depths of emotion unimaginable five years earlier.

'Keep Away' conveys a deeper sense of doubt. It's written as Lou's defence against charges of philandering, a brilliantly structured parade of ridiculous images as he attempts to prove his good intentions: "Here's a balloon, a rubber band and a bag/Why don't you blow them up if you think you've been had... I swear I'll keep away from dignity and pride/I'll keep away from abstracts, I'll keep it all inside/I'll just wrap me up in butter and melt me on a shelf/I'll fry in my own juices I'll become somebody else".

In the event, 'Love Is Here To Stay', and Reed wrote a kind of anthem to celebrate the fact - albeit one which was immediately satirised by the verses, which put him and Sylvia forward as a pair of opposites ("She likes her novels long/he's into comic books") who are "gilt-edged poly-morphous urban, but somehow it works".

Most of the album is devoted to the marriage, and the union in the pre-vious generation which cast a sickly shadow over Reed's own nuptials. But the subject of the record was, finally, Reed himself; and in the title track he approached the complexity of his everyday relationships with other people. Everyone is simply "growing up in public, with your pants down", a fate which Reed could understand better than most.

The mere fact that Lou could discuss his decade-long stroll through infamy and pain was a sign that he had learnt from the experience. The album's final song, 'Teach The Gifted Children', turned that learning process into poetry. Over music that weaved in and out of Al Green's 'Take Me To The River', Reed begged for the next generation to be shown the gifts of beauty and forgiveness, yet to be made aware also of anger and sin. It breathed warmth towards humanity, and hope for the future; it took love to turn Reed's years of twitching unease away from the expectation of disaster. 'Growing Up In Public' ended the first stage of his battle against the irresistible forces of fate; at last, it allowed Reed to think that the naturalist writers he had read might be wrong, that human character and destiny was not set in the blood, that he could final-ly choose life over death, hope over despair. But this was still the honeymoon. The succession of day after night would show whether the dawn was false or glorious.

'Growing Up In Public' was released in June 1980. That month, Reed brought his band to Europe for a brief Continental tour, where he effec-tively reprised the content of his shows the previous year, throwing his latest work into stark relief against the desperate scenario of 'Berlin'. The irony of Reed celebrating his second marriage by playing songs that reflected the traumatic collapse of his first can't have escaped him. In Paris, at the end of the tour, he invited old friend Garland Jeffreys up onstage to duet on 'Walk On The Wild Side' - a gesture that paid homage to the past (Jeffreys had once performed onstage with the Velvets and Eric Burdon at the height of the EPI) at the same time as Reed buried it.

Drugs were off limits on the 1980 tour; soon touring was off limits as well. For the remainder of the year, Lou's only public appearance was on screen, where he played the part of a manipulative and cantankerous rock manager in Paul Simon's wry autobiographical fantasy, 'One Trick Pony'. Reed apparently hated the experience, and the collaboration with Simon seemed an unlikely one. But both men were native Jewish New Yorkers and doo-wop fans who'd matured into semi-confessional song-writers, trying to force a teenage musical style squealing into adulthood.

And both shared with Woody Allen the dry self-mocking humour that is a New York trademark.

As Reed slowly approached 40, his outsider status in the rock world belied his veteran experience. Many of his contemporaries, like Paul McCartney and Pete Townshend, seemed unable to combine the ageing process with any form of grace, while others, like John Lennon, had opted out of the circus rather than walk bowed into head winds. Reed's closest partner in rock's gerontocracy was Bob Dylan, by 1980 emerged in a desperate struggle to convert the world to evangelical Christianity, and facing the narrow-minded opposition of the audience who had once cheered him for invoking the chimes of freedom.

Even in the middle of this crisis, however, Dylan continued to be revered as a rock guru - that was why his fans were so upset by his apparent shift away from his traditional values. For Reed, the situation was more complex. Every year, the legend of his four-year stint with The Velvet Underground gained another layer. The VU were now the accepted forefathers of the New Wave in Britain and America; if you didn't like the Velvets, then you were destroying your credibility.

With 'Street Hassle' long forgotten, however, and 'The Bells' and 'Growing Up In Public' quietly ignored, Reed's work as a solo artist had been boiled down to one perennial golden oldie, 'Walk On The Wild Side'. That - plus 'Heroin' and 'Sweet Jane' - was the reason why Lou Reed could sell out concerts in Europe or America. Few were coming to hear 'All Through The Night' or 'So Alone'.

Part of the problem was Reed's determination to edge his way into the black music mainstream. Ever since the dawn of punk had revived Reed's reputation, he had steadfastly ignored the new music's speed-freak rhythm and clamorous vocals. Instead, Lou had become a would-be soul singer, stretching his voice into ever more bizarre phrasing, and supporting himself with musicians who were more at home with funk than three-chord punk. At its worst, on tracks like 'Standing On Ceremony', the gap between Lou and his music became a canyon - the band walking sedately through a distant cousin of reggae, while Lou tried to fit trains of three and four syllable words into the spaces between the on-beats.

Looking back in 1982, Reed pinpointed the problem: "For the last few years, I was working with musicians who were into jazz and funk. I wasn't playing guitar on my records because I really couldn't play with those guys, being a simple rock and roll player. I thought it would be interesting to explore that direction, but there was a gap between me and them. You can hear it on the records. So I said, 'You've carried this experiment far enough. It's not working. The ideas are there and then they disappear, the music isn't consistent, you seem isolated, there's a certain confidence that's not there because you're not really in control.' So I dissolved the band."

With the band went Reed's commitment to free-form jazz, his desire to join Ornette Coleman in exploding rhythmic and melodic structure, his dream of becoming Al Green, his exploration of the limits of sound. In its place, for the moment, Lou offered nothing. For the first time since he had left The Velvet Underground, he elected to remain silent for more than a year. He took little part in the compilation of a critically acclaimed double album, 'Rock And Roll Diary', which traced his development from the first Velvet Underground album to the present day. After a Christmas 1980 show at the Bottom Line in New York, there were no records, no tours, no poetry readings: his only visible presence during 1981 was as lyricist on a record by, of all people, Kiss.

The link, as with Nils Lofgren in late 1978, was Bob Ezrin. Kiss, the comic book heroes of the American heavy metal scene, were working on a concept called 'The Elder', an exploration of the eternal struggle between Good and Evil which was originally planned to stretch over several albums. Paul Stanley of Kiss explained in 1980: "Lou was so into the project, that when we called him and explained it over the phone to him, he said, 'I'll get back to you in an hour'. And he called back an hour later with good basic lyrics to 'Mr Blackwell', 'World Without Heroes' and a lot of other stuff that hasn't been used yet."

"It's fascinating and flattering - not to mention the money - to be given a set of characters or whatever and be asked to write songs around them," Reed noted early in 1982. But though 'Music From The Elder' was released in November 1981, Reed's work on the project - three songs bearing his lyrics ended up on the album - had been completed more than two years earlier.

Lou and Sylvia continued to divide their time between New Jersey and the Village, where they continually bumped into the ghosts of Reed's past. Absent from the guest list at their wedding had been Andy Warhol; artist and protégé met in April 1981 for the first time in more than a year, and exchanged strained pleasantries. Warhol was not in the mood to be impressed by Sylvia: "She's nothing special, just a sexy little girl," he opined in his diary dictation the following morning, adding in a later entry, "His wife looks more Puerto Rican every time I see her."

The estrangement from the past was complete: Lou didn't mix much on the rock club scene any more, and anyway the energy of the Patti Smith/Television/Ramones triumvirate had long been dissipated. Warhol was as keen to gossip about Lou's new lifestyle as anyone: he noted that Lou had been seen in a notorious Village bar, and suggested: "Maybe he was just there picking up boys". But whatever Lou was doing these days, he was doing it in private, and the rock scene hardly noticed that he had gone.

1981 seems to have been the time when Lou made the decision to quit drinking. There had long been hints in his songs that the bottle uncorked violent emotions in his heart; during the early Eighties, Lou would reprise the subject in his work. He began attending Alcoholics Anonymous sessions in New York, and was still going several years later.

That year, Sylvia introduced him to a guitarist named Robert Quine - veteran of American punk band Richard Hell and The Voidoids, and also known to dabble on the fringes of the avant-garde. In Quine, Reed recognised a kindred spirit, "a guitarist who could play my way". Quine took the same short cuts as Lou: rather than playing conventionally up and down the scales, he leapt from one dissonance to another, unafraid to leave the connections unspoken. In his hands, as in Reed's, the guitar became an instrument of jagged, unsettling emotion; whether he played lyrically or atonally, Quine never settled for the easy option.

Reed had treated the guitar as little more than a stage prop since the end of the Velvets. For several tours, he'd abandoned the instrument completely; there was a delicious irony in his writing a would-be anthem like 'Rock And Roll Heart', and then scarcely touching the instrument that was the spirit of rock and roll. On 'Street Hassle', he had rediscovered some of the guitar's potential for noise, but there was little on record since 'White Light/White Heat' to suggest that Reed might be a major influence as a musician, as well as a songwriter.

Sparring with Quine seems to have renewed Lou's enthusiasm for the guitar. On recent albums he'd been content to let the keyboards of Michael Fonfara shape the music; Fonfara had even co-written the bulk of the 'Growing Up In Public' album, given the difficult task of providing danceable settings for Reed's weighty poetry. Now Reed once again began to write words and music himself, and all his new songs were guitar songs - equally viable with a band, or played solo.

"I keep a notebook," Reed explained when his next album was released. "I also write in my head a lot, or sometimes I'll write things out. It's much less a matter of doing the music first. Sometimes when that happens, it comes out of a riff. And what's a good riff? Sometimes you'll get locked into one, and in the end you don't come out with a good song, just a riff."

When he had assembled a body of songs, Reed recorded blueprints on cassette, playing a lightly amplified electric guitar. Then he called in a band - a simple three-piece support unit, which again was a decisive break from the much larger groups he'd taken on the road in the Seventies.

Besides Quine, Reed invited Fernando Saunders to play fretless electric bass, and Doane Perry on drums. "About a week before going in the studio," Reed noted, "I got together with the guitar player, and we ran down the songs together. I wrote it all out beforehand. Everyone knew the songs up to a point, but nothing was too structured."

To accentuate the aura of a fresh start, Reed elected not to continue his deal with Arista: instead, he returned to RCA, the label he'd left in 1976 with the bitterness of the 'Metal Machine Music' incident still sour in his mouth. In October 1981, Reed and his band gathered at RCA's New York studio, and recorded 'The Blue Mask' - which Lou immediately recognised as "my best album to date. This one was pretty much perfect - it came out the way it was supposed to."

Released early in the New Year, 'The Blue Mask' attracted the usual mixed response from the critics, most of whom assumed that Reed was taking a deliberate step back from his confrontational mode of the past. And the album did nothing to return Lou to the commercial mainstream which he'd abandoned with 'Metal Machine' Music.

Yet 'The Blue Mask' is one of Reed's masterpieces, cunningly constructed as a rebirth rather than a continuation, but with its best intentions torpedoed by Reed's desperate urge to reflect his inner turmoil. The album marked another changing of the tide in Reed's work. If the first three Velvet Underground albums were an exploration of sound and psyche, then 'Loaded' and his work through to 'Transformer' in 1972 represented a careful step back from the abyss, with Reed playing with exotic scenarios rather than inhabiting them. 'Berlin' inaugurated another change, and even through the darkest hours of the mid-Seventies, Reed's songs picked at his most vulnerable wounds. When his relationship with Rachel foundered, he entered a phase where there was no longer any visible gap between the Lou Reed who wrote the songs, and the Lou Reed who starred in them.

Reed was more conscious than anyone of the precarious balancing act he'd staged over the previous decade. And 'The Blue Mask' was meant from the start as a summary of the past, and a definite step into the future. Sylvia's original cover design cleverly played on the album title by placing a classic 'Transformer' era shot of Lou against a similar modern pose: look from one angle, and you saw the Lou of legend, from another and the man behind the mask became visible. (Typically, RCA managed to print the cover so that only the vintage picture could be seen.) Reed explained his purpose quite openly: "I'm very very image conscious, and I've tried to use it gracefully, to focus it. On this album I'm bringing all those Lou Reeds together, into one. But the basic image is and always has been - Lou Reed comes from New York City and writes rock and roll songs."

That simple statement would fast become a vocation, with Lou the John Cheever of rock, able to turn tiny segments of life - a chance remark, a cosy night in front of the fire, a motorcycle ride in the country - into a concise and witty short story, an exhibition of craft rather than soul. But on at least half of 'The Blue Mask', and part of the next album, 'Legendary Hearts', as well, Reed's sub-conscious knew too much to stay quiet. The tension between obsessive self-exposure, and the impersonal skill of the master storyteller, produced some of Lou's most brilliant, beautiful and sometimes terrifying writing; and Robert Quine was on hand to translate that anguish and passion into music.

The first seconds of track one - Saunders' bass sliding us into 'My House', Quine's guitar setting off in another direction, Reed's metallic rhythm holding him down - set the tone for the entire album. The intimacy and dialogue of the musicians left room for Reed to think; the songs sounded as if they were being born, not just performed. And as Reed's voice entered for the first time, midway between the desperate wavering of 'The Bells' and the cocksure recitation of 'Sweet Jane', the break from Reed's most recent work was immediately obvious.

'My House' found Lou and Sylvia in the New Jersey countryside. "The image of the poet's in the breeze", and the poet was Delmore Schwartz, reborn in the air which linked his Jersey refuge with Reed's, fifty miles or so to the East. "My friend and teacher occupies a spare room," Reed announced calmly, before revealing that the long-dead Schwartz had been contacted via a Ouija Board in Reed's farmhouse.

The incident was real, or so Lou claimed afterwards: "Something very strange happened. After a while we just had to stop, it was becoming too much for me to handle." But truth or invention, Delmore's miraculous presence allowed Reed to pay off his debts to "the first great man that I had ever met". His spirit hung over the house and the song, before blazing to life in the stridency of Quine's guitar playing over the final bars. But not before Reed had teased us with his irony: "I've really got a lucky life/My writing, my motorcycle and my wife." Having set his priorities straight, Reed was free to return full circle to the natural images of beauty with which he'd opened the song - the first hint in his work that some kind of solace existed outside the desperate clamour of the city.

'My House', an evocative display of "the spirit of pure poetry", represented one extreme of 'The Blue Mask'. The other surfaced in the title track. "Here are two people engaged in violent behaviour towards one another," Reed explained, "and it's an attempt at a salvation that they know can't occur and a redemption that doesn't exist. It's too much for them, they're past that, they're torturing each other, they're wearing dark blue masks."

The significance of the masks was known only to Reed, though it lent an extra twist of inhumanity to a horrifying account of obsessional pain and violence. The indifference with which Reed sang 'Venus In Furs', his first exploration of dependence on pain, gave an air of distance to Severin's sufferings at the hands of Wanda. But in 'The Blue Mask', there was no refuge from the blood and the screams. Reed and Quine forced brutal, savage chords from their guitars, and the song built from there - Reed close to screaming himself as the narrative reached its climax, and the two men rekindling the spirit of the second Velvets album as they squeezed out free-form flurries of notes and feedback.

The music itself evoked violence; but it had none of the ambiguity of the lyrics. At first, Reed's subject sounded like military torture - "They tied his arms behind his back to teach him how to swim... They stood over the soldier in the midst of squalor". But as the song grew more graphic, it became clear that the victim was a willing participant, boasting all the holy passion of a martyr at the stake: "He put a pin through the nipples on his chest, he thought he was a saint". The final image of the song - a finger severed, a stallion (an obvious phallic reference) "cut at his mount" - was less horrific, though, than the dubious status of Reed's narrator: "I've made love to my mother, killed my father and brother, what am I to do? ...Take the Blue Mask down from my face and look me in the eye/I get a thrill from punishment, I've always been that way." As much victim as torturer, Reed's character was bound into the dark contract of sado-masochism, and obsession knew no bounds: "When a sin goes too far it's like a runaway car, and cannot be controlled".

Powerful and hard to take, 'The Blue Mask' presented a scene far removed from the peaceful stroking of the muse in 'My House'. And the violence of Reed's delivery suggested that his own attitude to the subject was divided. Not since the poems Reed had written in 1975 had the poles of sex and physical pain been linked so blatantly.

'The Gun' - which Reed was careful to stress was "none of me" - repeated the connection, albeit in more conventional terms. Performed with a mixture of tension and total indifference, it presented a mugger, burglar, murderer, rapist - a man with the potential to do anything to his victims as long as he has a gun in his hand. Reed realised how close he was to fundamental urges of male domination: "I have found without exception that any guy who listens to that song reacts with universal fear. And it's dangerous for me too. If I do a song and there's a bad character or a drug character or something like that - sometimes it's me and sometimes it's not me - as I sing the song, I go through it. It's a really cathartic kind of thing in a lot of ways. It is acting. But doing these characters long enough - it gets to you. Some of those lyrics are very rough." The Blue Mask created terror with the directness of its language; on 'The Gun', Reed let the imagination conjure up its own horrors.

And that was precisely the problem that sparked 'Underneath The Bottle', the first song apparently inspired by Reed's strident efforts to stop drinking. Over one of his classic three-chord riffs, Reed set up the problem: "Liquor set me free/I can't do no work/The shakes inside me". From one verse to the next, he switched from determination to quit to the classic denial syndrome of the addict, convinced that all he needs to feel better is "a drink to relax me".

Delivered in a matter-of-fact voice that says 'This is the way I am, and nothing can change it', 'Underneath The Bottle' set Lou up as chief culprit in a cycle of self-abuse, and dragged a few laughs out of the situation along the way.

Likewise 'Women', the successor to 'A Gift on Coney Island Baby'. First time around, his boast to be "a gift to the women of the world" was rather undermined by his scathing comments on the female sex in *Creem*. By 1982, married two years - to a woman! - Lou was able to announce "I love women/I think they're great" with only the hint of a smirk. And the lyrics deserve a smile - Lou protesting that his indulgence in soft porn mags "was sexist, but I was in my teens", or suggesting that he might hire "a choir of castratis" (no American would say 'castrati', after all) "to serenade my love". It's a song Reed simply couldn't have written three years earlier.

These five songs - the first side of 'The Blue Mask' - ran the gamut from fear to love, violence to tranquility, evoking the spirits and demons which had inspired so much of Reed's work over the previous fifteen years. The remainder of the album offered a weaker brew. 'Waves Of Fear' allowed Quine to coax bleats and howls out of his guitar, while Reed paraded the dense, oppressive agonies of a panic attack, induced by alcohol or paranoia. 'On The Day John Kennedy Died' introduced a rare note of political awareness in Reed's work, though his idealistic reminiscences of his shock at JFK's killing were entirely free of irony. This was the Lou Reed who'd briefly expressed the wish in 1976 to play fund raising concerts for Jimmy Carter; by looking back to Kennedy as any kind of ideal, he was merely paying lip service to one of America's most durable modern myths.

Reed was far more impressive when he was dealing in uncertainty. 'The Heroine', included on the album in its original solo demo form when Sylvia suggested that this version was more evocative than the band's attempt, was a dense and faintly disturbing prolonged metaphor - with Lou, perhaps, as "the ship out of control", and Sylvia the heroine "locked in his defence... the pale ascendant strapped to the mast". More conventionally, Sylvia was the heroine of 'Heavenly Arms', the first entirely unambiguous love song Reed had ever released. Its tune harked back to 'Satellite Of Love' on 'Transformer', as if to highlight Lou's long, agonising progress from the sky-searching of 1972 to the achievement of heaven a decade later. The key note was hidden away in the middle of the song: "Only a woman can love a man in a world full of hate", Reed declared, and that was quite a statement coming from the creator of 'Coney Island Baby' and 'Street Hassle'. Reed used Sylvia's name as the entire lyric for the chorus - yet he still had Fernando Saunders sing the ultimate declaration of love over the fade, "Sylvia, you mean so much to me".

In the final account, Lou was just trying to be an 'Average Guy' - as he explained in the song which looked forward to his next two albums. Maybe this was an unconscious tribute to another of Lou's heroes, The Kinks' Ray Davies, who'd written countless hymns to the ordinary man struggling to come to terms with the complexity of life in the material world. Lou had loved The Kinks back when they were cranking out three-chord garage band riffs; he'd singled out 'The Great Lost Kinks Album', a collection of Davies's most eccentric and personal songs, as a favourite in the early Seventies; and then there was the weird rumour that 'Sister Ray' had been intended as an oblique reference to Ray Davies's camp behaviour onstage. 'Average Guy' followed the entire Davies ticket - "I'm average looking and I'm average inside/I'm an average lover and I live in an average place" - but inserted a single telling reference to Lou's own health: "I worry that my liver's big and it hurts to the touch".

"My goal has always been to make an album that would speak to people the way Shakespeare speaks to me, the way Joyce speaks to me," Reed noted to Robert Palmer of the *New York Times,* "something with that kind of power, something with bite to it." Shakespeare and Joyce created characters that were both specific to their times, and universal in their suffering and enjoyment of man's fundamental quests - for love, for understanding, for purpose and for God. Reed invested his examination of the limits of humanity in one character, and named him 'Lou Reed'. In 'The Blue Mask', he came closer to making Lou Reed into Everyman than ever before, and learnt something in the process. From now on, he would try to translate that learning into the craft of writing, without the need to flagellate in front of the crowd.

"I'm not going to tour anymore, period. It wasn't good for me. I wasn't happy with my band. Still, I did have fun. Now, I could possibly see playing New York, maybe one night at the Bottom Line. But as for 90 days and 89 cities, I can't do that any more. I used to drink a lot. And it would be hard for me to imagine getting through one of those tours without slipping back. And I don't want to do that."
(Lou Reed, 1982)

To promote 'The Blue Mask', Lou went on a publicity tour - and didn't drink. The studio sessions for the album had been strictly straight - no dope, no grass, and no alcohol too. Control was the order of the day, and that extended beyond Lou's personal habits to the managing of the media. Where Reed had once opened himself up to the psychodramas of one-on-one interviews, he now staged a series of mini-press conferences, in which journalists were wheeled in, six or eight at a time, and invited to ask questions about the album - nothing about Lou's personal life, please note, or The Velvet Underground, or his shift from Rachel to Sylvia. Scared of making a fool of themselves in front of their peers, few writers dared more than ask sycophantic queries about the making of 'The Blue Mask'.

Then it was back to New York, and New Jersey, and the hard slog of making a marriage work, and keeping off drink, and maintaining the flow of words and music. Already a keen exponent of solo basketball on his Jersey farm, Lou was now introduced by his brother-in-law to another schooling for the body - Wu-style Tai Chi Chuan, or Chinese boxing, a sport in which the ritual of the combat is as important as the outcome. "It's an aesthetic and physical discipline that I find exquisite," Lou revealed. "The discipline is in the ability to relax. It's very beautiful to watch." Watching and relaxing had not been hallmarks of Reed's art for many years; since the early Seventies, when he had 'collected' personalities, Warhol style, he had been too busy keeping himself alive, struggling to keep his head above the flow, to sit back passively and let life wash over him.

The new discipline was quickly apparent in his work; whether it was inspired by Tai Chi or not, Reed developed into an observer. This wasn't the voyeurism of which he'd constantly been accused since 'Heroin' in 1965; it was the skilled, trained observation of the writer, assembling material, shaping reality as he experienced it.

Implicit in the pose of the storyteller was simplicity. His aim was to let the characters reveal themselves through their stories, not to impose conclusions from above like a manipulative deity. And after the musical experimentation of the late Seventies, Reed was determined to return to basics.

"I've always liked those very basic, very simple rock and roll changes," he told Chris Bohn in early 1983. "I've never heard anything I like more than that. Not in opera, not in classical music, not in jazz nor in show tunes. Not movie music. Nothing. Nothing has impressed me as much as the most basic rock and roll chord change, and by that I mean, say, E to A. And to this day, when I hear that change done right - and it can be done wrong - I get an abnormal degree of pleasure from it. Wouldn't it be wonderful to put a melody over that, something that would stick like grease? And then wouldn't it be great if the lyrics also had some substance to them, were as simple and as elegant as that change from one chord to the other?"

That was Reed's new creative motto - simplicity and elegance. No more sprawling epics, like 'The Bells'; no lumbering collaborations between cumbersome lyrics and complex jazz rhythms; what Reed wanted was the lesson of Delmore Schwartz brought into music, simple words combined to evoke complex emotions. "It's very hard to keep it simple," Reed complained a year later; and equally hard to prevent simplicity slopping over into banality.

'Legendary Hearts', which Reed recorded in the final months of 1982, walked that line and never quite toppled off. The cover shot, conceived by Sylvia, was another mask - gleaming, metallic and fascistic, like the State Police in some science fiction dystopia, but then revealed on the back as nothing more sinister than Reed's bike helmet. Motorcycling through the back roads of Jersey had become one of Reed's methods of relaxation - hence the thick black leather of his jacket and gloves. And it directly inspired one of the most troubling songs on the new album, 'Bottoming Out'.

The album, which featured Quine and Saunders once again, with Fred Maher playing drums, had a lean, stripped-down quality which stepped away from the dramas of 'The Blue Mask'. It still left room for Reed to explore the darker edges of his psyche, however. A recurrent theme was the fragility of romance, and the complexity of the marriage contract. 'Bottoming Out' had Reed biking "down this winding country road" past the place where he'd crashed the previous week, and recollecting in some hope of tranquillity the fight which had sparked his reckless last ride: "If I hadn't left/I would've struck you dead/So I took a ride instead".

Over a tight, four-chord structure which he later repeated on 'There Is No Time' on the 'New York' album, Reed took a cold look at his "violent rage", then cut suddenly to another road, and another mood swing: "I'm drunk but my vision's good/And I think of my child bride". The memory didn't inspire conventional love and romance; instead, Reed sang morosely: "I aim that bike at that fat pothole/Beyond that underpass". Self-destructive, violent, desperate for another drink, the Lou Reed of 'Bottoming Out' was prepared to risk his own life to avoid risking anyone else's.

Remove the object of any obsession, and until the balance of mind is restored, the obsession simply doubles. Hence 'The Last Shot', another examination of the craving for alcohol, this time from the position of someone who has recognised that alcoholics are never cured, they just teach themselves not to drink alcohol. Ironic, self-mocking, yet touched with a terror of regression, 'The Last Shot' was this album's equivalent of 'Underneath The Bottle' - albeit from a step further down the road towards a cure.

Despite this hint of progress, 'Legendary Hearts' was an album tinged with depression, a subdued account of marital life rather than a celebration. The title track was a beautifully constructed ballad, hinged around a circular series of chords that left us right back where we started from. But the message was apologetic: "I can't live up to this/I'm good for just a kiss/Not legendary love". And the weary reference to "promises to keep/I never should have made" was far removed from the spicy sensuality of 'Heavenly Arms' on 'The Blue Mask'.

Much of the album shared the same faintly regretful tone - 'Turn Out The Light', for instance, with its moody guitar riff topped by lyrics which pleaded the transience of all emotions; or 'Make Up Mind', effectively an extended pun, which had a sting in the tail: "Are you laughing at me in your sleep tonight/Leaving me behind/Why don't you make up your mind".

But the song which cut closest to the bone was 'Betrayed', not only for its startling confession about marital discord - "Three of us lie in this bed/Night of infamy... Her father's in her head/And quick she turns/And slaps my face/And with her eyes open wide she screams/I hate you I hate you I hate you/But she's looking right past me" - but also in its sorrowful belief in the inevitability of the human character, the impossibility of escaping upbringing and family blood. Given Reed's attitude towards his family, and his interest in the harrowing sagas of Hubert Selby Jnr., who drags his characters through hell in the name of irresistible fate, this was an admission soaked in regret.

Amidst songs like these, which left even Robert Quine sounding subdued, faint lights of hope passed almost unnoticed. Only 'Martial Law' escaped from the album's prevailing mood. Over Robert Quine's only noticeable guitar riff on the album, Reed created a new pose - "the marshal in this city", come to impose law and order in the name of non-violence. For Reed to invent himself as a bastion of the law, with a mission to stop husbands and wives arguing in the early hours, was a neat way of diffusing the tension of the moment.

Even outside the house there was little to celebrate. 'Home Of The Brave' was an ironic reflection on America, where you can't walk a block without risking violence and crime; Lou even threw in a gloomy chorus of the Sixties soul standard by Arthur Alexander, 'Everyday I Have To Cry', to ram the message home.

Yet the album, a collection of regrets and painful admissions that life was more difficult to control than he'd thought, still ended with a tiny statement of hope - a city fantasy which blatantly followed the example of Goffin and King's song for The Drifters, 'Up On The Roof'. In their 'Rooftop Garden', the Reeds could look down on the world below and reflect, "What a lovely couple are you and I". As a hint of salvation for the future, it was a touching way to end an album that had slowly ground down any of the faint optimism of 'The Blue Mask'.

'Legendary Hearts' was hardly a message to gladden the heart of any Lou Reed fan, yet its very existence was proof that Reed still valued honesty above deceit. His critical stock was at an all-time low, however, with reviewers competing to damn Reed for his irrelevance and refusal to remake the first Velvets album. Taking 'Rooftop Garden' as his theme, a reviewer in the London paper *Melody Maker* lashed Reed for being "so out of touch and unreal that it's shocking", for sounding "disgustingly out of his head", for producing work that was "so worthless... crass and childish", and for creating "the most insultingly appalling release in years by any major artist". Like John Lennon before him, Reed found himself reviled for the simple act of growing older, and acting his age. When his critics required him to fake the debauchery of the Sixties and Seventies, rather than reflect the more subtle ambiguities of the Eighties, it's little wonder that Reed eventually elected to step back from his work and write songs that had their origins in craft rather than the confessional.

It was the new Reed, not his uncontrollable ancestor, who eventually took the decision to return to live work. He began, as predicted, at the Bottom Line in New York, with a show that was filmed for subsequent video release. In the audience that night was Andy Warhol, who noted, "Lou's lyrics you can understand now, and the music was really loud. He did a lot of familiar songs, but you didn't recognise them, they sounded different." Insofar as they did, that was down to the interplay between Reed and Robert Quine, whose subdued performance on 'Legendary Hearts' was belied by the sparky ebullience of his work onstage with Lou. The shows dipped into his recent catalogue, but also exhumed several gems from the Sixties, like 'Sunday Morning', 'New Age' and a closing medley of 'Rock And Roll' and 'Sister Ray'.

While Britain and America continued to treat Lou Reed as an amusing leftover from the past, other territories greeted him as a superstar. That's why in September 1983, Reed, Quine, Saunders and Maher made the trip to Italy, for a week of shows in huge arenas. Part of the deal was that the local branch of RCA Records would tape the shows for a live album, which was duly issued as a double set - 'Live In Italy', which was sensible enough - early in 1984, but only in Europe.

'Live In Italy' wasn't the finest possible record of the Reed/Quine partnership, but it was still a powerful, if slightly anonymous, live album. Reed invested fire in 'Kill Your Sons', as if the scars of the past would never disappear, while Quine helped him create a storm of guitar noise on a memorable medley of 'Some Kinda Love' and 'Sister Ray'. Reed was presenting effectively a greatest hits show - half Velvets, half solo, with the obligatory 'Walk On the Wild Side', 'Heroin' and 'Sweet Jane' - but performed with sufficient grace to give the concerts a craftsmanlike air. Reed was now close to a predictable rock and roll career, with an annual album/tour cycle accompanied by music that was merely a consolidation of what had gone before.

Gradually, Reed had been assimilated into the rock mainstream. Apart from friends like Genya Raven and Garland Jeffreys, or Bob Ezrin contacts like Nils Lofgren and Kiss, nobody in the late Seventies approached Reed for superstar collaborations. Into the early Eighties, as Reed's life and work became less extreme, that situation changed. Paul Simon had shown the way by requesting Lou's presence in 'One Trick Pony'. Now the makers of an appalling animated movie called 'Rock And Rule' asked Lou to contribute two songs for the soundtrack; he obliged with 'My Name Is Mok' and 'Triumph', both apparently leftovers from the sessions for 'Growing Up In Public'.

Soundtrack work was an obvious development for Reed's career, as his cinematic writing qualities had been noted as early as the first Velvets album. 'Berlin' was promoted, after all, as a "film for the ear", and Reed's name had also been raised in connection with movie ventures by Andy Warhol and Terry Southern. But no-one dared to sink a substantial portion of a Hollywood budget into a songwriter whose name was still linked with excess and outrage. Instead of scoring, say, a movie by Martin Scorsese or Brian de Palma, Reed was invited to contribute soundtrack songs to a strange collection of films through the mid-Eighties, none of which added any great lustre to his career.

Lou may have hated the process of filming 'One Trick Pony', but his typecast performance as a stoney-faced music business hard-man showed that he was quite capable of satirising his own image on screen. He repeated the process in *Get Crazy,* where he had a hilarious cameo role as a rock star who gets lost en route to a New Year's Eve gig that allowed Lou to perform 'My Baby Sister' - a charmingly coy teen ballad that unveiled an entirely new Reed persona, the sentimental elder brother with his eye out for his little girl. "Pick a melody from one to ten/I'll make a rhyme up and then we'll try again", Reed sang, light years away from the gloom of the 'Legendary Hearts' songs.

To the John Travolta/Jamie Lee Curtis vehicle *Perfect,* Lou contributed 'Hot Hips' - an endearingly inane three-chord dance song in the style of his Pickwick throwaways of 1964. Before the movie was premièred, Reed turned up on MTV, rock's visual substitute for the crassness of all-hit radio. He'd already made a video clip for 'Don't Talk To Me About Work' from 'Legendary Hearts': now here was 'I Love You Suzanne', kicking off with a quote from The Contours' early Sixties dance classic, 'Do You Love Me', and then powering through a three-chord guitar sequence that was the essence of high school rock. The video showed Lou in performance, leathered and menacing as ever - and then suddenly the street punk was transformed into a disco king, break-dancing his way through a bewildering set of contortions and dance-floor moves. The clip was hilarious, even more so when Reed swore blind that he'd done all the dancing himself; and its constant exposure on MTV introduced Lou to teenage America for the first time since 'Sally Can't Dance' a decade earlier.

Reed needed a hit record. He'd delivered RCA his most consistent album in years, and watched it die a brief, unnoticed death. 'Legendary Hearts' proved equally out of sync with the market. By 1984, Reed's stature as a rock legend did nothing to sell his latest product; instead it signalled that his greatest work was strictly in the past. And to anyone who hadn't registered The Velvet Underground's reputation, Lou Reed was just another name, not even a trademark of sleaze like it had been in the Seventies.

'I Love You Suzanne' had no pretensions towards art, but it was a great pop record, and the novelty value of the video clip helped it into the charts. The move seems to have been quite deliberate: Reed approached his 1984 album, 'New Sensations', with commercial appeal uppermost in his mind. Robert Quine wasn't available for the sessions, so Reed handled the guitar work himself. He fleshed out the sound with keyboards, horns and backing singers - all restrained enough, but still a step back from the sparse, exposed sound of his last two albums.

It was the aural impact that preoccupied Reed's attention during the sessions. With few exceptions, the 'New Sensations' songs cooled down the passions and pains of his recent work; what Lou wanted this time out were "certain sounds that I heard on the radio - a certain kind of bass drum thing, for instance - that were really strong and exciting". And to achieve it, Lou entered into what he described as "a relationship with the engineer that was more involved than I would normally like to have", to the extent that John Jansen ended up the project's co-producer. The sound on the radio was loud, booming, each instrument swathed in echo, and the delicate interplay of the musicians was sacrificed for the sake of volume. 'New Sensations' took twice as long to make as 'Legendary Hearts', and Reed emerged with a record that was a perfect reflection of state-of-the-art studio techniques *circa* 1984.

For once, Sylvia Reed didn't design the album cover; perhaps she should have done, as the finished shot of little-boy-Lou sat with legs splayed in front of a giant monitor screen did nothing to help the project's artistic credibility. Like the cover, the album was a deliberate step out of the darkness. For every song on previous albums about the complexity of human emotions, here was one which reduced ideas to catch-phrases. After repeated instalments of angst and self-analysis, the removal of the confessional Reed was shocking; it felt like a sell-out. If you were hooked on Lou's soap-opera, then 'New Sensations' was his way of changing the channel.

It might not have been a major album, but that didn't make it a bad one; Reed was now too much of a craftsman for that. The best of the 'New Sensations' songs were scenes from the life, little episodes and adventures of the kind that make up the average day. And alongside throwaways like 'My Red Joystick', half innuendo, half disco slickery, there was a subtle jab like 'Turn To Me', which took the conventions of the supportive soul ballad and whirled them on their head: "If your father is freebasing/And your mother turning tricks/That's still no reason you should have a rip/Remember I'm the one who loves you/You can always give me a call".

The title track was Reed's manifesto, a roll-call of New Year resolutions for the cleaned-up rock star that ends up a love song to his motorbike. And like most of the album, it was set to music so gentle that it nearly wasn't there: no Lou Reed album has a softer guitar sound. 'Doin' The Things That We Want To' set Lou up as contemporary and fan of Sam Shepherd and Marty Scorsese, who had their own visions of love in the city to sell. More significantly, the song inspired Shepherd and Bob Dylan to write 'New Danville Girl', one of Dylan's most remarkable songs of the Eighties.

For that alone, 'New Sensations' deserves to survive. Perhaps its nearest equivalent was 'Loaded', the fourth Velvets album which had signalled Lou's abdication from the centre of the maelstrom. But while 'Loaded' was stained with cynicism, 'New Sensations' wrapped its commercial sheen round fragments of life - the macho posing of 'My Friend George', the ambiguous blessing of a night 'High In The City', beset by drug-crazed hoodlums and bums. And while Reed had made the Velvets' 'Ride Into The Sun' a wide-eyed voyage of fantasy, 'Fly Into The Sun' nearly two decades later was a clear-sighted acceptance of the imminent apocalypse, delivered without passion or grief. Equally powerful and unexpected was 'What Becomes A Legend Most'. Over electric violin and delicate guitar, Reed turned the Blackglama advertising slogan - Andy Warhol used the ad in a silkscreen a year later - into a wry update of 'New Age', a tender evocation of a star ageing into a myth. Maybe that's how he saw himself.

Amidst this unexpected lightness of touch, one song tolled a familiar tale. 'Endlessly Jealous' was a sober reckoning of that familiar couple, power and love - the narrator trying to restrain himself from violence, as the throb of jealousy twists his thoughts into anger and guilt. One new sensation, at least, wasn't so novel after all.

ELEVEN

"Just because I write about what I write about doesn't mean I don't care about what's going on around me. The days of me being aloof about certain things are over."
(Lou Reed, *Rolling Stone*, 1986)

LIKE AN EAGER DÉBUTANTE, LOU REED came out into rock society in 1984. After three solid albums, and four years without a breath of scandal to his name, Reed was accepted by his peers. That August, he lined up alongside James Brown, George Clinton, Peter Wolf and Madonna on the artists' panel of the New Music Seminar in New York, to discuss the impact of new technology on rock, and the implications of the $30 ticket ceiling scaled on The Jacksons' American tour.

A fortnight later, Lou showed up at the MTV Awards, steadfastly ignoring Andy Warhol further down his row. He taped a loving, though still acerbic, version of Kurt Weill's 'September Song' for an all-star tribute album to Brecht's composer. That was the first time he'd ever released a song written by someone else; weeks later he repeated the gesture, under the guidance of producer Phil Ramone, when he recorded the unashamed disco groove 'My Love Is Chemical' for *White Nights*, a bizarre ballet thriller starring Mikael Baryshnikov.

All this was grist to the superstar mill; Sting or Jackson Browne might have done the same. So too the ever more frequent appearances on MTV, where he submitted to interviews from the network's banal hosts, filmed station IDs and trailers, and even appeared in an hour-long special in the Rock Influences series. That allowed him to invite some influences of his own, The Chantelles, to perform their girl group classic 'Maybe', backed by Lou and his band.

Leaving behind another video clip, this time for 'My Red Joystick', Reed then went on tour through America, Australasia and Europe to promote a record that was proving to be his biggest-seller since the mid-Seventies. In comparison with Michael Jackson's 'Thriller', 'New Sensations' scarcely sent a blip through the system; but for Lou any chart placing was tantamount to paydirt.

With Robert Quine mercifully restored to the band, which was swollen to a five-piece by the retention of Peter Wood from the album sessions, Reed staked out a workmanlike, predictable passage around the world's concert halls, mixing extracts from his Eighties albums with the expected crop of Velvets classics. Despite the extra ornamentation provided by Wood's keyboards and occasional accordion, though, there was little evidence on this tour of Lou's latest musical love - rap music.

Lou was a natural rap fan - he'd been selling his own variation on the theme since 1966. Any genre that encouraged words to come flowing across the radio was bound to meet with his approval, especially when the required delivery was Reed's patented semi-spoken drawl. "Some of the rap groups coming out of New York are touching on things that interest me," he declared late that year, "and there's some pretty good writing to be found in rap music." Like the punk bands at CBGB's in '75 and '76, rap offered Reed a rekindling of the spirit. In the music of Run DMC and Afrika Bambataa he found the voices of the street - sassy, fast and certain, spewing out puns and metaphors, threats and insights, all for the love of the word and the rhythm.

Not that he forgot the third element of the Lou Reed trilogy: the image. Early in 1985, Reed was offered an advertising contract by the manufacturers of Honda scooters - small fry, against the broad Harleys that Reed favoured between his thighs, but a deal nonetheless. The very idea of Lou Reed, prophet of bisexuality and drug masturbation, being used to market any product on TV and in the magazines would once have been hilarious. By 1985, it was just another career move.

Announcing the deal to the world, Honda's PR division waxed eloquent. They were going, they said, to "take a walk on the wild side, to portray the spirit of adventure and excitement involved in scootering". Mr Neil Leventhal, Honda's Motor Scooter Manager, proclaimed proudly: "Reed is an innovator - one of the pioneers of new music. His music is unique and experimental - much like scooters." And he wrote it with a straight face - the same expression with which Lou cashed the cheque.

In May 1985, television viewers could watch a quick-cut assembly of shots designed to reproduce the feel of an underground film. Over the sound of 'Walk On The Wild Side', here was Lou, posed across his scooter outside the Bottom Line, or overlooking the Hudson River docks, with the slogan: "Don't settle for walking". "Who else could make a scooter hip?" Lou boasted the following year when he signed a deal to advertise American Express cards. And when it came to the morality of advertising, he had few qualms in exploiting a system that was willing to finance his work in return for the use of his image. Besides, who had clean hands? "Look who's recording you - the same companies who manufacture missiles," Lou noted. "You could really start tearing it apart."

The videos on MTV, the Honda and Amex ads - they added up to a complete reversal of Reed's career. He was enjoying his highest media profile for a decade, and none of the coverage was negative. The summer of 1985 also saw the release of a 'new' Velvet Underground album,

'VU', which gathered up ten of the leftover cuts from their sojourn with MGM. Some of the tapes had previously surfaced on bootlegs, but they were presumed officially lost until archivist Bill Levenson had the bright idea of looking in the vaults while he was preparing tapes for reissues of the original Velvets albums.With Lou Reed's tacit approval - there were even rumours that he contributed some secret guitar overdubs - the MGM tapes were remixed and presented to the world in an arty package accompanied by respectful annotation and photographs from the Factory. Polygram serviced radio stations with a promo single of 'I Can't Stand It'; and then there was talk of a Velvets reunion.

The plan was modest enough - the original members would regroup to shoot a video for 'I Can't Stand It' (a record that John Cale hadn't even played on), and then there would be a handful of small but prestigious live shows around the world. Lou Reed, who had first approached Cale with the offer of a collaboration a decade earlier, dismissed the talk with a curt "It'll never happen". But for a while, all four members expressed interest in the project, until echoes of past disagreements - probably between Sterling Morrison and Reed, whose relationship seemed the shakiest of the four - raised their head.

So the reunion came no further than an album of archive recordings - a second, 'Another View', surfaced in 1986 - and the involvement of Reed, Cale, Tucker and Morrison in the filming of a London Weekend Television special on the band's history in the *South Bank Show* series. Cale, Tucker, Morrison and Nico were all filmed in the TV company's studios; Cale and Nico even indulged in some nostalgic performances for the cameras. Reed, meanwhile, kept his distance: he agreed to be filmed only in front of a graffiti-clad New York building, and then kept his feelings hidden behind shades and clichés.

Missing from the revival, which was part celebration, part wake, was the pale figure of Andy Warhol. To his diarist, Pat Hackett, Warhol exposed his pain at the way in which he had been ostracised from the negotiations around the reunion. Hadn't the Velvets been his band? Where would they be today without him? "And I mean, I just don't understand why I have never gotten a penny from that first Velvet Underground record," Warhol whimpered. "That record really sells and I was the producer! Shouldn't I get something? I mean, shouldn't I?" And over the next few days he considered ways he could make something out of his investment in the band - not that he needed the money, but it was only fair, I mean, wasn't it?

More important to Andy was the love of his disciples; and throughout the Eighties he had felt increasingly estranged from Lou Reed. "What I can't figure out is when Lou stopped liking me," he told his diary. "I mean, he even went out and got himself two dachshunds like I had and then after that he started not liking me, but I don't know exactly why or when. Maybe it was when he married this last wife, maybe he decided that he didn't want to see peculiar people." And then, the rat, Lou didn't even want to get back with the Velvets - now that could have brought Andy some money, and they could have asked him to make the video, couldn't they?

Warhol wasn't approached for any of the Velvets projects in 1985. He didn't appear on the *South Bank Show*; he wasn't given the task of assembling a collection of Velvet Underground footage for a commercial video release. That job fell to Ben Edmonds, who'd done similar work on a Doors retrospective. But the Velvets' video history was abandoned for lack of original source material. And with it, for the moment, went the remaining hopes for any reunion of the band.

None of the Velvets was represented at the Live Aid concerts in July 1985 (the only Reed reference was Bono's ad-libbing to 'Walk On The Walk Side' during the last few bars of 'Bad', U2's set closer); but rock's shift from non-conformism to charity work sparked a similar turn in Lou Reed's career. Any cynicism about the motives behind the Live Aid venture - centred around the worldwide exposure that acts received for their latest releases in return for giving up a Saturday afternoon to help the starving - was overcome by the scale of the public response to the disaster. For a generation of musicians who had been left stranded by the collapse of the radicalism of the Sixties, Live Aid suggested a way in which they could give their careers some kind of moral justification. California had housed campaigns to save the whale, or halt nuclear power, since the early Seventies; but Live Aid, and the human rights crusades which followed, cut across factional boundaries.

Lou Reed had maintained a critical distance from kneejerk rock politicking ever since the Central Park rallies of 1967. His public backing for Jimmy Carter in 1976 was never translated into action; since then, he'd evidenced more interest in sexual and personal politics than in the machinations of party cliques and national egos. And personal politics could, as Lou had pointed out, last you a lifetime.

Of all things, Reed was radicalised by owning a second home in the New Jersey countryside. As he told David Fricke in *Rolling Stone*, he had a cynical city-dweller's view on the country: "I'd show up out there and go, 'What the fuck is going on? It's raining here. What is this, another weekend with rain?' Finally, they sat me down to tell me the facts of life, such as there are farmers out there and they're getting killed by the drought. I became aware of what weather means, besides New Yorkers going away for the weekend."

At Live Aid, Bob Dylan compounded the felony of a monumentally poor performance by asking that the world devote some time to the plight of the American farmers, as well as the starving millions of Africa. His comments seemed perversely ill-timed: Africa was dying, America merely had problems meeting its mortgage payments. But from his remarks grew the institution of Farm Aid, an annual concert held to raise funds for the families of those American working men whose loans had been foreclosed by banks who didn't recognise the concept of compassion. Willie Nelson and Neil Young headed the relief effort; and Lou Reed was one of those who answered the call in the autumn of 1985, joining a remarkable array of American voices spanning the breadth of post-1955 musics.

A few weeks later, Reed lent his support, and his voice - just one line on the record - to the formation of Artists United Against Apartheid, a multi-racial effort headed by 'Little' Steven Van Zandt which began with a record ('Ain't Gonna Play Sun City') and ended with a video, a book, and eventually a concerted campaign to force the release of the South African nationalist leader, Nelson Mandela. "I couldn't not be vocal about apartheid," Lou Reed explained, especially as his close friend, the salsa performer and noted political songwriter Ruben Blades, was active in the movement.

Ruben Blades' inspiration, and the comradeship of other rock stars working towards the same aims: together they refocused Reed's career. Lou wasn't willing to sacrifice his art to the cause; his writing lacked the moral certainty of the sloganeer. So there would be no woolly collection of political songs, no soundtracks for rallies or picket lines. But it was equally impossible for Reed to write without considering the wider context of his work - the fact that he lived in a country which controlled the system whereby Africa was starved of its natural resources, which gave covert support to the racist régime in South Africa, which financed the building of terrorist forces against governments that failed to meet American approval. Merely by existing and working within that society, Reed was lending a silent vote to the forces of repression and exploitation. When so many of his peers were preparing to march, it would have been callous not to join them.

For Lou, however, writing had always come from experience. So the songs on 'Mistrial', his next solo album issued in the summer of 1986, contained no catch-all recipes for universal enlightenment. The outside world shadowed several of the tracks, but only insofar as it affected Lou himself. His prime exposure to the currents of the time came through television - the medium which had introduced him to a new audience, and brought him the pictures of the starving and oppressed. Yet television represented more than a tool for education or record promotion. It had become the constant companion to the youth of America, providing their values, fuelling their fantasies, twisting their perspectives into one long wreckage of fist fights and horror movies. And Lou Reed - creator of real life horrors from 'Heroin' to 'The Bells' - didn't like what he saw.

'Video Violence' stated the case quite plainly: from dawn to dusk, the hapless TV viewer was greeted with slashers and rapists, so it was no wonder that "the currents rage so deep inside us". And down the street there are snuff movies, another *Nightmare On Elm Street*, or a topless dancer strutting for dollar bills while Madonna blares off the jukebox. For most of the song, Lou sounded like a representative of one of those parents' groups who were trying to sanitise rock and roll, because the kids don't have the moral strength to choose for themselves. Then he cut the picture to some "good working stiff", paying lip service to a TV evangelist while beating his woman black and blue, and placed the moral lesson in his mouth. Either way, it was patronising as hell. The indifference and élitism behind that "good working stiff" suggested that Reed's politics had a way to go to reach democracy.

Certainly his moralism had never been so overt. On 'The Original Wrapper', he set up the same scenario again - father and baby assaulted by the TV, and meanwhile "the murderer lives while the victims die/I'd much rather see it an eye for an eye/a heart for a heart/a brain for a brain". This was Old Testament justice, not the liberal Christianity of the rock radicals. And it spelled out all the moral lessons that had been implicit in 'Berlin', say, where Caroline gets what she deserves, the dirty rotten slut; or 'Sally Can't Dance', with the heroine reaping the reward for her loose lifestyle; or the *Attitudes* poems, one slice of bad faith meriting another. We're back again to the American naturalists, convinced that morality and fate were bound up in one explosive parcel, that sin and poverty were marked out before each man was born, his task simply to fulfil the savage demands of his destiny.

An eye for an eye, a tooth for a tooth: that was the sentence Reed had demanded for Valerie Solanas after the Warhol shooting. But at home, the game had to be played by different rules. Album after album through the Eighties, he confessed in public to his sins - and each time he begged for a second chance, for the light of rehabilitation. 'Don't Hurt A Woman' replayed the familiar story: "I was angry/I said things I shouldn't say/But please don't turn your back". Set to music that was tender and endlessly sad, Reed offered himself up for forgiveness. This time, he said like a typical man, things would be different.

Mostly, though, 'Mistrial' steered clear of grand statements. On 'New Sensations', he had subjugated his lyrics to the quest for the sound. 'Mistrial' repeated the mistake, with Lou and co-producer/bassist Fernando Saunders conjuring up a synthesised brew that was faithful to the day it was made, and dated just as quickly. Most of the tracks used computerised percussion instead of drums; sometimes the bass was played on a synthesiser; there was scarcely a hint of the two guitars/bass/drums which Reed had used as a holy trinity in the past. In keeping with his new public image, the album was commercial too, up to a point, and most of the songs would have sounded at home on MTV.

But all too often, the songs said nothing - throwaways like 'No Money Down', 'I Remember You' and 'Spit It Out', which were all sauce and no meat. 'No Money Down' looked great on MTV: the video clip ended with Lou reaching up to tear his own face to shreds, like one of the horror movies he fingered on 'Video Violence'. But like the weakest songs on his last album, they reeked of craftsmanship for its own sake.

Elsewhere there were moments of humour - 'The Original Wrapper', for instance, which not only lived up to the pun in its title (what was Reed doing on 'Sweet Jane' or 'Walk On The Wild Side' but inventing rap music?) but also took on the black kids at their own game, with a lyric stuffed full of political jibes, wordplay, and sexual innuendo. "Check that sausage before you put it in the waffle", Reed snapped as a one-man anti-AIDS campaign.

Then there was 'Mama's Got A Lover', a wonderfully vicious song with a savage twist in the last line: "She's starting a new chapter/I wish she was on the last page". You were dying for Lou to confirm that it was all true, but as usual he maintained a discreet silence.

For those who loved 'The Blue Mask' and 'Legendary Hearts', there was just 'Tell It To Your Heart' - superbly crafted, as ever, in its evocation of the transience of love, and the need to keep communication open if a relationship is to survive.

Such insight was the exception on 'Mistrial', an album which was nothing more than another instalment in a career. Lou Reed had become an institution - he produced his records for 'Sister Ray Enterprises Inc.' and his songs were published by 'Metal Machine Music Inc.' - and rock institutions issued regular albums as a matter of course.

After 'New Sensations' and 'Mistrial', Lou Reed albums were less an event than a familiar presence from the past, dropping by to let you know he was still alive.

RCA certainly didn't treat Reed any differently from the rest of their roster. They prepared a horribly contrived promo tape called 'He's Got A Rock And Roll Heart', which centred round an anodyne MTV interview; then there was the usual variety of remixes, special editions and the like, the common currency of the multinational media corporation. And Reed also turned up on the David Letterman Show to use TV to promote 'Video Violence'.

The song was also a staple in his live shows that summer, as part of the Amnesty International benefit tour which played stadium concerts across America and Europe. Reed lined up alongside Sting, U2, Jackson Browne, Bryan Adams, Peter Gabriel, Joan Baez and the Neville Brothers - almost the entire membership of rock's liberal wing, preaching the gospel of tolerance and freedom in the name of the organisation which campaigns for political prisoners, regardless of their creed, colour or opinions. Aside from 'Walk On The Wild Side', Reed treated audiences to a short set of material from his last two albums, before joining in the ensemble performances of songs like 'Biko' or 'I Shall Be Released'. Along the way he composed a song for the cause called 'Voices Of Freedom' - again sparked by his friendship with Ruben Blades - which he débuted at the European shows, and also performed at a smaller Amnesty benefit in London, *The Secret Policeman's Third Ball*.

Funniest of Reed's extra-curricular activities during 1986 was his performance of the Sam and Dave hit 'Soul Man' for the film of the same name. Sam Moore reprised his lead role from the original record; Lou added his Brooklyn monotone to the choruses. The effect was hilarious, and it gave Lou his first hit record in Britain since 1973. There was a video to accompany the record, as there usually was these days; later in the year Lou asked another ex-Warhol protégée, Baby Jane Holzer, to appear in one of his videos for 'Mistrial'. Andy Warhol found out, two days after his former lover had died from AIDS: in his final reference to Lou in his diaries, he noted: "I hate Lou Reed more and more, I really do, because he's not giving us any video work." The world was gradually leaving Andy behind.

Billy Name, official photographer and designer for the Factory in the Sixties, was now a deputy sheriff in Poughkeepsie, and he invited the

Warhol cronies - Malanga, Ingrid Superstar - up for a reunion. Warhol couldn't face it. Meanwhile, Victor Bockris, who'd already collaborated with Malanga on *Uptight*, a visually stunning account of The Velvet Underground, was prowling through Warhol's past, interviewing colleagues, friends and acolytes for a definitive Warhol biography. Not for the first time, Warhol wondered whether he really had died back in 1968. He was suffering more pain from his wounds; his stomach and groin ached consistently. Eventually he could not escape from hospital. His gallbladder was swollen, threatening gangrene; yet the operation to remove it passed without complications, and Warhol ought to have recovered. Instead, in circumstances that raised questions about the standard of care at New York Hospital, Warhol died on the morning of February 22, 1987. Doctors attempted to resuscitate him, but were hampered by the onset of rigor mortis; Andy had lain dead for an hour or more without hospital staff noticing.

When the news was announced, many assumed it was the ultimate Warhol hoax. At the funeral, some waited for Andy to stroll in and announce another pop-art con trick. Instead, he was buried alongside his mother in Pittsburgh. Warhol's death cast a shadow over the Factory clique; even as they had outgrown him, they remained his pupils, and his disappearance - the thought that Andy was no longer there to reassure them that they were wonderful, that he loved their work - forced them to re-examine their relationship with him. For Lou Reed, the vague undertone of guilt was doubled when Warhol's diaries were published after his death. There on the page was Andy's hurt - Lou had ignored him at the MTV Awards, failed to invite him to the wedding, used someone else to make his videos. Like an errant son, Reed had, in Andy's eyes, let him down. Now the son had to live with his memories, his mixed emotions, and the exposure of his treason.

Guilt and sin were, once again, on the surface in late 1986 and early 1987. Reed was collaborating with Ruben Blades on the latter's first English-language album, 'Nothing But The Truth'. "Lou and I finished a draft for a song about a son coming back to a painful reunion with his parents," Blades explained. "We were both emotionally exhausted... I almost had an anxiety attack that night." While Blade distractedly leafed through a book in Reed's Jersey home, Lou played a melody - "hauntingly beautiful, but also very angry, like an electric Irish lullaby" - on his guitar in the music room above. Blades began to write some lyrics to fill the void, and from this indirect partnership came 'The Calm Before The Storm', an apocalyptic, ominous ballad to which Reed added the title line.

Elsewhere, Lou acted as editor to Blades' work, rewriting the painfully honest love song, 'Hopes On Hold', and adding a fresh perspective to the brilliant 'Letters To The Vatican', a sly and sad vignette of homelessness and false illusions. He also lent his band to the recording sessions, playing on and producing versions of all three songs, though Blades chose to re-record 'Hopes On Hold' in a milder arrangement for the album.

Otherwise Reed's only recording activity in 1987 was episodic. He came up with another movie song - 'Something Happened', this time, for the film *Permanent Record*, a lengthy guitar freak-out with minimalist lyrics. And he was enticed into performing with stand-up bassist Rob Wasserman - a remarkable technician whose fluent, jazz-based style sparked a response from Lou. The pair performed an ad hoc interpretation of the classic Sinatra saloon song, 'One For My Baby', which wound up on Wasserman's album 'Duets'. The collaboration stuck; Wasserman, like guitarist Mike Rathke with whom Lou had worked on the Blades project, was put on retainer for Lou's next record.

After completing four albums for RCA, Reed decided not to re-sign with the label. He'd given then an ultra-commercial album, 'New Sensations', and they'd failed to make it go gold. 'Mistrial' was not only a last shot at superstardom; it also doubled as a contract fulfilment. When it flopped, Reed began negotiating elsewhere.

He wound up at Sire, which was in retrospect the obvious choice. Seymour Stein's indie label had handled New York New Wavers like The Ramones, Richard Hell and Talking Heads; Reed knew that Stein would have no misconceptions about the nature of the artist he was taking on. And now Sire was affiliated to the giant WEA group, guaranteeing all the advantages of distribution and marketing that only a major label could bring. True, Sire already had Madonna, and there was no way Reed would out-sell her. But his name still brought prestige to any label, and the Sire deal ensured that his work would not be ignored. It took more than a year to finalise the contract, and when it was signed, Reed had to agree to promote his records more conscientiously than he had done in the past. In return, he was promised the full support of his label, and artistic independence.

All Reed had to do was focus his work. The purgative self-analysis of 'The Blue Mask' and 'Legendary Hearts' had been succeeded by the professional discipline of 'New Sensations' and 'Mistrial'. Growing up in public was no longer an issue: Reed had already done it. His new work had to encompass his extended vision of the world: no longer a backdrop for his own psycho-dramas, it had become a theatre of injustices and hardships, in which Reed - as a white male in the most powerful nation on earth - had a villain's role, whether he liked it or not. He needed a subject outside his own life, but which still grabbed his heart. He found it outside his front door, on the streets of New York.

TWELVE

"I can't do anything outside of New York. It's death."
(Lou Reed, 1974)

IN 1985, LOU REED WAS ONE OF A series of prominent New Yorkers asked to contribute to a *New York* magazine series entitled "What I Like About New York". His answer? "Freedom, endless opportunities in everything - films, Chinese culture, people, places, things - a city of wonderful, impossible mixtures and energies. The only city in the world deserving the name. What I don't like - crime, traffic, a criminal subway system, a city government that is oblivious to the plight and feelings of the poor, the minorities, the homeless... Antiquated criminal-justice system; antiquated civil-service & union rules, regulations and membership; second-rate public-school system."

New York - "The only city in the world deserving the name", if 'city' is a synonym for a cauldron of racial tensions and firecracker ethnic violence, a haven of artistic experimentation and liberation, a Manichaean juxtaposition of the extremes of wealth and poverty. Born and educated in the city, and then adopted by Greenwich Village when no other community in the world would have sustained him and his musical cohorts, Lou Reed had been playing out a passionate love affair with New York for more than forty years. Yet distance, in the shape of his Jersey farmhouse, had lent an air of objectivity to his infatuation. Breathing the relatively fresh air of New Jersey, riding his bikes along uncluttered side roads between fields and rivers, Reed saw New York for what it is - the embodiment of the modern technological world, in all its shiny lustre and rotting decay.

Through the Seventies and, more especially, the Eighties, the greatest city on earth stumbled from one financial crisis to the next, while brokers gambled and won millions by day and bag ladies and crack addicts stalked the streets by night. Wander haplessly out of your zone at any hour, and you were likely to be snatched as prey by youths bred in despair. Enter the subway, a nightmarish, Dantesque journey into the earth's bowels, and you waited for the clamorous arrival of a train streaked with war-paint; and you watched and wondered which of your fellow passengers was the maniac who might push you under the rails.

Through the busiest and most prosperous city streets, designer-clad office workers stepped unseeing over the bodies of down-and-outs, some dead, some merely waiting for death. On the sidewalks twitched young men wired on drugs, waiting for the provocative glance that might trigger their inbred need to kill. And above the maze of pedestrians and cabs rose the skyscrapers, eternal icons of a city built on dreams, and now fuelled by a nightmare.

That was Lou Reed's deteriorating New York at its darkest - filthy, diseased and reeling uncontrollably towards Armageddon. There was a second New York - home of CBGBs and the Factory, the apartments of the Upper East Side and the tolerance of Christopher Street, galleries and lofts, recording studios and the Bottom Line. And that was the city that had kept Lou Reed sane. But increasingly you could not reach one version of New York without daring the streets of the other.

There was a political dimension to the battle for the heart of the city - one which Reed might never have noticed a decade earlier. Federal government policies starved the city of cash; Reagan's Republicans cut back State welfare programmes and benefits, and left the penniless city to staunch the blood.

Some of Reed's fellow rock stars made desperate moves to help. Charity is never the answer to poverty; it simply dresses the wounds. But it was all that rock singers had to offer, and the gesture and its attendant publicity was worth more than the cash. In December 1987, Paul Simon staged a benefit show at Madison Square Garden for the New York Children's Health Project, with funds earmarked for a medical van which could tour the city helping homeless children. One of rock's most stellar concert bills was assembled for the occasion, and Lou Reed appeared after an achingly passionate set by Ruben Blades, to perform 'Walk On The Wild Side' backed by a chorale which included Debbie Harry and Grace Jones. An hour or so later, he was back onstage, as part of an all-star vocal group - Billy Joel, Ruben Blades, Bruce Springsteen, Paul Simon - behind Dion for a rowdy but enthusiastic 'Teenager In Love'. The occasion bore fruit later on, when Dion invited Lou to appear on his comeback album, 'Yo Frankie'. The same month, Lou took the stand at the New York Society for Ethical Culture, speaking out on behalf of Amnesty's worldwide campaign of writing letters to political prisoners. The cause was different, but the commitment was the same. Reed wasn't buying any liberal ticket wholesale; he'd have murderers executed in Central Park, and broadcast it live on TV - and what about the crackpots Castro sent over from Cuba, how come we didn't send some of ours back in return?

Since JFK, he'd never trusted politicians - there was Jesse Jackson, preaching the liberation of the poor, alongside Louis Farrakhan, and what would he do with the Jews? What was that line about hymie town?

The suspicion of Jackson evolved into 'Good Evening Mr Waldheim'; the desire for retribution against criminals into 'Hold On'. Paul Simon's benefit concert for the homeless spawned 'Dirty Blvd'; then there were the Vietnam veterans slumped behind cardboard signs begging quarters in the rain; the annual Halloween Parade through the Village, shadowed by the fear of AIDS ("How can anybody gay keep their sanity?", Reed asked in 1978); the used syringes washing up on the Jersey shore; the dealers catching children in street-corner crossfire; the junkies hustling for their next fix.

New York - beacon of a new civilisation built on the dream of spiritual renewal in the innocence of the New World, now mangled into a concrete zoo fed on greed and despair - was the subject of his songs, to be approached with rage, with disillusionment, with the cynical, cocksure humour that runs through the city like a nerve. The result was an album of insight and compassion, grim realism and spiritual questioning, bitter portraits and savagely witty asides: 'New York', the finest work of Lou Reed's career.

There's not an album like it in rock - nothing where the music and the lyrics bite so hard, where the poetry has been reworked again and again without losing the spontaneity of the streets, where every line resounds with meaning, with the sound of a lone voice that was both Everyman and a slightly crabby songwriter from Brooklyn. "What New York is about, over and above what I'm singing about," Reed explained to Sean O'Hagan in 1989, "is the use of language"; and he had never been so precise and so free, his images and metaphors tumbling free-form off the tongue with the rhythm of natural speech, hardened and sculpted into the resonance of great poetry. Reed set it all to the simplest song structures - almost the whole album played around those three basic rock'n'roll chords which had scored his career - and tightened the music like a screw, stripping away unnecessary decoration. Every note, every lyrical aside, counted; for the first time in his life, Reed had achieved the perfect compression of language and music into a seamless whole.

Aware of the need to make a grand statement - the kind he'd evaded when he signed with Arista in 1976 - Reed fashioned his song cycle into a musical novel. That was a conceit, to be sure, but a justified one: this was one concept album where the concept didn't force itself upon the songs, but evolved naturally out of them.

The music was the creation of Reed and guitarist Mike Rathke, who as a friend of Sylvia's sister had jammed occasionally with Lou without anyone treating it as an audition. On bass, Reed called in Rob Wasserman, who handled a fretless electric model that was bare and bony like a ship's mast after a storm. And on drums, doubling as Reed's co-producer, was Fred Maher - veteran of 'Legendary Hearts' and 'New Sensations'. That was the band - no keyboards, choirs or horns, no outside producer searching for an obvious hit single. For a year or more, Reed evolved the songs - spending nights in front of his word processor, editing and compressing his lyrics till they could get no closer to the image that had inspired them. "I really hate rewriting," he noted when the album was released, and he might have added that his last couple of records proved the point. On 'New York', the rewriting was as vital as the original concept: it turned an interesting record into a great one.

Like Delmore Schwartz, Reed searched for "Precision - To visualise the Word; to verbalise the Thing/To Seek the Generality and Yet to Find/The Just Example which convinces all/To take an Attitude, To Criticize/To argue pro and con". In the past, the first line of an album had often set the tone - the aggressive self-mockery of 'Street Hassle' for instance ("Hey if it ain't the Rock and Roll Animal himself"), or the pastoral, supernatural aura of 'The Blue Mask' ("The image of the poet's in the trees"). With 'New York', Reed began with a crisp flurry of imagery - "Caught between the twisted stars the plotted lines the faulty map that brought Columbus to New York" - which laid the scene for the rest of his album. With the "plotted lines" of his "faulty map", Columbus had sown the seeds for a city caught on a distorted axis, watched by "twisted stars"; and here, while "the earth squeals and shudders to a halt", comes Romeo Rodriguez, stunted hero of 'New York's first song, 'Romeo Had Juliette'.

New York's star-cross'd Latin lovers search for romance while outside "the crack dealers were dreaming of an Uzi someone had just scored", and the brains of one of the city's finest mingle with the dirt and refuse on the side of the street. And to keep the Italian connection, "Manhattan's sinking like a rock... they said it was like ancient Rome". The Shakespearian tragedy is set in motion; none can stay its hand.

Down in the Village, it's time for the 'Halloween Parade' - and past Reed's apartment on Christopher Street cruise the clones and fairies, the proud inheritors of New York's liberal-minded tradition, the successors to the "fags on speed" of the Warhol Sixties. This year, though, their costumes fail to hide the oppressive fear of AIDS - the media-styled 'gay plague' used by moralists as evidence of divine retribution. "You'll never see those faces again," Reed mutters, before admitting: "The past keeps knock knock knocking on my door/And I don't want to hear it anymore".

And unstated, Reed conjures up the ghosts of the recent past - Warhol, Nico, Ondine, each loss diminishing those who remain.

Meanwhile the boy Pedro sits in some doss-house euphemistically named a hotel, fated to repeat the sins of his father - a prize theme in Reed's work, given dignity in 'Dirty Blvd' by the clear-sighted social vision of the writing. The boulevard represents freedom - the chance to watch the movie stars at Lincoln Center, or "the TV whores calling the cops out for a suck". And in the most vitriolic language he's ever used on record, Reed defaces the symbol of the American spirit: "Give me your tired, your poor, I'll piss on 'em/That's what the Statue of Bigotry says".

'Endless Cycle' repeats the legacy of brutality and poverty - the inescapable inheritance of misery and despair. The song takes us back to the American tragedies of Theodore Dreiser or Upton Sinclair - any scenario where men are forced to pit themselves against a destiny that has been pre-determined since birth, in a pointless struggle that they cannot hope to win. After this, the cure-all warning of 'There Is No Time' has little effect: while Fred Maher's drums pound and the guitars rage, Reed's insistence that "This is a time for action because the future's within reach" rings curiously hollow.

'The Last Great American Whale' widens the horizons into the realms of parable. "Jeez, what a great title," Reed commented when he recalled the origins of the song; elsewhere he'd quipped, "Give me a good title and I'm home free". "I wrote the first version and it was horrible," he continued, "but I'm not interested in whether it's good or bad, I just want the thing written out. Then I will go someplace with it." Where Reed went was into a magical tale of natural power and the sullen destructiveness of man, forever threatened by what he cannot control. The whale - "they say he didn't have an enemy" - is his Edenic symbol of goodness; it perishes in a Christ-like act of salvation, wasted by "some local yokel member of the NRA (who) kept a bazooka in his living-room". And Reed shifts from the mythic to the all-too-real - America's shores polluted by chemicals and poisoned rats, by today's natives who'll "shit in a river/dump battery acid in a stream". Having made the point, he moves on, with a quip borrowed from John Mellencamp: "Stick a fork in their ass and turn them over, they're done".

After that, the 'Beginning Of A Great Adventure' has to be viewed with more than a little irony. Over a walking jazz bass line concocted by Mike Rathke, Reed spiels out his thoughts about the responsibilities or otherwise of parenthood, reciting a hilarious set of possible names for the child, and fantasising how he could build "a little liberal army in the woods" to counter the "redneck lunatics... with their tribe of mutant inbred piglets with cloven hooves". It may be the beginning of a great adventure, but it's one encircled by the lessons of 'Dirty Blvd' and 'Endless Cycle'.

To sire a child, or rebuild a continent, you need a Busload Of Faith to get by; as Lou says, "You can depend on the worst always happening", if nothing else. And in a brilliant couplet that replays the grim heritage of Reed's race, Lou slapped at the liberal conscience: "You can't depend on the goodly hearted/The goodly hearted made lampshades and soap".

Turn on the morning news, and it's a catalogue of tragedy twinned with farce; no wonder Lou says he's 'Sick Of You' to a lobotomised President, or his arms-deal lackeys, to nuclear meltdowns and "hypos in the cabbage". You can laugh that off, more or less, until the violence creeps under your own front door; then all you can do is 'Hold On', while the drug dealers wave their Uzis at cop cars and there are "blacks with knives and whites with guns fighting in Howard Beach".

And Jesse Jackson is standing for president as the disciple of Martin Luther King, an apostle of peace and freedom up on a platform alongside Louis Farrakhan. In 'Good Evening Mr Waldheim', Reed's politics jump from liberalism to a vague form of Zionism - "Does that include the PLO?" - fingering the Austrian leader who can no longer recall his Nazi past, and the Pontiff who prefers the pressgang legitimacy of South American generals to the Christian Marxism of tortured priests. Reed outraged Jackson's backers, and those who urged freedom for the Palestinians herded into squalid homelands; but if you didn't buy Lou's ticket, then "there's no ground common enough for me and you".

Common ground - that was a concept that troubled Reed, whether it was Jackson building bamboo bridges across the racial divide, crack dealers igniting gang warfare on the streets of Lou's hometown, or the ragged legacy of Vietnam. "I was drafted and I got out of it, as crazy," Lou recalled. "But that's not something to be proud of. I managed to get out of it, as almost everybody I knew did. But I think about it. There's a moral dilemma that goes along with that." And it spawned 'Xmas In February', a Vietnam Vets movie in three episodic scenes. In brutal, telling images - the chemical defoliant Agent Orange "spread against the sky like marmalade", the soldier's "fingers mixed with someone's crop" in the South East Asian rice fields - Reed introduces his veteran, and then takes him home, to fight for work against those who evaded the draft and didn't lose their prime, or their limbs, fighting "the war that wasn't won". Abandoned to poverty and neglect, the Vietnam vet has no boundaries between peace and war: "He's the guy on the street with the sign that reads, 'Please help send this Vet home', but he is home, and there's no Xmas in February".

The policeman of the world, divine agent of democracy and justice, America is a 'Strawman', "going straight to the devil"; and Reed's song, set to a lumbering progress of metallic guitars, lays out the charge sheet. On one side is the 'Home Of The Brave', ready to finance "another million dollar movie"; on the other, "you who have so little", the beneficiaries of Live Aid and a score of charity appeals, each a withered finger in the gaping hole of the fragile dam that keeps the peoples of Ethiopia and the Sudan from starvation and disease.

Faced with the endless parade of emaciated babies, tortured prisoners, the poor, the dying, the homeless, Reed can only wave humanity aside, and contemplate the divine in all its uncertain glory. In 'Strawman' he waits ironically for "a minor miracle", like "a flaming sword or maybe a gold ark floating up the Hudson", proof that we really are God's chosen people, that there is someone or something up there that gives a shit after all.

Someone is up there, on the Cross - "lying banged and battered, skewered and bleeding", in Scorsese's harrowing interpretation of *The Last Temptation Of Christ*. 'Dime Store Mystery' is the ironic title of Reed's final song on New York, a stunning evocation of belief and unbelief and uncertainty, the division between soul and body, the all-too-real flesh that bears the nails on the Cross, or - like Andy Warhol (honey), to whom the song is dedicated - lies decaying in a coffin in St. Patrick's Cathedral, no-one's idea of a Saint or a Messiah, but a Catholic nonetheless, a believer in the divine, now facing the denouement of "the Mysteries of Life... shrieking, screaming, whispering", while outside the cathedral beggars wait for Veterans Day and the city lies, caught between the twisted stars, the plotted lines, the faulty map that brought Columbus to New York. Which is where we began.

New York is all of this and more. "This is no time for circumlocution/This is no time for learned speech", Reed announces early in the album, and his poetry is laden with images, each as lean and sharp as a stiletto knife. And the music is equally precise, whether it's Reed launching 'There Is No Time' with a growl of feedback, or Maureen Tucker pounding the erratic heartbeat of the album's two mighty metaphors, 'Last Great American Whale' and 'Dime Store Mystery'.

Reed had touched these themes before - what else had he been attempting since 1965 but a ballad of the city streets? - but never with such accuracy, or such effect. He'd toyed with social comment, but never channelled it into art. He'd laid out the mechanics of the needle and the spoon, but never pulled the camera back to pinpoint the pressures that led men to drugs, to addiction and to despair. And while the music offered nothing new - "You can't beat two guitars, bass, drum," as Reed noted on the album jacket - never had it been so closely aligned to the rhythm of the words, such an organic part of songwriting. Reed knew he had produced his best work, and for once the critics agreed with him. And as if to prove that his knife had cut to the bone, Reed's lyrics were seized by the censors - not in America, where it was thought poor taste to criticise Jesse Jackson, though it wasn't yet illegal; but in Italy, where not just the words, but the philosophical concepts behind them, were deemed blasphemous. The album appeared there without a lyric sheet; elsewhere, Reed's stunning assemblage of words testified to the richness of a record without parallel in rock history.

The fragments of The Velvet Underground still carried a mythic force in the late 1980s, even if they were revered more for their past than their potential. Doug Yule had been unable to capitalise on the kudos of playing in Reed's band back in 1975; Sterling Morrison had long since opted for a career as an academic. Maureen Tucker sank into family life after the demise of the Velvets: she was rediscovered by devotees of the band in 1980, and proceeded to revive her musical career with records that survived more on goodwill than on any artistic merit.

John Cale and Lou Reed, joint linchpins of the band's sound, were struggling to hold their place in rock's pantheon. Reed's status as a major artist was recaptured by the 'New York' album; but Cale had long since resigned himself to life on the margin, and a cult following for his experiments with minimalist styles of songwriting and composition.

Then there was Nico - at best a semi-detached member of the Velvets, yet indissolubly linked with the band since their first album. Domiciled in Manchester for most of the Eighties and intermittently addicted to heroin, she occupied a strange role as the patron saint of the underground. Successive generations of rock mavericks, from Jim Morrison and Iggy Pop to The Buzzcocks, Sex Pistols and beyond, consulted her like a seer; and in her cool, enigmatic way, Nico bestowed her grace upon them all. With her relentlessly barren musical landscape, that icy voice backed by the eerie drone of her harmonium, she hovered like a ghost over rock's dilettante left-field. Each new set of admirers showed her off to their audiences; without fail, her gloomy music was greeted with catcalls or, from ruder gatherings, bottles. Nico responded, as ever, with a mixture of acerbic language and utter calm.

There were constant rumours of penury and addiction; Nico never ballooned and decayed like that other Sixties pop queen of hedonism, Anita Pallenberg, but neither did she imitate Anita's determined return to health. In July 1988, Nico was on an ill-judged fitness kick: after cycling in Ibiza, over-dressed in oppressive heat, her body was found by the side of the road. She had suffered a cerebral haemorrhage, perhaps after she had struck her head in a fall. Her death, like Warhol's the year before, wrapped another layer of embalming cloth around the restless corpse of the Factory years.

No-one was as oppressed by the legend of the Factory as its former inhabitants, few of whom had ever managed to escape the association. So it was only fitting that the death of Warhol, a man who seemed to vanish like a Cheshire cat after his shooting in 1968, should leave such an enormous void in their lives. John Cale, for one, began work on a lasting tribute - an instrumental work, prompted by a suggestion from the artist Julian Schnabel early in 1988. For a couple of months, Cale laboured at the project; but he needed reassurance that his music was equal to the task. With Warhol dead, there was only one man who shared Cale's artistic debt, and who understood his music well enough to be able to comment. And so it was that in May 1988, John Cale contacted Lou Reed, and asked him to listen to the work in progress.

After Cale and Reed had swapped recent work, it was only natural that they should make music together. "It began as just the two of us throwing ideas around," Cale explained, "but gradually it turned into songwriting." The subject of the songs was obvious from the start: Andy Warhol.

The second half of 1988 thus became the most creative period of Lou Reed's life. He finished up the songs for the 'New York' album, and then recorded them with Fred Maher, Michael Rathke and Rob Wasserman; and at the same time he and Cale wrote and arranged fourteen 'Songs For Drella'. "John and I just rented out a small rehearsal studio for three weeks and locked ourselves in," Reed told Bill Flanagan of *Musician*. "I was really excited by the amount of power just two people could do without needing drums," Cale added, "because what we have there is such a strong core idea that the simpler the better."

In January 1989, the month 'New York' was sent out to reviewers, Reed and Cale staged two performances of their Warhol suite at St. Ann's Church in Brooklyn, under the auspices of the Brooklyn Academy of Music. 'Drella' was at this stage still being described as a "work in progress": there were plans for the suite to be orchestrated that summer, more songs to be written, and the completed work to be unveiled at the Brooklyn Academy's 1989 Next Wave Festival in November.

"'Songs For Drella' is a brief musical look at the life of Andy Warhol," ran the programme notes for the initial performances, "and is entirely fictitious". What the audiences at St. Ann's Church saw was Reed playing electric guitar, Cale perched behind a variety of electronic keyboards, and occasionally venturing out to scythe at his trusty electric viola; a handful of slides of Warhol's work and habitat, projected behind them; and towering over the proceedings, a solitary portrait of the artist, a reminder of the spark which had fused the partnership between two of rock's most idiosyncratic talents.

What they heard were fourteen songs - mostly written by Reed, as Cale acknowledged ambiguously in the notes for the 'Drella' album: "Although I think he did most of the work, he has allowed me to keep a position of dignity in the process". Clearly not all of the bitterness of the Velvets' years had been dissolved. "We're bringing a lot of baggage to the project," Cale confirmed before the initial concerts, and besides the strains of his relationship with Reed, there was also the uneasy mix of love and regret with which both musicians viewed their mentor.

Alongside the "look at the life of Andy Warhol" which the 'Drella' programme promised, the suite had a second subject: the exorcism of Lou Reed's guilt. Reed had taken the accusatory entries in *Andy's Diaries* to heart. 'Songs For Drella' offered two viewpoints: the first was Warhol's, with Reed and Cale sympathetically presenting Andy's defence against the charges of triviality and laziness which had been levelled against him since his death; and the second was unmistakably Lou Reed's.

"We never quite clarified what our attitude was toward Andy speaking all the time," Cale admitted to Bill Flanagan. In the event, 'Songs For Drella' - its title a reference to the coy nickname given Andy in the Factory - began with Cale's piano banging out a faintly ludicrous music hall tempo, and Reed acting out Warhol's awkward childhood in a 'Small Town'. As ever in Lou's work, an upbringing was something to escape from; as his 'Andy' put it, "There's no Michelangelo coming from Pittsburgh", and the near-albino Warhol needed the safety of New York as a haven for his unsettling appearance and inclinations. 'Open House' drops us in the city, with Andy drawing shoes for a living, the consummate commercial artist. The song, underpinned by Cale's ominous keyboards, establishes Warhol's inability to deal with human contact: "You scared yourself with music," Reed has him say, "I scared myself with paint". And terror remains an intrinsic part of Warhol's relations with the world thereafter.

With 'Style It Takes', Reed and Cale offer us Warhol the artist - presenting a pitch to backers or dealers, perhaps, hawking portraits, films, a range of ready-made superstars, anything in return for cash. "I've got a Brillo box and I call it art", Andy quips; and like the title says, he has the style it takes.

But is art anything more than style - or simple productivity? Did Warhol's ethos reduce the creative process to a parody of the production line, decorated in the finery of chic society? Cale and Reed might have explored this issue, and with it the depth of Warhol's art: instead, 'Work' evades the question, and introduces the suite's second character, Lou Reed. Back in the early Seventies, Lou had noted that Warhol taught him that "the most important thing is work", and the line turns up unchanged in 'Drella'.

Beyond Warhol's production line techniques, however, the song digs gingerly at the suite's secret message of guilt. Reed describes how he fired Warhol as the Velvets' manager; and though moments later he confesses that he still uses Andy's approval as a touchstone for his work, it's the sense of regret that lingers.

With the focus returned from Lou to Andy, Reed and Cale throw another angle on Warhol's art. 'The Trouble With Classicists' points a finger at the pre-conceptions artists bring to their work, regardless of their school or philosophy. In Warhol's eyes, they are all "too wrapped up in style", unlike the graffiti artists on the street (whom he canonised in his final years), outsiders from the art establishment just as Warhol fondly viewed himself. Warhol could reduce art to 'Faces And Names', though he never felt able to live up to his own reputation. Like the next song, 'Images', this piece highlights the method of his work, silk-screening the same iconic portrait, of a star, an accident, or Andy himself, over and over; and then offering a choice of meanings and interpretations in the way he augments or distorts the original image.

'Starlight' moves Warhol from static images to film, and pinpoints the slender gap between reality and fiction in Andy's movies: "You know that shooting up's for real/That person who's screaming, that's the way he really feels". Not that Warhol takes any responsibility: 'It Wasn't Me' is Andy's answer to the perennial accusation that he manipulated and exploited his camp followers. "You never saw me take any drugs", Andy says in the original lyric, "I never said burn up and die". Right on schedule, from the Factory lift steps Valerie Solanas, shouting that Andy is controlling her life; and Lou Reed reappears to proclaim 'I Believe', a ferocious call for biblical retribution. Once again, though, Reed stings himself in the tail: the song ends with Andy crying out, "Why didn't you visit me?" after the shooting. Twenty years on, the accusation still cuts to the bone.

'Nobody But You' returns us to the shattered body of Andy Warhol, for the most oblique and ambiguous song in the suite. Stripping away the silver and pancake mask for a second, Andy unveils his regrets, his constant self-loathing; and then, in the final, shocking line of the song, he turns the hatred on his audience: "All my life, it's been nobodies like you". It's a verdict closer to Reed's persona than to Warhol's; and it's a rare hint in 'Songs For Drella' that the artist's attitude to his work and his public might be less than benign.

'Slip Away' and 'Forever Changed' illustrate the post-shooting Warhol - 'Slip Away' exposing his fear that once he cut himself off from the craziness of the street, he would lose the inspiration for his work; 'Forever Changed' proving the point, with Andy admitting "I lost myself and never came back". And in the final lines of the song, the scene shifts delicately from Warhol's restless globe-trotting in his final years to the New York Hospital, with "The whole thing quickly receding/My life disappearing". And all that's left is Lou Reed, talking to Andy's memory, still familiar enough to announce himself with a simple, 'Hello It's Me'. Sentimental and, as ever, apologetic, the song brings us back to St. Ann's

Church, and the emptiness left by the death of the man whose portrait hung over the St. Ann's Church stage.

'Songs For Drella' left much unsaid. It presented Warhol as an artist without history, who arrived fully developed on the New York scene, rode it like a mysterious colossus, and then suddenly vanished, leaving behind little more than the memories of the cow wallpaper and the silver foil that decorated the Factory. There was no hint of Andy's debt to the Pop Art pioneers; little criticism of his haphazard approach to art, the catch-all policy which produced as much dross as gold; no sense that after Andy abandoned visual art in the mid-Sixties, he was little more than the sum of his assistants and hangers-on, that his most important role in his last twenty years was as a blank canvas over which they - Reed and Cale certainly, then later Paul Morrissey and the graffiti artists - could sketch their own ideas. And as for Warhol the political naïve, the social élitist, the "urban idiot savant" of the *Diaries*: 'Songs For Drella' drew a discreet groundsheet over his head.

Lou Reed had always sought to distance himself from autobiographical interpretations of his work; once again, he declared that 'Drella' was "entirely fictitious", and the words "A Fiction" were added for its appearance on vinyl. Delighted with the artistic merit of their collaboration, and the critical reaction to their two live shows in January 1989, Reed and Cale vowed to meet again later in the year and rework the 'Drella' suite. For the moment, Cale returned to cult obscurity, while Reed set out to promote 'New York'.

The album won consistently favourable reviews, most critics insisting that it was the finest work of his solo career; and Lou capitalised on the moment. He began touring in March with six nights at the St. James Theater on New York's Broadway, and then took the show to similarly compact theatres across America and Europe. In keeping with his view of 'New York' as a single, unified work, he devoted the first half of his shows to a performance of the entire album, in exactly the same order as the record; then he indulged himself, and the audience, in the second half, throwing in favourites like 'Satellite Of Love' and 'Walk On The Wild Side' alongside a duet with Rob Wasserman on 'One For My Baby', and a remarkable rearrangement of 'The Original Wrapper' which at last caught the full concept of the song.

Two or three of the more insularly American of the 'New York' songs were dropped from the European shows - notably and most regrettably 'Good Evening Mr Waldheim', as if no-one outside the States had ever heard of Jesse Jackson; but otherwise these concerts were as commanding, and as rigorously controlled, as anything in his career.

After the album and the tour came the video - or videos, as Lou had already shot promo clips for 'Dirty Blvd' and 'Romeo Had Juliette'. The full-length concert video captured the intensity and concentration of the live performances, and then punctured the atmosphere by inserting a few seconds' silent pause between each song, as if the director thought that 'New York' was a book of short stories, not a novel.

Missing from the video, and the album, was 'The Room', an instrumental cut included (under duress) on the English single release of 'Dirty Blvd'. "They kept saying, 'Don't you have anything you left off? Why should somebody buy the single if they've already got the album?',", Lou explained to Bill Flanagan. "I said, 'When they put *Moby Dick* out do you think they said, "In the paperback version, let's leave out Chapter 13"?' Anyway, I didn't have anything. Then I said, 'I remember one little jam Mike and I did that was great fun. Maybe I can find it on cassette'." What emerged was four minutes of guitar noise, that - in the tradition of Cale's 'Loop' or the more accessible moments of Reed's own 'Metal Machine Music' - followed a vaguely classical structure without a hint of compromise. And the title was another reminder of Hubert Selby's harrowing fantasy of imprisonment and revenge.

In August, Lou set out on another American tour - this time with none other than Maureen Tucker as his support. Just before the 'New York' sessions, he'd performed on her album 'Life In Exile'; she reciprocated with her two cameo roles on Lou's record. She repeated her parts during several of Lou's shows, but the tour was cut short when Lou broke his ankle slipping on the stairs from the stage after a soundcheck.

Maintaining his high public profile that summer, Reed made cameo appearances on new records by Dion, Simple Minds, his former bassist Fernando Saunders (for whom he wrote a song called 'Opposites Attract') and Tom Tom Club, with whom he performed 'Sweet Jane', 'Femme Fatale' and Talking Heads' 'Psycho Killer' at a CBGBs club show in September.

By now, Reed was back in New York with John Cale, who had just completed his setting of Dylan Thomas poems, 'Words For The Dying'. Talking earlier in the year, Reed had let slip his desire to write a song called 'Dear Diary' for the 'Drella' project. In rewriting the lyrics for 'Hello It's Me', Lou had added a telling line: "Your *Diaries* are not a worthy epitaph". An inane and trivial account of social engagements, with each minor expenditure listed for tax purposes, *Warhol's Diaries* were a monument to the shallowness of his final years, when a fleeting glimpse of a Hollywood star at a party was an event, and art merely an occasional pastime. Warhol failed to tell his amanuensis, Pat Hackett, about the death of his former lover, Jon Gould, from AIDS in September 1986; and he let slip nothing about his declining health in the early weeks of 1987.

Reality made only brief impact on the *Diaries,* in fact, and Reed's fear that Warhol would be remembered for this weighty book rather than his art was well-placed. Yet at the same time, he was nagged by the printed evidence of Andy's growing annoyance at his behaviour, his sense of being betrayed by a long-time confidant. Another plan for the 'Drella' project had been announced in April: "We're gonna have a dream sequence, write a dream for him, a fun thing." Eventually, Reed chose to combine 'Dear Diary' and the dream sequence, and deal with his own guilt, all in one song. The result was the single masterpiece of 'Songs For Drella' - 'A Dream'.

Though Reed bridled when critics suggested that he'd simply copied entries from Warhol's diary, the song did include many verbatim quotes from Andy's daily confessions. But in a brilliant piece of writing, Lou reassembled complaints and anecdotes from the ten-year span of the *Diaries* into a single, overwhelming nightmare. 'A Dream' harps on Warhol's deepest fears - his health, his lack of artistic inspiration, the worry that his friends might love him for his name rather than himself. And with savage self-analysis, Reed weaved into this desperate, pathetic monologue all the diary entries which recorded his own distancing from Warhol, leaving John Cale to recite Andy's final verdict: "I hate Lou, I really do." Then the dream turns cloudy, and finally black, and Warhol finally crosses the line between knowledge and confusion, and the unsettling guitar and keyboard accompaniment fades away. It's great writing, but it would be nothing without Cale's sad, resigned delivery, which leaves us unwilling witnesses to Warhol's private despair.

'A Dream' was the only piece which Cale and Reed added to 'Songs For Drella' during 1989, though they tightened up the arrangements of several songs, and Reed rewrote many of the lyrics. Some of the changes were minor - Warhol's father became a construction worker rather than a coalminer in 'Small Town', for instance - others more significant. In the sole reference to The Velvet Underground, on 'Style It Takes', Cale was finally persuaded to sing that their music 'grates' rather than 'breaks'; he resisted the apparent slur in the original performances. And Reed's line about the unworthiness of the *Diaries* replaced the rather lame "They auctioned off your life and that's a fact" in the suite's final song. More significantly, Cale and Reed altered the order of the songs: 'Slip Away' was placed before the shooting, and given the subtitle 'A Warning'; while 'Starlight' was moved away from 'Images', which had a similar arrangement.

'Songs For Drella' was given its official première at the Opera House of the Brooklyn Academy Of Music on November 30, 1989; three further performances were staged over the next four nights. At the last, Maureen Tucker came on stage for a three-quarters Velvets reunion on 'Pale Blue Eyes', which turned the Warhol tribute almost full circle.

The next day, Reed and Cale repeated the entire 'Drella' cycle for the cameras, in preparation for a 1990 video release. The footage was riveting, even without the added stimulus of an audience: Reed was as deadpan and professorial as ever as he coaxed feedback from his guitar, while Cale was the archetype of the eccentric composer as he pummelled or stroked his piano, or flayed at his electric viola. The music was more elegant than their previous recordings together, as the album (also cut in December 1989) revealed; but at times The Velvet Underground myth was an almost visible third participant on stage. As Cale and Reed shot each other emotionless glances between songs, the unspoken text testified to the healing of their wounds; and the pathos of 'A Dream' was given a double edge when the camera honed in on Reed's impassive face as Cale recounted Andy's bitter farewell to his former protégé.

The 'Songs For Drella' album, issued in May 1990, didn't equal the commercial impact of 'New York'; very much a whole rather than a collection of songs, it was hardly radio-friendly, as the jargon goes. But it attracted similar ecstatic reviews to Lou's previous album, and left observers wondering how he would be able to match the bite and lyrical power of 'New York' and 'Drella' in his subsequent work. At a time when Lou's contemporaries like Bob Dylan and Neil Young were being acclaimed for their strongest albums in years, Reed's return confirmed that the rock hierarchy might, against all the odds, be able to age with some kind of grace, that the passing decades might bring greater knowledge which could in turn be channelled into greater art.

Maturity was the watchword behind Reed's flurry of activity as the 'Drella' album was released. In April, he was asked by a new literary magazine to interview Hubert Selby Jnr., "a writer I really admire", author of several novels which helped shape Lou's attitude towards his own characters. "I really wanted to meet him all my life, so I said yes," Lou revealed; strangely, the finished interview was rejected less than a fortnight after their encounter. By then, Reed was in London, where he appeared at the second Nelson Mandela concert at Wembley Stadium. The first had pleaded for the ANC leader's release; the second celebrated the day when Mandela and his wife had walked hand in hand through the prison gates past a phalanx of press and South African police, to end 27 years of martyrdom to the causes of equality and freedom.

Reed never got to meet Mandela; he watched his speech from backstage on a TV monitor. Earlier in the afternoon, he had performed two of the songs from 'New York' - 'The Last Great American Whale' and 'Dirty Blvd' - backed only by his own guitar. Alone of all the performers, Reed made no effort to ingratiate himself with the worldwide audience by performing trite songs of freedom; neither did he patronise Mandela with a fatuous welcoming speech. Reed's presence was message enough, and the grim symbolism of his songs acted as an oblique metaphor of Mandela's own struggles.

From London, Reed flew to Prague, capital of newly liberated Czechoslovakia. Less than six months after the suitably named 'Velvet Revolution' which had ended the Communist régime, the country was still in ferment, as remnants of the Old Guard, apostles of the Catholic and Orthodox churches, and libertarians jostled for position. Before the revolution, Prague had been a fairytale city kept under almost imperceptible martial law. Unlike the rest of the Eastern bloc, Czechoslovakia was not buried beneath posters and icons boasting the superiority of Marxism-Leninism. The reality of the repression became apparent only when you spoke to the people - in their fear of the ever-present secret police, or their tales of barren shops, and luxury goods reserved for the Communist élite.

By night, this beautiful mediaeval city was all but deserted. On the Charles Bridge which linked Old and New Prague, small groups of students and teenagers gathered at regular intervals, swapping tentative songs of liberation. All else in the Communist capital was quiet, and apparently orderly; only the procession of alcoholics who stumbled their way home every evening hinted at the pressures of life under occupation.

Reed had come to Prague for a meeting with Vaclav Havel - a play-wright who, by refusing to compromise his ideals and his art, had become first a political prisoner under Czechoslovakia's harsh cultural régime, and then in the bizarre and exultant events of the final weeks of 1989, the country's first post-Communist President. Havel had been approached for an interview by the magazine *Rolling Stone*: Havel agreed, but only if he could choose the interviewer.

In 1968, the young Czech writer had visited New York; having marched through the streets of the city in anti-Vietnam protests that would have been clubbed to a halt in his native land, he returned to Prague, clutching a prized copy of the Velvets' 'White Light/White Heat'. Rock music was effectively outlawed in Czechoslovakia, as an unwelcome outpost of the decadent West; and the Velvets' music became a talisman for bands like The Plastic People of the Universe, who underwent years of harassment, even imprisonment, in the name of art and freedom. For Havel and the artists of Czechoslovakia, Reed represented the voice of freedom. For Lou, Havel showed that art could not only reflect society, it could - must - change it.

Schooled on tales of the cold war, Lou suspected everyone he met in Prague; only in Havel's presence did he relax. The pair swopped anec-dotes about censorship and repression; and Reed quizzed the President about his 'criminal' past, and his transformation into a hero of the free Czech people. Havel asked if Reed would play in a private club for him and his friends that night; Reed demurred at first - "I'm a very private person", he protested - then agreed as a personal favour for his fellow playwright. And at the Gallery that night, Reed watched, touched and bemused, as Czech bands played Velvet Underground songs with preci-sion and passion.

Inspired by the moment, he came to the stage and performed some of the songs from 'New York' alone on guitar; then he joined the Czech band Pulnoc in reprising some of the Velvets' classic numbers. "It was as if Moe, John and Sterl were right there behind me, and it was a glori-ous feeling," Reed wrote in his account of the visit.

Lou's essay, half Hemingwayesque reportage, half verbatim transcript of his conversations with Havel, was once again rejected by the maga-zine that had commissioned it, though the more ambitious *Musician* picked up the rights. The writing had the dry, brief authenticity of Reed's lyrics, as Lou recalled his visit to the stunningly evocative Jewish ceme-tery in the city centre. Jews were traditionally restricted to a few hundred square yards of the city; the dead had to be buried in layers, each pathetic gravestone concealing bodies ten or twenty deep. With the plaques seem-ingly thrown at random into the ground, bent at angles or forced into tight rows like prisoners in a death camp, the Jewish cemetery is almost unbearably moving to visit. For Reed, a Jew becoming ever more aware of the consequences of persecution, the sight must have left an indelible mark.

The *Musician* piece was revealing in other ways. Reed made a point of emphasising his refusal to drink alcohol; it was a detail he noted as a badge of pride. Freedom from self-abuse had left Reed able to explore the world outside his own psyche: now he recalled that at the start of his career, "I had been concerned with, among other things, demonstrating how much more a song could be about than was currently being written."

In the Sixties, the limits had been expanded to take on drugs and sexual perversion, plus the grim cycle of power and guilt played out in relationships. Now, after his involvement in the Mandela concert, and his visit to the reclaimed city of Prague, Lou was learning new boundaries to cross. He concluded: "So the VU albums and my own are implicitly about freedom of expression - freedom to write about what you please in any way you please." Reed had extended that freedom from the darkest emotions of his own heart to the blackest facets of contemporary urban life, and beyond; after Prague, it seemed unlikely that he would ever be able to ignore the outside world again.

THIRTEEN

IN THE LATE AFTERNOON OF JUNE 15, 1990, two musicians strolled onto an open-air stage in the French countryside, twenty miles from Paris. One clutched an electric guitar; the other took up position behind a simple display of electronic keyboards. Lou Reed, clad in his uniform shades, leather jacket and blue jeans nodded curtly at his companion; and John Cale, hair shaved severely above his ears, fringe flopping decadently over his eyebrows, began to play their canny evocation of Andy Warhol, 'Style It Takes'. As the wind swirled the sound off the stage and up into the hills beyond, Reed and Cale moved gently into 'Slip Away'. "Still there's no more Billy Name," Reed sang, as Billy Name stood entranced in the audience beside fellow survivors of the Factory. As the duo began 'Nobody But You' and then 'Forever Changed', they began to ride the music, responding to each other's rhythm, living the songs as much as playing them. Then Reed whispered his farewell to Warhol, 'Hello It's Me', the crowd applauded politely, and Lou stepped away from the microphone.

Glancing briefly behind him, he resumed his place, and announced: "We have a little surprise for you. I'd like to introduce Sterling Morrison - and Maureen Tucker." There was a moment of stunned silence, before the audience realised that they were about to witness something that, according to Lou Reed, could never happen: a reunion of the original Velvet Underground.

The occasion was the grand opening of the Andy Warhol Exposition, a majestic celebration of the artist's art and times which was staged under the auspices of the Cartier Foundation in Jouey-en-Josas. The organisers had not only assembled an unrepeatable collection of Warhol's work, including films like the *Symphony Of Sound* portrait of the Velvets in rehearsal which had remained unseen for almost 25 years; they had also succeeded, through their devotion to the cause, in persuading the remnants of the Factory empire to attend. Plane tickets were sent out to Billy Name, to Nat Finkelstein, to Ultra Violet; and to the four original members of The Velvet Underground. When they arrived at the festival site, the Velvets were overwhelmed by what they saw; though they insisted to the last minute that a reunion was impossible, they realised that it would be churlish not to respond in kind to the efforts of the organisers. And so it was that Reed, Cale, Morrison and Tucker occupied the same stage for the first time since the late summer of 1968.

There were no rehearsals, merely the briefest of soundchecks, and an instant decision that they should perform the song which epitomised the popular image of The Velvet Underground: 'Heroin'. As Cale's electric viola howled out a discordant drone, Reed and Morrison's guitars locked instantly into that two-chord cycle, and Tucker pounded at her bass drum with the finality of the grim reaper. For nine minutes, the Velvets rode the waves of the song, Tucker hurrying the others in her excitement, Reed missing out lines as he glowed in the sheer aura of the sound. Then it was over: the final crescendo of Cale's feedback died away; Reed picked one last arpeggio; and the Velvets drifted slowly off stage, unable themselves to believe what had happened. Afterwards, they swopped reminiscences, and made vague plans to work again in the future; they dined together that night and the next, and left France more united than they had been since the heyday of the Exploding Plastic Inevitable in 1966.

Since then, Cale and Reed have played a further 'Songs For Drella' show in Japan, on Lou's first tour as a solo artist. Lou also brought his one-man-band to Liverpool, for the controversial tribute concert to John Lennon organised by Yoko Ono. Alongside the likes of Kylie Minogue and Wet Wet Wet, Reed played stark, almost acoustic versions of two of Lennon's finest songs: 'Mother', the inspiration for Lou's own analysis of the bitter heritage of shared blood, 'Families', and 'Jealous Guy', a lyric that would have fitted comfortably on to Lou's apologetic albums of the early Eighties.

On MTV Lou appeared in a bizarre station ID, quoting the dagger speech from *Macbeth*. In New York, he wrote a song for the ailing songwriting legend Doc Pomus, then spoke at his memorial service.

In Canada, meanwhile, archivist Rob Bowman began the painstaking task of compiling a triple-CD retrospective of Lou's solo work, holding hours of interviews with Reed, and enduring his subject's changes of heart over what rare treasures should be unveiled to the public. Simultaneously, Lou prepared a collected edition of his lyrics, with both projects sharing a title taken from the veteran Velvets theme, 'Some Kinda Love: Between Thought And Expression'. Back in New York in the New Year, Lou took Rob Wasserman, Fred Maher and Mike Rathke back into the studio for an album recorded without overdubs, and provisionally scheduled -under the title 'Magic And Loss'- for the autumn of 1991. And the echoes of the Velvets' reunion still resound: as I write the final pages of this book in April 1991, word reaches me that Maureen Tucker has been recording with Sterling Morrison and John Cale, and that Sylvia Reed has been commissioned to provide the cover artwork for the project. Is this a second Velvets reunion smuggled in under the guise of a Tucker solo album? By the time you read this, all should have been revealed.

It is tempting to view this burst of nostalgic energy - the 'Drella' project, the collaboration with Tucker, the sunny summer afternoon in France - as the end of one karmic cycle of death and rebirth, the comfortable conclusion to a dazzling and often meandering career. If Lou Reed were to die tonight, that's what we would be left with: the tale of a musical and lyrical explorer who ventured far into the margins of experience, and then gradually clawed his way back into the mainstream, ending his career neatly in a rapprochement with his fellow travellers of the past.

Lou Reed celebrates his 50th birthday in 1992. In the iconography of rock, he might as well be Methuselah; in any other genre of art you care to imagine, he is in his prime. Rock music was invented as an expression of youth, a gesture of savage revolt against the stale orthodoxies which had prevailed since the end of the Second World War. It became, like every revolution before it, less a single act than a state of mind. Leon Trotsky espoused the cause of Permanent Revolution, a rigorous form of Marxism-Leninism which would continually root out its own bourgeois tendencies and reaffirm its basic faiths. But his dream foundered beneath the stolid realism of Josef Stalin and his secret police. Rock began with similar ambition; its Permanent Revolution entailed eternal youth, perhaps, a constant search for the cutting edge, for a music that would offer both a critique of society, and an inspiration for its future growth.

It was a vision that sparked rock's pioneers, from Elvis Presley to The Beatles, The Rolling Stones to, yes, The Velvet Underground. They all envisaged a break with the past, and then a world rebuilt in their own image. But what begins as an act of revolution soon becomes a career, and in turn each of rock's teen rebels has become a pillar of the establishment, or been propelled through a car windscreen, crushed in a plane wreck, or found stiff and bloated in a Memphis or Paris bathroom.

For the young, growing old is a sin, a fate too distasteful, too unhip, to contemplate. Pretty soon it becomes a vocation, then a source of pride. The rock archetype of this process is Pete Townshend: writing "Hope I die before I get old" when he was barely out of his teens, and then surviving to a ripe age as a grand old man of English letters. And in Lou Reed's career, the same inevitable journey has taken place. In 1966, Reed lived and wrote for the moment; by the late Seventies, he was hustling for his place in the pantheon of posterity, alongside William, Fyodor and the rest of the classics.

Approaching fifty, then, Lou Reed is far from complete: his story has, *Deus vult*, twenty or thirty years to run. The pleasure of growing old(er) alongside rock's pioneers is seeing who continues to grow, and who follows the almost irresistible temptation to settle for what they have already become. Look at Bob Dylan, Neil Young, Joni Mitchell, Lou Reed, and you see artists who have refused to settle into companionable early senility. Restless, forever dissatisfied, they continue to plunge blindly into the currents of the future, swallowing as much water as they push aside, yet still immersed in the struggle which breeds life, rather than floating gently in living inertia.

As each decade has passed, Lou Reed has narrowed his horizons, and honed his vision. In the Sixties, he was ready to take on the world, creating manic soundscapes that could topple buildings or push a civilisation closer to the edge. In the Seventies, he concentrated on pushing himself to the limits, using himself as a guinea-pig for the wildest implications of the drug-quaffing, taboo-breaking rock culture. Waking one day and finding himself - surprise! - still alive and thinking, he began to lash out at the forces that had moulded his own personality, the family background that he had left behind but was unable ever to escape.

In the Eighties, Reed stepped back from the abyss, and studied his own reactions - the itching need to self-destruct, the rival urge to lose himself in the simplicities of love, his growing awareness of the complexity of human relationships. And having built himself a solid rock on which to stand, he then sharpened his claws as a writer. He began to exercise the skills he'd fashioned so painfully over the previous 25 years, aiming them at specific targets - the simmering cauldron of New York City, for instance, or the tangled legacy of Andy Warhol.

On one level, Reed's art has become more mellow, less extreme; even the feedback extravaganza of 'The Room' during the 'New York' sessions was kept under control. On another, his work is more precise and effective than ever before: on 'New York' and 'Songs For Drella', his words not only flowed, elegantly and with consummate grace, but they bit - savagely - with a ferocity and purpose that he could never have achieved with the Velvets, as the Rock'n'Roll Animal, even as the anxious newly-wed of 'Legendary Hearts'. And his music has changed to reflect the sharp passions of his writing: neither 'New York' nor 'Drella' has an ounce of spare flesh. Each phrase, each chord, has a purpose; in an age when technical skill has allowed musicians the gift of endless self-indulgence, Reed has drawn his bowstring tighter and tighter. No longer self-indulgent autobiography, Lou's work has the certainty of the master craftsmen, topped with the spontaneity of genius.

Reed's often tortuous progress towards artistic enlightenment has produced a canon of work which few rock musicians can rival. Consistency has never been his strength, at least until recent years; the writer of albums like 'Berlin' and 'Sally Can't Dance' was scarcely conscious of what he was producing, or why. On 'Street Hassle', 'The Bells' and 'Growing Up In Public', Reed staked out a new-found maturity, and then struggled to find the music to do it justice. Only with 'The Blue Mask', that painful document of self-discovery, did Reed's lyrical growth reach an understanding with his music. And the shock of recognition proved so profound that for most of the Eighties, Lou shied away from the implications of what he had found.

There's a fascinating series of books called *The Critical Heritage,* each one devoted to a writer whose place in literary history seems immovable. They gather together contemporary reviews of new work by figures like Wordsworth and Coleridge, Henry James and Charles Dickens - immediate responses to 'classic' books, written by critics who didn't have the benefit of hindsight, and who certainly never imagined that a century or more later, their petty stings would come back to haunt them. In these anthologies, books which are now renowned as masterpieces - Henry James' *The Bostonians,* Herman Melville's *Moby Dick,* Dickens' *Bleak House* - are reviewed not as timeless classics, but as contemporary fiction, subject to all the hasty generalisations of the working journalist. It is shocking, almost blasphemous, to see these epic works handled so rudely; yet it is a useful reminder of the yawning gap between the artist's immediate audience, and the more balanced judgement of posterity.

Rock musicians, and authors too, live and work in the present. Just as James, Melville and Dickens were judged work-by-work as jobbing writers rather than unchallenged classics, so musicians like Lou Reed have to suffer the abuse of critics who have their own narrow expectations of his work. Study Lou Reed's collected reviews, and you have an essay in disappointment: whenever Lou has apparently settled into one role, he has had the unnerving habit of shifting sideways, backwards or, in his glory days, ahead.

It is part of the artist's function to unnerve and disappoint, to keep one step ahead of other people's preconceptions. The artist should satisfy his own soul, and at the same time he may enrich the lives of his audience, if they are willing to be enriched. By laying himself bare in public, then examining the implications of what happens when one human being reaches out and touches another, and finally venturing out to explore the workings of the society in which he lives, Lou Reed has fulfilled his calling as an artist.

But his final duty is to himself, and to his own sense of growth and adventure. Tai Chi, in which Reed has schooled himself over the last decade, offers the notion of perpetual birth, death and rebirth, each cycle accompanied by the gaining of knowledge. That is a reassuring concept for an artist about to complete fifty years of life, and it offers the hope that Lou Reed might escape the premature senescence which is the fate of most popular artists, and continue to produce art that enlightens, amuses, enrages and extends his audience, and himself, just as his work over the last twenty-five years or more has done. Posterity will judge whether Reed belongs alongside Shakespeare and Dostoevsky; meanwhile, there is still a 'work in progress' sign on his door.

CODA: MAY 1992

THE ORIGINAL DRAFT OF THIS BOOK was written during the lengthy pause in Lou Reed's career between 'Songs For Drella' and the multi-media blitz that accompanied the January 1992 release of 'Magic And Loss'. The latter album seems to have completed a cycle, rather than sent it careering through another spin. On the most obvious symbolic level, 'Magic And Loss' deals with finality – with the certainty of death, which (apologies to believers of all faiths) is still as final a metaphor as I care to think about.

Reed chose to celebrate the end of his fiftieth year with a record that stared unwaveringly at the shadow of his own mortality. He used the deaths of two personal friends as a way of confronting his own demons, unearthing fear, courage, respect and evasiveness in almost equal proportions. The album also completed a trilogy of decay, with each instalment growing ever more specific. 'New York' charted the decline of a civilisation and a city; 'Songs For Drella' used Andy Warhol's shooting and ultimate death as a statement on the accepted values of the Sixties; finally 'Magic And Loss' brought it all close – too close, for some tastes – to home.

In 1975, Lou had used the release of 'Metal Machine Music' as a sly piece of media manipulation, which within a year saw him released from what he saw as onerous management and record contracts. Playing to the lowest expectations of his audience, he convinced the outside world that he had leaned too far over the edge of the precipice, and had slipped to his doom – while all the time he remained carefully in control of his actions, his art, and the way they were presented to the public.

That same desire to influence the reception of his work informed every stage of the release of 'Magic And Loss'. Advanced cassettes of the album were offered to sympathetic journalists in the autumn of 1991, months before the planned release date. Word spread that this was Reed's masterwork, the culmination of his post-1989 renaissance. By January 1992, when the record was actually available to the hoi polloi, the climate was such that almost any record from Reed would have been greeted favourably.

Best of all, as far as Lou was concerned, he was now being treated on his own terms. Years of insisting that he be seen as a writer rather than a rock star finally paid off, and almost without exception – Adam Sweeting in *The Guardian* newspaper in London was a brave and/or stubborn hold-out – the British and American press united in reverential praise of this most literary and literate of rock writers, whose work escaped the narrow preoccupations of the genre.

Did 'Magic And Loss' match its advance publicity? Yes, for seriousness of intent and execution, yes again for cohesiveness and internal unity, but perhaps not as a matching of music and lyrics, or as a justification for using the conventions of rock'n'roll to approach the almighty forces of death and destiny.

"Between two Aprils, I lost two friends. Between two Aprils, magic and loss," read Lou's brief explanatory note for the album. The cause, in both cases, was cancer. One friend, already mentioned in these pages, was Doc Pomus: legendary (for once, the word seemed justified) R&B songwriter and singer, creator of pop and soul hits for The Drifters, Elvis Presley and many more, and a convincing blues singer himself, despite being restricted by a severe attack of polio to a wheelchair for the last thirty years of his life. Wildly humorous and equally affectionate, Pomus seems to have inspired love in all those who knew him: Reed, as we've already seen, read a lesson at his April 1991 memorial service.

The second inspiration for 'Magic And Loss' was at first named as Lincoln Swados, described as a former room-mate of Reed's at Syracuse University in the early Sixties, and also apparently the subject of the harrowing 'Home Of The Brave', which appeared on the 'Legendary Hearts' album in 1983. "He once tried to commit suicide by jumping in front of a train," Reed said of his friend, "and then had to live to tell about it."

A month later, the album appeared: "Dedicated to Doc and especially to Rita". 'Rita', so Reed told Melody Maker in January 1992, was "a friend, the last name wouldn't mean anything to you". On the record was a song called 'Dreamin'', its lyrics referring to one of his two inspirations; in a touching image, Reed sang: "If I close my eyes I can smell your perfume, you look and say, 'Hi babe'." This character, then, was female – or at least perfumed – and close enough to Reed to call him "babe". "My God," a friend said to me excitedly when the album was released, "it must be Rachel. Rachel and Rita – it's obvious." Perhaps too obvious, in fact, as Reed was probably doing nothing more than investing his real-life characters with fictional attributes, emotions and roles. He does, after all, see himself as a rock storyteller. But the switch from Lincoln Swados to 'Rita' was intriguing, especially in the light of Reed's statement elsewhere that Swados died of starvation in his New York apartment, rather than of cancer like 'Rita'.

"There's only a couple of big themes, and death is one of them," Lou announced when the album was released. Its subject, he declared, was "how you deal with loss – it's a celebration of friendship and transcendence".

Friendship had rarely surfaced in Reed's past work; his narrators, whether they were actors or voyeurs, usually operated alone. Transcendence, though, could be the secret message of his last decade, with its stunning conversion of despair and self-abuse into hope and self-knowledge. And it's that magical transformation which he intended as the subject of 'Magic And Loss', that certainty that even within the bleakest of fates there lies a spiritual or intellectual notion of rebirth. The album, he stated finally, was intended as "cleansing for the soul".

With each track given a mystical symbol, and a subtitle – 'The Thesis', 'The Situation', 'The Summation' – 'Magic And Loss' had something of the air of a seventeenth century morality tale, a pilgrim's progress tracked through a landscape of science, faith and despair. Like the entire concept and presentation of the album, Reed's choice of terrain invited charges of pretentiousness, which were inevitable once he elected to face the eternal and the mortal within the hour-long span of a 1990s rock record.

So it was in keeping with the spirit of the project that the album began with 'Dorita', a mock-symphonic guitar instrumental whose title combined the names of the two victims. Weighty, florid and deliberately pompous, 'Dorita' was claimed by its creator as the guitar orchestration that he'd been promising ever since 'Metal Machine Music' and 'The Bells'. Tongue very firmly removed from cheek, Reed described the rise and fall of guitars as "an evocation of the human spirit in pure sound". If that wasn't apparent to the listener, then at the very least 'Dorita' announced something of intended significance to follow.

Faced with the problem of relating two similar tragedies, Reed followed the lead set by 'Dorita' and made them one. The victims' individual characters are recognisable: the memorial service for Doc Pomus is the subject of 'Goodby Mass', while the songwriter's scabrous, self-mocking humour is a reference point in several of the songs. And we've already noted the feminine mystique that tugs at Reed's memory in 'Dreamin''. Pomus and Rita are, for the most part, compressed into one single 'you', a representative of man's mortality whose importance is measured by its effect on Reed.

The same basic novelistic techniques which Lou used on 'Songs For Drella' – the sudden shift of perspective or persona, the viewing of characters from within and without, the multiple visions of the same event – reappear on 'Magic And Loss'. Simple though they are, they're still startling within the context of a rock record. You could use a film analogy as well: with a series of lingering close-ups separated by jump-cuts, Reed takes us from the hospital bed to the funeral service and the cremation, and then leaves us for over half the album with memories of the past, worked out through a succession of reactions – grief, anger, aggression and finally transcendent acceptance of the inevitable. That painful progression from pain to guilt to rage, and finally to the realisation that life must continue, is the lesson of 'Magic And Loss'. You can either applaud Reed for showing us the wound open to the bone and allowing us to watch it heal, or deplore his attempts to create significant art out of a universal experience.

Like an existentialist Smokey Robinson, Reed's lyrics on 'Magic And Loss' are replete with paradox, often matching the stark, switchback quality of the guitar riffs which provide their fragile musical support. 'What's Good' (also included on the soundtrack of the latest Wim Wenders movie) teases us with a succession of non-senses, before bringing the story back to the point: "What good was cancer in April/Why no good, no good at all". "Life's good," the song concludes, "but not fair at all", and it's that juxtaposition between pain and pleasure which underpins the album.

The lyrics bend just as easily from humour – "that mix of morphine and dexedrine," Reed notes on 'Sword Of Damocles', "we use it on the street" – to cold, bleak descriptions of suffering that make no attempt to place the discreet veil of poetry between the ravaging pain of the cancer victim and the unwavering eye of the witness. After the burial and cremation, Reed escorts us through a cycle of songs subtitled 'Escape', 'Regret' and 'Revenge' – the last of these being 'Warrior King', one of the toweringly aggressive rockers which have become a Reed speciality over the last decade. "The narrator pictures the disease as a person and himself as the Warrior King," Reed explained like a college lecturer. "The Warrior King seems like the only character powerful enough to beat something as all-powerful as this enemy." He blusters, swaggers and threatens, as terrifying as the public image of Reed himself faced with an un-cooperative interviewer: it's a side of his own character that Lou obviously uses as a ploy, like a Samurai let loose on a parade of paper tigers. On 'Magic And Loss', its appearance is as unwelcome and untidy as the proverbial china-shop bull; bereavement sometimes takes people that way.

After 'Revenge' comes 'Reverie Gone Astray' in the form of 'Harry's Circumcision', the strangest, funniest, least explicable song on the album. For five minutes we escape the constant shadow of cancer and embark on a familiar psychodrama. Harry is also the name Reed's favourite novelist, Hubert Selby Jnr., gives to many of his interchangeable heroes, which is probably not a coincidence. In himself, he recognises "the cheeks of his mother, the eyes of his father", and with the same blank rage that is one of Selby's trademarks he decides to alter his inheritance with a razor's edge. As with 'The Gift' twenty-five years earlier, the horror of the story is undercut (not a bad choice of word, perhaps) by Reed's black humour: in his role as narrator, he can't resist playing a God with a passion for cheap jokes.

Then it's back to the dull litany of grief, a repetition of an earlier song ('Power And Glory') which is meant to suggest the transformation from despair to hope, and then a title track which has to live up to all the symbolic importance of its subtitle: 'The Summation'.

Using an extended metaphor of fire – fire as a trial, fire as a means of destruction, fire as the vehicle for a phoenix-like rebirth – the song attempts to find a level-headed acceptance of the universal inevitable that is almost Buddhist in its simplicity. "There's a little bit of magic in everything," Reed concludes, "and then some loss to even things out". The loss and magic of the rest of the album happened in reverse order; here it's as if Reed sees us all treading on some cosmic wheel of karma, experiencing fragmentary moments of magic and then doomed to endure loss as part of the same cyclical fate. It's meant to inspire hope, I suppose, or at the very least the promise of relief. Instead, I find its urbane, open-armed greeting of life's inevitability repressive and false. "This isn't a bleak record," Lou asserted in one of his carefully structured promotional interviews for the album; but the underlying message of his title track belies the claim.

"It's all craft," Reed dropped as an aside in an interview, and the comment explained a lot. It took a craftsman – and an ambitious one, at that – to attempt to face and even conquer the sting of death. Reed's skill and experience as a writer are evident in every verse, in each rewritten and finely honed phrase and image. What's missing, though, is inspiration: possibly because death is the opposite of imagination, possibly because Reed was restricted by his self-imposed framework. 'Magic And Loss' is a highly impressive, often affecting piece of work; but it lacks the light touch of the unconscious, the air of surprise, that marks out his best records, even when they're as plotted as 'New York' or 'Songs For Drella'. For once, Reed promised more than he could deliver.

In concert, there was no mistaking the seriousness of Lou's intentions. His early 1992 shows were arranged in two sections: the first, preceded by a solemn announcement that latecomers would not be admitted, was devoted to the entire 'Magic And Loss' suite; the second to extracts from his previous two albums. What followed was closer to a classical recital than a rock concert, with Reed and his customary core of musicians moving dispassionately through the death saga without a word or gesture to the audience. The 'New York' and 'Songs For Drella' episodes were equally free from improvisation: wherever possible, the musicians tried not to stand between the audience, and The Words. At the end of each segment, Reed and the band bowed tightly to the audience like a mutant string quartet.

Musically faultless though the sets were, they mostly lacked soul, or any hint of the unexpected. The exceptions were provided by the Legendary Little Jimmy Scott, a little-known blues singer who had added some unearthly vocal lines to 'Power And Glory'. His visual presence proved to be as diverting, and unconventional, as his contribution to the record. Twisting his body like an aged cobra, he painfully brought his eerie vocals to the surface, as if some part of his soul was being excised in the attempt. When he was brought back to the stage for Reed's otherwise perfunctory encores, he gave the perennial 'Satellite Of Love' a hint of life that had seemed extinct decades ago.

It was a rare moment of relief, even if it hardly qualified as light. Otherwise, Reed's stance in the early months of 1992 was as a literate artist, utterly in control of his career. The previous autumn, he'd begun a series of poetry readings in New York's Central Park, and by March 1992 the showcase reached the semi-classical environs of London's South Bank. Clad in his professional black, Reed recited selections from *Between Thought And Expression*, the long-promised anthology of his writings that was published in America just before Christmas, and in Britain to coincide with the concert tour.

The book was touted as "a collection of lyrics that I feel can stand alone from the music for which they were originally written". With some interesting exceptions, they charted the range of his career and writing styles, from the street poetry of the Velvets' albums through his initial homages to Eliot and Schwartz, a brief glimpse at the glam and horror years of the early Seventies, and then a solid concentration on the period of renaissance after 1980. To most of the lyrics, Reed added a line or two of explanation, terse and often witty. He owned up to his shock therapy, his family strife, his battles with drugs and the bottle and his aggression; he even admitted that the sado-masochistic psychodrama of 'The Blue Mask' was a "self-portrait". But there was no Rachel: the yearning final section of 'Street Hassle' was discarded, 'Coney Island Baby' was omitted, and all references to Reed's much-publicised dalliance with New York's gay underground were excised.

The same omission was obvious on the three-CD retrospective given the same title as the book, which eventually surfaced in March 1992, more than a year behind the original schedule. Compiler and annotator Rob Bowman was allowed, in notes that seemed as if they'd been heavily edited by their subject, to refer to 'Coney Island Baby' as "the grandest love song of his career", but not to admit that it was written for and dedicated to Lou's mid-Seventies transvestite companion.

The boxed set, by the standards of such things, was unspectacular: while Bob Dylan's 'The Bootleg Series' offered three CDs of entirely unissued material, Reed's 'Between Thought And Expression' could muster only a handful of rarities, the most intriguing being the 'Take No Prisoners' out-take 'Here Comes The Bride'. The rest was routine, leaving the booklet – even in its expurgated state – as the main attraction. In it, Bowman revealed for the first time that the 'Berlin' album had been edited down from two albums to one at the insistence of RCA; and he provided valuable new information about the circumstances of Reed's recording debut with the Shades/Jades.

Attractively packaged and sequenced though it was, 'Between Thought And Expression' seemed to squeeze some of the life out of Reed's work, canonising it rather than letting it breathe. For the real, vital Lou Reed, you had to turn to Maureen Tucker's 1991 album, 'I Spent A Week There The Other Night', an enchantingly passionate rant about lack of money, the boredom of work and other everyday evils that hit much closer to home than all the grand designs of 'Magic And Loss'. On the opening track, the punky 'Fired Up', the waters parted at the end of a chorus and into the chasm fell a sparking, fearsome monster – a Lou Reed guitar solo cranked up to an intensity that he hadn't mustered on record since the second Velvets album. "I was proud of that," Tucker told me. "I just told him that's how I wanted him to play! I love to hear him do that." And Tucker also succeeded in creating the unimaginable, a new Velvet Underground recording – nearly, anyway, as 'I'm Not', a lengthy drone piece with John Cale's viola central to the sound, featured all four original members plus extra musicians. Tucker downplayed the significance of the occasion: "It wasn't planned as a great reunion, and the four of us were never together at one time"; but the track seemed to draw a neat line beneath the doubtful promise of a full-scale VU reunion.

Reed's guitarwork on Tucker's album demonstrated that the fire could be lit when required or inspired, though the raw energy of his solos would have been ill-suited to the delicate structures of his recent concept albums. "There are novels and plays, and this is at least the equal of those – maybe a bit more," Reed exaggerated wildly when 'Magic And Loss' was released. "I'm interested in writing a book, but not about me," he added.

Between Thought And Expression wasn't that book, though it did extend beyond his lyrics to include his interviews with Vaclav Havel and (for the first time in print) Hubert Selby Jnr. Both featured the unmistakeable prose style of Lou Reed, as unique a print as his singing voice, and as uncompromising. With his music increasingly limited by the confines of his literary visions, perhaps the time has come for Reed to separate the two – to return to his rock'n'roll the risk and fierce energy of his work on 'Fired Up', and to point his literary ambitions towards printed prose, perhaps in the form of the Great American Novel which he has been threatening to create in his music for more than twenty-five years.

DISCOGRAPHY

JADES U.S. SINGLES

LEAVE HER FOR ME *(Reed)*/
SO BLUE *(Reed)*
Time 1002 1958

LEAVE HER FOR ME
(Reed)/BELINDA
Dot 1958

PICKWICK ERA RECORDINGS

THE OSTRICH *(Vance/Sims/
Reed/Phillips)*/SNEAKY PETE
(Vance/Sims/Reed/Phillips)
by The Primitives
Pickwick 1001 Late 1964

SOUNDSVILLE
Design DLP 187 Early 1965
LP contains the following tracks
with known Reed connections:
You're Driving Me Insane *by The
Roughnecks*/Johnny Won't Surf No
More by Jeannie Larimore/I've Got
A Tiger In My Tank *by*
The Beachnuts/Cycle Annie *by*
The Beachnuts

TELL MAMA NOT TO CRY
(Vance/Sims/Reed/Phillips)/
MAYBE TOMORROW
(Vance/Sims/Reed/Phillips)
by Robertha Williams
Uptown 707 1965
Maybe Tomorrow was also issued
with the singer credited as Ronnie
Dickerson.

WHY DON'T YOU SMILE NOW
(Vance/Cale/Reed/Phillips)/(Don't
Put All Your Eggs In One Basket)
by The All Night Workers
Round Sound 1 1965
Why Don't You Smile Now was
also covered in 1965 by Donnie
Burks on U.S. Decca, and The
Downlines Sect on U.K. Columbia.

OUT OF SIGHT
Design DLP 269 c1967
LP contains Cycle Annie
by The Beachnuts

VELVET UNDERGROUND U.S. SINGLES

ALL TOMORROW'S PARTIES
(Reed)/I'LL BE YOUR MIRROR
(Reed)
Verve 10427 October 1966
Promo copies exist in picture sleeve;
it is uncertain whether this single was
ever available commercially.

SUNDAY MORNING *(Reed)/*
FEMME FATALE *(Reed)*
Verve 10466 December 1966

WHITE LIGHT/WHITE HEAT
(Reed)
HERE SHE COMES NOW
(Reed)/Morrison/Cale/Tucker)
Verve 10560 March 1968
Promo copies exist; probably not
issued commercially.

HERE SHE COMES NOW
(Reed/Morrison/Cale/Tucker)
I HEARD HER CALL MY NAME
(Reed)
Verve 10560 March 1968
Promo copies exist; probably not
issued commercially.

WHAT GOES ON *(VU)/*
JESUS *(VU)*
MGM 14057 1969
Promo copies exist; probably not
issued commercially.

WHO LOVES THE SUN *(VU)/OH*
SWEET NUTHIN' *(VU)*
Cotillion 44107 1970

VELVET UNDERGROUND
U.K. SINGLES

WHO LOVES THE SUN *(VU)/*
SWEET JANE *(VU)*
Atlantic 2091 088 April 1971

CANDY SAYS *(VU)/*I'M
WAITING FOR THE MAN
*(Reed)/*RUN RUN RUN *(Reed)*
MGM 2006 283 June 1973

SWEET JANE *(VU)/*
ROCK AND ROLL *(VU)*
Atlantic K 10339 August 1973

WHITE LIGHT WHITE HEAT

*(Reed)/*HEROIN *(Reed)/*VENUS IN
FURS *(Reed)/*I'M WAITING FOR
THE MAN *(Reed)*
Polydor POSPX 398 (12″) 1981

HEROIN *(Reed)/*VENUS IN FURS
*(Reed)/*WAITING FOR THE MAN
*(Reed)/*RUN RUN RUN *(Reed)*
Polydor POSPX 603 (12″) October
1982

WAITING FOR THE MAN
*(Reed)/*HEROIN *(Reed)*
Old Gold OG 4049 (12″) March
1988

VENUS IN FURS *(Reed)/*ALL
TOMORROW'S PARTIES *(Reed)*
Old Gold OG 4051 (12″) March
1988
All Tomorrow's Parties is an
alternate mix, also available on the
CD release of the Velvets' début
album.

VELVET UNDERGROUND
U.S. ALBUMS

THE VELVET UNDERGROUND
AND NICO
Sunday Morning *(Reed)/*I'm
Waiting For The Man
*(Reed)/*Femme Fatale *(Reed)/*Venus
In Furs *(Reed)/*Run Run Run
*(Reed)/*All Tomorrow's Parties
*(Reed)/*Heroin *(Reed)/*There She
Goes Again *(Reed)/*I'll Be Your
Mirror *(Reed)/*Black Angel's Death
Song *(Reed/Cale)/*European Son
(Reed, Cale, Morrison, Tucker)
Verve 5008 March 1967

WHITE LIGHT/WHITE HEAT
White Light/White Heat *(Reed)/*The
Gift *(Reed/Morrison/Cale/Tucker)/*
Lady Godiva's Operation *(Reed)/*
Here She Comes Now *(Reed/*
*Morrison/Cale/Tucker)/*I Heard

Her Call My Name *(Reed)*/Sister Ray *(Reed/Morrison/Cale/Tucker)* Verve 5046 December 1967

THE VELVET UNDERGROUND
Candy Says *(VU)*/What Goes On *(VU)*/Some Kinda Love *(VU)*/Pale Blue Eyes *(VU)*/Jesus *(VU)*/ *Beginning To See The Light/I'm Set Free (VU)*/That's The Story Of My Life *(VU)*/Murder Mystery *(VU)*/ Afterhours *(VU)*
MGM SE 4617 March 1969
Copyright in all the above songs was awarded to Lou Reed after a legal battle.

LOADED
Who Loves The Sun *(VU)*/Sweet Jane *(VU)*Rock and Roll *(VU)*/ Cool It Down *(VU)*/New Age *(VU)*/Head Held High *(VU)*/ Lonesome Cowboy Bill *(VU)*/ I Found A Reason *(VU)*/ Train Round The Bend *(VU)*/ Oh Sweet Nuthin' *(VU)*
Cotillion SD 9034 September 1970
Copyright in all the above songs was awarded to Lou Reed after a legal battle.

LIVE AT MAX'S KANSAS CITY
I'm Waiting For The Man *(Reed)*/Sweet Jane *(Reed)*/Lonesome Cowboy Bill *(VU)*/Beginning To See The Light *(VU)*/I'll Be Your Mirror *(Reed)*/Pale Blue Eyes *(VU)*/Sunday Morning *(Reed)*/ New Age *(VU)*/Femme Fatale *(Reed)*/Afterhours *(VU)*
Cotillion SD 9500 May 1972

VELVET UNDERGROUND
Candy Says *(Reed)*/Sunday Morning *(Reed/Cale)*/Femme Fatale *(Reed)*/ White Light/White Heat *(Reed)*/ Jesus *(Reed)*/Heroin *(Reed)*/ Beginning To See The Light *(Reed)*/ Here She Comes Now

(Reed/Morrison/Cale/Tucker)/ Afterhours *(Reed)* (MGM GAS 131) 1972
For the first time, this album credited songs from the third and fourth Velvets LPs to Lou Reed, rather than the Velvet Underground. It also credited Sunday Morning to Reed and John Cale for the first time.

SQUEEZE
Polydor 2383 180 February 1973
Lou Reed had no involvement in this VU album, which was essentially a Doug Yule solo project.

LOU REED AND THE VELVET UNDERGROUND
That's The Story Of My Life *(VU)*/Sister Ray *(Reed/Morrison/ Cale/Tucker)*/Lady Godiva's Operation *(Reed)*/Heroin *(Reed)*/ Sunday Morning *(Reed)*/All Tomorrow's Parties *(Reed)*/ There She Goes Again *(Reed)*/ White Light/White Heat *(Reed)*/ Femme Fatale *(Reed)*
Pride PRD 0022 1973

LIVE 1969
I'm Waiting For The Man *(Reed)*/ Lisa Says *(Reed)*/What Goes On *(Reed)*/Sweet Jane *(Reed)*/We're Gonna Have A Real Good Time Together *(Reed)*/Femme Fatale *(Reed)*/New Age *(Reed)*Rock And Roll *(Reed)*/Beginning To See The Light *(Reed)*/Ocean *(Reed)*/Pale Blue Eyes *(Reed)*/Heroin *(Reed)*/ Some Kinda Love *(Reed)*/ Over You *(Reed)*/Sweet Bonnie Brown; It's Just Too Much *(Reed)*/ White Light/White Heat *(Reed)*/ I'll Be Your Mirror *(Reed)*
Mercury SRM 2-7504 (double album) April 1974
This album once again credited

songs from the third and fourth Velvet albums to Lou Reed, rather than the VU.

VU
I Can't Stand It *(Reed)*/Stephanie Says *(Reed)*/She's My Best Friend *(Reed)*/Lisa Says *(Reed)*/Ocean *(Reed)*/Foggy Notion *(Reed)*/Inside Your Heart *(Reed)*/One Of These Days *(Reed)*/I'm Sticking With You *(Reed)*
Polygram 823 299 February 1985

ANOTHER VU
We're Gonna Have A Real Good Time Together *(Reed)*/I'm Gonna Move Right In *(VU)*/Hey Mr Rain (Version I) *(VU)*/Ride Into The Sun *(VU)*/Coney Island Steeplechase *(VU)*/Guess I'm Falling In Love (Instrumental Version) *(VU)*/Hey Mr Rain (Version II) *(VU)*/Ferryboat Bill *(VU)*/Rock And Roll (Original Version) *(Reed)*
Polygram 829 405–1 1986

THE BEST OF THE VELVET UNDERGROUND
Waiting For The Man *(Reed)*/ Femme Fatale *(Reed)*/Run Run Run *(Reed)*/Heroin *(Reed)*/All Tomorrow's Parties *(Reed)*/I'll Be Your Mirror *(Reed)*/White Light/White Heat *(Reed)*/Stephanie Says *(Reed)*/What Goes On *(Reed)*/Beginning To See The Light *(Reed)*/Pale Blue Eyes *(Reed)*/ I Can't Stand It *(Reed)*/Lisa Says *(Reed)*/Sweet Jane *(Reed)*/Rock & Roll *(Reed)*
Polygram 841 164 1989

VELVET UNDERGROUND U.K. ALBUMS

All track listings identical to U.S. releases unless stated

THE VELVET UNDERGROUND AND NICO
Verve SVLP 9184 October 1967

WHITE LIGHT/WHITE HEAT
Verve SVLP 9201 June 1968

THE VELVET UNDERGROUND
MGM C 8108 April 1969

LOADED
Atlantic 2400 111 March 1971

ANDY WARHOL'S VELVET UNDERGROUND FEATURING NICO
I'm Waiting For The Man *(Reed)*/ Candy Says *(VU)*/Run Run Run *(Reed)*/White Light/White Heat *(Reed)*/All Tomorrow's Parties *(Reed)*/Sunday Morning *(Reed)*/ I Heard Her Call My Name *(Reed)*/Femme Fatale *(Reed)*/Heroin *(Reed)*/Here She Comes Now *(Reed/Morrison/Cale/Tucker)*/There She Goes Again *(Reed)*/Sister Ray *(Reed/Morrison/Cale/Tucker)*Venus In Furs *(Reed)*/European Son *(Reed/Morrison/Cale/Tucker)*/Pale Blue Eyes *(VU)*/Black Angel's Death Song *(Reed/Cale)*/Beginning To See The Light *(VU)*
MGM 2683 006 December 1971

LIVE AT MAX'S KANSAS CITY
Atlantic K 30022 August 1972

SQUEEZE
Polydor 2383 180 February 1973

LOU REED AND THE VELVET UNDERGROUND
I'm Waiting For The Man *(Reed)*/Sister Ray *(Reed/Morrison/ Cale/Tucker)*/Lady Godiva's Operation *(Reed)*/Who Loves The Sun *(VU)*/All Tomorrow's Parties *(Reed)*/There She Goes Again

(Reed)/White Light/White Heat
(Reed)/Femme Fatale *(Reed)*
MGM 2315 256 October 1973

THE VELVET UNDERGROUND
White Light/White Heat *(Reed)*/
What Goes On *(VU)*/Venus In Furs
(Reed)/That's The Story Of My Life
(VU)/Here She Comes Now
(Reed/Morrison/Cale/Tucker)/
Beginning To See The Light *(VU)*/
Jesus *(VU)*/Run Run Run *(Reed)*/
Some Kinda Love *(VU)*/The Gift
(Reed/Morrison/Cale/Tucker)/
I'm Set Free *(VU)*/I Heard Her Call
My Name *(Reed)*
MGM 2354 033 1976

LIVE 1969
Mercury 6641 900 (double album)
February 1979

VU
Polydor POLD 5167 March 1985

THE VELVET UNDERGROUND
BOXED SET
Polydor VUBOX 1 1968
Includes first three albums, plus VU
and Another VU.

ANOTHER VU
Polydor POLD 5028 February 1987

THE BEST OF THE VELVET
UNDERGROUND
Polydor 841 164-1 1989

OTHER V.U. RECORDINGS

EAST VILLAGE OTHER-
ELECTRIC NEWSPAPER
ESP 1034 1966
LP contains Noise By
The Velvet Underground

ANDY WARHOL'S INDEX 1967
Book including flexidisc featuring
Loop by the Velvet Underground
(John Cale solo recording)

THE VELVET UNDERGROUND
Polydor 843 885 2 1990
French boxed set including the
band's first three LPs, VU, plus a
four-track CD single, including Ride
Into The Sun (studio take)/One Of
These Days (live)/I'm Sticking With
You (live)/Pale Blue Eyes (live); all
four tracks are previously unreleased

LOU REED U.S. SOLO SINGLES

GOING DOWN *(Reed)*/
I CAN'T STAND IT *(Reed)*
RCA 0727 1972

WALK AND TALK IT *(Reed)*/
WILD CHILD *(Reed)*
RCA 0784 1972

WALK ON THE WILD SIDE
(Reed)/PERFECT DAY *(Reed)*
RCA 0887 1972

SATELLITE OF LOVE *(Reed)*/
WALK AND TALK IT *(Reed)*
RCA 0964 1973

VICIOUS *(Reed)*/
GOODNIGHT LADIES *(Reed)*
RCA AFBO 0054 1973

HOW DO YOU THINK IT FEELS
(Reed)/LADY DAY *(Reed)*
RCA AFBO 0172 1973

SWEET JANE *(Reed)*/
LADY DAY *(Reed)*
RCA AFBO 0278 1974

SALLY CAN'T DANCE *(Reed)*/
VICIOUS *(Reed)*
RCA PB 10053 1974

SALLY CAN'T DANCE *(Reed)*/
ENNUI *(Reed)*
RCA PB 10081 1974

CHARLEY'S GIRL *(Reed)*/
NOWHERE AT ALL *(Reed)*
RCA PB 10573 1976

CRAZY FEELING *(Reed)*/
NOWHERE AT ALL *(Reed)*
RCA PB 10648 1976

I BELIEVE IN LOVE *(Reed)*/
SENSELESSLY CRUEL *(Reed)*
Arista 0215 1976

STREET HASSLE *(Reed)*/
STREET HASSLE *(Reed)*
Arista (12″) 1978

CITY LIGHTS *(Reed/Lofgren)*/
I WANT TO BOOGIE WITH YOU
(Reed/Fonfara)
Arista 04311 1979

THE POWER OF POSITIVE
DRINKING *(Reed/Fonfara)*/
GROWING UP IN PUBLIC
(Reed/Fonfara)
Arista 0535 1980

MY RED JOYSTICK/MY RED
JOYSTICK (Remix)
RCA (12″) 1983

SOUL MAN *(Hayes/Porter)*/
non-Reed Recording
A&M 1986
A-side by Sam Moore & Lou Reed
Also available as a 12″ single

MY LOVE IS CHEMICAL

THE ORIGINAL WRAPPER
(3 versions) *(Reed)*
RCA PW 14427 (12″) 1986

ROMEO HAD JULIETTE *(Reed)*/
BUSLOAD OF FAITH

(Live) *(Reed)*
Sire 9 22875-7 1989

LOU REED U.K. SOLO SINGLES

WALK AND TALK IT *(Reed)*
WILD CHILD *(Reed)*
RCA 2240 August 1972

WALK ON THE WILD SIDE
(Reed)/PERFECT DAY *(Reed)*
RCA 2303 November 1972

VICIOUS *(Reed)*/
SATELLITE OF LOVE *(Reed)*
RCA 2318 March 1973

CAROLINE SAYS I *(Reed)*/
CAROLINE SAYS II *(Reed)*
RCA APBO 0221 February 1974

SWEET JANE *(Reed)*/
LADY DAY *(Reed)*
RCA APBO 0238 April 1974

SALLY CAN'T DANCE *(Reed)*/
ENNUI *(Reed)*
RCA 2467 October 1974

CHARLEY'S GIRL *(Reed)*/
NOWHERE AT ALL *(Reed)*
RCA 2666 March 1976

ROCK AND ROLL HEART
(Reed)/SENSELESSLY CRUEL
(Reed)
Arista 105 April 1977

STREET HASSLE *(Reed)*/
WAITING FOR THE MAN *(Reed)*/
VENUS IN FURS *(Reed)*
Arista 12198 (12″) July 1978
Tracks 2 & 3 by The Velvet
Underground

WALK ON THE WILD SIDE
(Reed)/PERFECT DAY *(Reed)*
RCA GOLD 5 May 1979

CITY LIGHTS *(Reed/Lofgren)/*
SENSELESSLY CRUEL *(Reed)*
Arista 307 October 1979

WALK ON THE WILD SIDE
*(Reed)/*VICIOUS *(Reed)*
RCA GOLD 523 August 1981

I LOVE YOU SUZANNE *(Reed)/*
VICIOUS *(Reed)*
RCA 417 May 1984

I LOVE YOU SUZANNE *(Reed)/*
VICIOUS *(Reed)/*
WALK ON THE WILD SIDE
(Reed)
RCA RCAT 417 (12″) May 1984

SEPTEMBER SONG
non-Reed recording
A&M AM 283 October 1985

NO MONEY DOWN *(Reed)/*
DON'T HURT A WOMAN *(Reed)*
RCA 501 June 1986

NO MONEY DOWN (Extended
Mix) *(Reed)/*NO MONEY DOWN
(Dub) *(Reed)/*DON'T HURT A
WOMAN *(Reed)*
RCA RCAT 501T (12″) June 1986

WALK ON THE WILD SIDE
*(Reed)/*VICIOUS *(Reed)*
Old Gold OG 9634 October 1986

DIRTY BLVD *(Reed)/*
THE LAST GREAT AMERICAN
WHALE *(Reed)*
Sire W 7547 February 1989

DIRTY BLVD *(Reed)/*THE LAST
GREAT AMERICAN WHALE
*(Reed)/*THE ROOM *(Reed/Rathke)*
Sire W 7547T (12″) February 1989

WHAT'S GOOD *(Reed)/*THE
ROOM *(Reed/Rathke)*
Sir W 0090 (7″) March 1992

WHAT'S GOOD *(Reed)/*THE
ROOM*(Reed/Rathke)/*HARRY'S
CIRCUMCISION *(Reed)/*A
DREAM *(Reed/Cale)*
Tracks 3 & 4 are poetry readings.
Sire W 0090CD (CD) March 1992

LOU REED U.S. SOLO ALBUMS

LOU REED
I Can't Stand It *(Reed)/*Going Down
*(Reed)/*Walk And Talk It
*(Reed)/*Lisa Says *(Reed)/*Berlin
*(Reed)/*I Love You *(Reed)/*Wild
Child *(Reed)/*Love Makes You Feel
*(Reed)/*Ride Into The Sun *(Reed)/*
Ocean *(Reed)*
RCA LSP 4701 May 1972

TRANSFORMER
Vicious *(Reed)/*Andy's Chest
*(Reed)/*Perfect Day*(Reed)*Hangin'
Around *(Reed)/*Walk On The Wild
Side *(Reed)/*Make Up
*(Reed)/*Satellite Of Love
*(Reed)/*Wagon Wheel *(Reed)/*New
York Telephone Conversation
*(Reed)/*I'm So Free *(Reed)/*
Goodnight Ladies *(Reed)*
RCA LSP 4807 November 1972

BERLIN
Berlin *(Reed)/*Lady Day *(Reed)/*
Men Of Good Fortune *(Reed)/*
Caroline Says I *(Reed)/*How Do You
Think It Feels *(Reed)/*Oh Jim
*(Reed)/*Caroline Says II *(Reed)/*The
Kids *(Reed)/*The Bed *(Reed)/*Sad
Song *(Reed)*
RCA APL 10207 July 1973

ROCK'N'ROLL ANIMAL
Intro *(Hunter)/*Sweet Jane
*(Reed)/*Heroin *(Reed)/*White Light/
White Heat *(Reed)/*Lady Day
*(Reed)/*Rock and Roll *(Reed)*
RCA APL 10472 February 1974

SALLY CAN'T DANCE
Ride Sally Ride *(Reed)*/Animal
Language *(Reed)*/Baby Face *(Reed)*/
N.Y. Stars *(Reed)*/Kill Your Sons
(Reed)/Ennui *(Reed)*/Sally Can't
Dance *(Reed)*/Billy *(Reed)*
RCA APL 10611 August 1974

LOU REED LIVE
Vicious *(Reed)*/Satellite Of Love
(Reed)/Walk On The Wild Side
(Reed)/Waiting For The Man
(Reed)/Oh Jim *(Reed)*/
Sad Song *(Reed)*
RCA APL 10959 March 1975

METAL MACHINE MUSIC
Metal Machine Music Parts 1 to 4
(Reed)
RCA CPL 21101 (double LP)
July 1975

CONEY ISLAND BABY
Crazy Feeling *(Reed)*/Charley's Girl
(Reed)/She's My Best Friend
(Reed)/Kicks *(Reed)*/A Gift*(Reed)*/
Ooohhh Baby *(Reed)*/Nobody's
Business *(Reed)*/Coney Island Baby
(Reed)
RCA APL 10915 December 1975

ROCK AND ROLL HEART
I Believe In Love *(Reed)*/Banging
On My Drum *(Reed)*/Follow The
Leader *(Reed)*/You Wear It So Well
(Reed)/Ladies Pay *(Reed)*/
Rock and Roll Heart *(Reed)*/
Chooser And The Chosen One
(Reed)/Senselessly Cruel *(Reed)*/
Claim to Fame *(Reed)*/Vicious
Circle *(Reed)*/Sheltered Life
(Reed)/Temporary Thing *(Reed)*
Arista AL 4100 October 1976

WALK ON THE WILD SIDE
Sweet Jane *(Reed)*/White Light/
White Heat *(Reed)*/Sally Can't
Dance *(Reed)*/Nowhere At All
(Reed)/Coney Island Baby *(Reed)*/
Satellite Of Love *(Reed)*/Wild Child
(Reed)/I Love You *(Reed)*/How Do
You Think It Feels *(Reed)*/New
York Telephone Conversation
(Reed)/Walk On The Wild Side
(Reed)
RCA APL 12001 1977

STREET HASSLE
Gimme Some Good Times *(Reed)*/
Dirt *(Reed)*/Street Hassle *(Reed)*/
I Wanna Be Black *(Reed)*/Real
Good Time Together *(Reed)*/
Shooting Star *(Reed)*/Leave Me
Alone *(Reed)*/Wait *(Reed)*
Arista AB 4169 Febraury 1978

TAKE NO PRISONERS
Sweet Jane *(Reed)*/I Wanna Be
Black *(Reed)*/Satellite Of Love
(Reed)/Pale Blue Eyes *(Reed)*/
Berlin *(Reed)*/Waiting For The Man
(Reed)/Coney Island Baby
(Reed)/Street Hassle *(Reed)*/
Walk On The Wild Side *(Reed)*/
Leave Me Alone *(Reed)*
Arista AL 8502 (double LP)
November 1978

THE BELLS
Stupid Man *(Reed/Lofgren)*/Disco
Mystic *(Reed/Suchorsky/Fogel/
Fonfara/Boles)*/I Want To Boogie
With You *(Reed/Fonfara)*/With You
(Reed/Lofgren)/Looking For Love
(Reed)/City Lights *(Reed/
Lofgren)*/All Through The Night
(Reed/Cherry)/Families *(Reed/
Boles)*/The Bells *(Reed/Fogel)*
Arista AB 4229 April 1979

GROWING UP IN PUBLIC
How Do You Speak To An Angel
(Reed/Fonfara)/My Old Man *(Reed/
Fonfara)*/Keep Away *(Reed/
Fonfara)*/Growing Up In Public
(Reed/Fonfara)/Standing On

Ceremony *(Reed/Fonfara)*/So Alone *Reed/Fonfara)*/Love Is Here To Stay *(Reed/Fonfara)*/The Power Of Positive Drinking *(Reed/Fonfara)*/ Smiles *(Reed/Fonfara)*/Think It Over *(Reed/Fonfara)*/Teach The Gifted Children *(Reed/Fonfara)* Arista AL 9522 April 1980

ROCK'N'ROLL DIARY
Waiting For The Man *(Reed)*/White Light/White Heat *(Reed)*/I Heard Her Call My Name *(Reed)*/Pale Blue Eyes *(Reed)*/Beginning To See The Light *(Reed)*/Sweet Jane *(Reed)*/Rock And Roll *(Reed)*/ Heroin *(Reed)*/Femme Fatale *(Reed)*/Walk On The Wild Side *(Reed)*/Berlin *(Reed)*/Men of Good Fortune *(Reed)*/The Kids *(Reed)*/ Coney Island Baby *(Reed)*/ Temporary Thing *(Reed)*/ All Through The Night *(Reed/ Cherry)*/So Alone *(Reed/Fonfara)*/ How Do You Speak To An Angel *(Reed/Fonfara)*/Keep Away *(Reed/ Fonfara)*/Street Hassle *(Reed)* Arista AL 8603 (double LP) November 1980
First nine recordings are by The Velvet Underground

THE BLUE MASK
My House *(Reed)*/Women *(Reed)*/ Underneath The Bottle *(Reed)*/ The Gun *(Reed)*/The Blue Mask *(Reed)*/Average Guy *(Reed)*/ The Heroine *(Reed)*/Waves Of Fear *(Reed)*/The Day John Kennedy Died *(Reed)*/Heavenly Arms *(Reed)* RCA February 1982

LEGENDARY HEARTS
Legendary Hearts *(Reed)*/Don't Talk To Me About Work *(Reed)*/Make Up Mind *(Reed)*/Martial Law *(Reed)*/The Last Shot *(Reed)*Turn Out The Light *(Reed)*/Pow Wow

(Reed)/Betrayed *(Reed)*/Bottoming Out *(Reed)*/Home Of The Brave *(Reed)*/Rooftop Garden *(Reed)* RCA 1982

NEW SENSATIONS
I Love You Suzanne *(Reed)*/ Endlessly Jealous *(Reed)*/My Red Joystick *(Reed)*/Turn To Me *(Reed)*/ New Sensations *(Reed)*/Doin' The Things That We Want To *(Reed)*/ What Becomes A Legend Most *(Reed)*/Fly Into The Sun *(Reed)*/ My Friend George *(Reed)*/High In The City *(Reed)*/Down At The Arcade *(Reed)* RCA APL 14998 1984

MISTRIAL
Mistrial *(Reed)*/No Money Down *(Reed)*/Outside *(Reed)*/Don't Hurt A Woman *(Reed)*/Video Violence *(Reed)*/Spit It Out *(Reed)*/ The Original Wrapper *(Reed)*/ Mama's Got A Lover *(Reed)*/ I Remember You *(Reed)*/Tell It To Your Heart *(Reed)* RCA AFL 17190 1986

NEW YORK
Romeo Had Juliette *(Reed)*/ Halloween Parade *(Reed)*/ Dirty Blvd *(Reed)*/Endless Cycle *(Reed)*/There Is No Time *(Reed)*/ Last Great American Whale *(Reed)*/ Beginning of a Great Adventure *(Reed/Rathke)*/Busload Of Faith *(Reed)*/Sick Of You *(Reed)*/ Hold On *(Reed)*/Good Evening Mr Waldheim *(Reed)*/Xmas In February *(Reed)*/Strawman *(Reed)*/ Dime Store Mystery *(Reed)* Sire 9 25829 1989

SONGS FOR DRELLA
Smalltown *(Reed/Cale)*/Open House *(Reed/Cale)*/Style It Takes *(Reed/ Cale)*/Work *(Reed/Cale)*/Trouble

With Classicists *(Reed/Cale)/*
Starlight *(Reed/Cale)/*Faces And
Names *(Reed/Cale)/*Images
*(Reed/Cale)/*Slip Away (A Warning)
*(Reed/Cale)/*It Wasn't Me
*(Reed/Cale)/*U Believe *(Reed/Cale)/*
Nobody But You *(Reed/Cale)/*
A Dream *(Reed/Cale)/*Forever
Changed *(Reed/Cale)/*Hello It's Me
(Reed/Cale)
Sire 9 26140 1990
Performed by Lou Reed/John Cale

MAGIC AND LOSS
Dorita *(Reed)/*What's Good *(Reed)/*
Power And Glory*(Reed/Rathke)/*
Magician *(Reed)/*Sword Of
Damocles *(Reed)/*Goodby Mass
*(Reed)/*Cremation *(Reed)/*Dreamin'
*(Reed/Rathke)/*No Chance *(Reed)/*
Warrior King *(Reed)/*Harry's
Circumcision *(Reed)/*Gassed And
Stoked *(Reed/Rathe)/*Power And
Glory Part II *(Reed/Rathke)/Magic
And Loss (Reed/Rathke)*
Sire 7599 26666 February 1992

BETWEEN THOUGHT AND EXPRESSION
I Can't Stand It *(Reed)/*Lisa Says
*(Reed)/*Ocean *(Reed)/*Walk On The
Wild Side *(Reed)/*Satellite of Love
*(Reed)/*Vicious *(Reed)/*Caroline Says
I *(Reed)/*How Do You Think It
Feels *(Reed)/*Oh Jim *(Reed)*Caroline
Says II *(Reed)/*The Kids *(Reed)/*Sad
Song *(Reed)/*Sweet Jane *(Reed)/*Kill
Your Sons *(Reed)/*Coney Island
Baby *(Reed)/*Nowhere At All
*(Reed)/*Kicks *(Reed)/*Downtown Dirt
*(Reed)/*Rock And Roll Heart
*(Reed)/*Vicious Circle *(Reed)/*
Temporary Thing *(Reed)/*Real Good
Time Together *(Reed)/*Leave Me
Alone *(Reed)/*Heroin *(Reed)/*Here
Comes The Bride *(Reed)/*Street
Hassle *(Reed)/*Metal Machine Music
*(Reed)/*The Bells *(Reed/Fogel)/*

America *(Key)/*Think It Over
*(Reed/Fonfara)/*Teach The Gifted
Children *(Reed/Fonfara)/*The Gun
*(Reed)/*The Blue Mask *(Reed)/*My
House *(Reed)/*Waves Of Fear
*(Reed)/*Little Sister *(Reed)/*
Legendary Hearts *(Reed)/*The Last
Shot *(Reed)/*New Sensations *(Reed)/*
My Friend George *(Reed)/*Doin' The
Things That We Want To *(Reed)/*
The Original Wrapper *(Reed)/*Video
Violence *(Reed)/*Tell It To Your
Heart *(Reed)/*Voices Of Freedom
(Reed)
RCA PD 90621 (3-CD boxed
set) April 1992

LOU REED SOLO U.K. LPs
(All tracks identical to U.S. releases
unless stated)

LOU REED
RCA SF 8281 July 1972

TRANSFORMER
RCA LSP 4807 November 1972

BERLIN
RCA RS 1002 October 1973

ROCK'N'ROLL ANIMALS
RCA PL 10472 February 1974

SALLY CAN'T DANCE
RCA PL 10611 September 1974

LOU REED LIVE
RCA RS 1007 March 1975

METAL MACHINE MUSIC
RCA CLP 21101 (double LP) July
1975

CONEY ISLAND BABY
RCA RS 1035 January 1976

ROCK'N'ROLL HEART
Arista ARTY 142 November 1976

WALK ON THE WILD SIDE
RCA PL 12001 April 1977

STREET HASSLE
Arista SPART 1045 April 1978

VICIOUS
Vicious *(Reed)*/Charley's Girl
(Reed)/I Can't Stand It *(Reed)*/
Ride Sally Ride *(Reed)*/Lady Day
(Reed)/Kill Your Sons *(Reed)*/
Perfect Day *(Reed)*/Walk And
Talk It *(Reed)*/Crazy Feeling *(Reed)*/
Caroline Says II *(Reed)*
RCA NL 42731 January 1979

TAKE NO PRISONERS
RCA XL 03066 (double LP) March
1979

THE BELLS
Arista SPART 1093 October 1979

CONEY ISLAND BABY
RCA INTS 5082 (reissue) March
1980

GROWING UP IN PUBLIC
Arista SPART 1131 May 1980

ROCK'N'ROLL DIARY
Arista DARTY 8 (double LP)
December 1980

TRANSFORMER
RCA INTS 5061 (reissue) February
1981

LOU REED LIVE
RCA INTS 5071 (reissue) February
1981

ROCK'N'ROLL ANIMAL
RCA INTS (reissue) May
1981

BERLIN
RCA INTS 5150 (reissue)
October 1981

THE BLUE MASK
RCA RCALP 6028 June 1982

LEGENDARY HEARTS
RCA RCALP 6071 May 1983

LIVE IN ITALY
Sweet Jane *(Reed)*/Waiting For The
Man *(Reed)*/Martial Law *(Reed)*/
Satellite Of Love *(Reed)*/Kill Your
Sons *(Reed)*/Betrayed *(Reed)*/Sally
Can't Dance *(Reed)*/Waves Of Fear
(Reed)/Average Guy *(Reed)*/White
Light/White Heat*(Reed)*/White
Light/White Heat *(Reed)*/Some
Kinda Love; Sister Ray *(Reed;*
Reed/Morrison/Cale/Tucker)/Walk
On The Wild Side *(Reed)*/Heroin
(Reed)/Rock And Roll *(Reed)*
RCA PL 89156 (double LP, issued
only in Europe) January 1984

NEW SENSATIONS
RCA PL 84998 April 1984

CONEY ISLAND BABY
RCA NL 83807 (reissue) June 1984

LOU REED LIVE
RCA NL 837752 (reissue) June
1984

TRANSFORMER
RCA NL 83806 (reissue) June 1984

MISTRIAL
RCA PL 87190 April 1986

BERLIN
RCA NL 84388 (reissue) June 1986

ROCK AND ROLL ANIMAL
RCA NL 83664 (reissue) June 1986

SALLY CAN'T DANCE
RCA PD 80611 (reissue) 1987

WALK ON THE WILD SIDE
RCA PD 83753 (reissue) 1987

MISTRIAL
RCA NL 90253 (reissue) October
1988

NEW YORK
Sire WX 246 February 1989

RETRO
Walk On The Wild Side *(Reed)*/
Satellite Of Love *(Reed)*/I Love You
Suzanne *(Reed)*/Wild Child
(Reed)/How Do You Think It Feels
(Reed)/Lady Day *(Reed)*/Coney
Island Baby *(Reed)*/Sweet Jane
(Reed)/Vicious *(Reed)*/Sally Can't
Dance *(Reed)*/Berlin *(Reed)*/
Caroline Says II *(Reed)*/Perfect Day
(Reed)/Kill Your Sons *(Reed)*/
White Light/White Heat *(Reed)*
RCA PL 90389 1989
CD edition includes two bonus
tracks, Waiting For The Man and
Heroin

SONGS FOR DRELLA
Sire 7599 26140 April 1990
Performed by Lou Reed/John Cale

MAGIC AND LOSS
Sire 7599 26666 March 1992

BETWEEN THOUGHT AND
EXPRESSION
RCA PD 90621 (3-CD boxed
set) April 1992

RELATED RELEASES
(All albums unless otherwise stated)

CHELSEA GIRL
Verve 5032, US; MGM 2353 025,
UK 1967
By Nico
*Reed plays guitar, and is composer
of* It Was A Pleasure Then, Little
Sister, Wrap Your Troubles In
Dreams *and title track.*

WILD ANGEL
RCA APL1-1306, US 1976
By Nelson Slater
Produced by Reed who also
contributed guitar/piano/backing
vocals. Tracks: Wild Angel/
Dominating Force/Sad About
It/Here's A Heart/Memory
Girl/Things Have Happened
Strange/We/A Good Time Was Had
By All/Complete The Story Now

URBAN DESIRE
20th Century T 562, US; 20th
Century BTH 8002, UK 1978
By Genya Ravan
Lou sings on Aye Co'lorado

NILS
A&M SP 4756, US; A&M AMLH
64756, UK 1979
By Nils Lofgren
Reed co-composer of I'll Cry
Tomorrow, A Fool Like Me and I
Found Her

ESCAPE ARTIST
Epic 36983, US; Epic EPC 84808,
UK 1980
By Garland Jeffreys
Reed contributes backing vocals

MUSIC FROM THE ELDER
Casablanca 7270, US; Casablanca
6302 163, UK 1981
By Kiss
Reed co-composer of Mr Blackwell,
World Without Heroes and Dark
Light

GET CRAZY
United Artists (US only) 1983
Soundtrack
Reed contributes My Baby Sister

Sun CITY
EMI-Manhattan MT 7 (single) 1985
By Artists United Against Apartheid

Reed one of many featured vocalists.
Also available on 12″ single and LP.

SOUL MAN
A&M SP 3903, US; A&M AMA 3903, UK 1986
Soundtrack
Includes Reed and Sam Moore performing title track.

THE SECRET POLICEMAN'S BALL (THE MUSIC)
Virgin 7-90643, US; Virgin V 2458, UK 1987
Live compilation
Includes Reed performing Voices Of Freedom, and included on vocal chorus of Biko.

NOTHING BUT THE TRUTH
Elektra 9-60754, US; Elektra 960 754-2, UK 1988
By Ruben Blades
Reed co-wrote and co-produced Letters To The Vatican and The Calm Before The Storm, playing guitar on both tracks and singing on The Calm Before The Storm. He also co-wrote Hopes on Hold.

DUETS
MCA 42131 1988
By Rob Wasserman
Reed sings and plays on One For My Baby

HEY MERSH! (Tucker)
50,000,000,000,000,000,000,000 Watts MOE 6 (12″ single) 1989
By Maureen Tucker
Reed plays guitar and performs backing vocals

LIFE IN EXILE AFTER ABDICATION
50,000,000,000,000,000,000,000 Watts MOE 6 1989
By Maureen Tucker
Reed plays guitar on Hey Mersh! and Pale Blue Eyes, and performs backing vocals on Hey Mersh!

CASHMERE DREAMS
Grudge 4501 1989
By Fernando Saunders
Reed composer of Opposites Attract

STREET FIGHTING YEARS
Virgin SP 3927, US; Virgin MINDS

1, UK 1989
By Simple Minds
Reed sings on This Is Your Land

YO FRANKIE
Arista AL 8549, US; Arista 209766, UK 1919
By Dion
Reed Sings on King Of The New York Streets

BOOM BOOM CHI BOOM BOOM
Sire 9-25888, US; Fontana SFLP 8, UK 1989
By Tom Tom Club
Reed sings and plays guitar on Femme Fatale

I SPENT A WEEK THERE THE OTHER NIGHT
New Rose ROSE 273 CD (France) 1991
By Moe Tucker
Reed plays guitar on Fired Up and (with the original members of the Velvet Underground) I'm Not.